# WRITING
## *Fundamentals*
### Second Edition

Joseph T. Lyons
St. Lawrence College

Prentice-Hall Canada Inc., Scarborough, Ontario

# For Diane

*...once more with feeling*

**Canadian Cataloguing in Publication Data**

Lyons, Joseph T. (Joseph Thomas), 1935-
  Writing fundamentals

Includes index.
ISBN 0-13-969585-0

1. English language—Rhetoric. 2. English
language—Rhetoric—Problems, exercises, etc.
I. Title.

PE1408.L96 1986    808'.042    C85-099088-2


© 1986 Prentice-Hall Canada Inc.
  Scarborough, Ontario.

Prentice-Hall, Inc., Englewood Cliffs, New Jersey
Prentice-Hall International, Inc., London
Prentice-Hall of Australia, Pty., Ltd., Sydney
Prentice-Hall of India Pvt., Ltd., New Delhi
Prentice-Hall of Japan, Inc., Tokyo
Prentice-Hall of Southeast Asia (Pte.) Ltd., Singapore
Editora Prentice-Hall do Brasil Ltda., Rio de Janeiro
Prentice-Hall Hispanoamericana, S.A., Mexico

ISBN 0-13-969585-0

   3   4   5   6   IG   91   90   89   88

Production Editor: David Jolliffe
Designer: Gail Ferreira
Cover Design & Paste-up: Janet Eidt
Compositor: Fleet Typographers
Production: Sheldon Fischer
Printed and bound in Canada by Gagne Printing Ltd.

The report, "Simulated Thermal Effluent into Lake Ontario"
by J.B. Silburn is printed by permission of the author
and the Ministry of the Environment, Province of Ontario.

# Contents

# CHAPTER 12  Writing a Report  224

# Preface

Although the second edition of *Writing Fundamentals* has significant content changes, its format and rationale remain the same. It is still designed for both community college and pre-university students who need the structural discipline of applied communications. And it still asks the user to problem solve by constructing outlines, writing unified paragraphs, and by correcting and revising defective sentences and paragraphs. Indeed, many of the content changes were suggested by student users of the first edition as well as by their writing teachers. Here are the major changes in this edition:

1. More sentence correction exercises in each chapter (from 20 to 30).

2. New paragraph revision exercises.

3. New recognition exercises for parts of speech (Chapter 1).

4. Punctuation chapter expanded to include a new comma rule section and a new section on parentheses and brackets with attendant exercises.

5. Chapter on outlines expanded with new exercises.

6. More diction and usage examples.

7. Simplified exercises in the paragraph chapter.

8. New chapter on Report Writing (Chapter 12).

9. Answers to exercises in the back of the book (Appendix) for self-marking.

10. A separate packet of exercises for added drill.

The organizational strengths of the first edition of *Writing Fundamentals* have been maintained and its utilitarian focus re-emphasized: the text continues to be a functional tool for classroom instruction, not a benign handbook for student reference. It recognizes the time constraints placed upon English teachers, and deals realistically with the problem-solving process of revision that every student must confront in his or her own writing. Here are the continuing strengths of the text.

1. The writing style is clear, precise, and economical. The language does not patronize or talk down to readers, and the diction and vocabulary are appropriate for mature, post-secondary students.

2. The relationship between sentence correction and paragraph revision continues to be close and obvious.

3. There is a strong emphasis on skill development. From the discussion of grammar as a relationship between words, phrases, and clauses, to that of outlining as the organizational foundation for paragraphs, essays, and reports, the text requires students to continually apply what they learn. Therefore they are confronted not by isolated linear exercises, but by a skill progression that is both challenging and thoughtful.

4. The Canadian orientation of the text is natural, logical, and unintrusive, and the language is non-sexist.

5. The text is comprehensive. It contains all the necessary skills to allow students to write unified and coherent exposition. Consequently the teacher does not have to supplement it with additional skill material. Nor is the teacher "locked in" to a rigid pattern of programmed instruction, but can use the text prescriptively to suit the needs of students working on different skill levels.

6. The text is flexible. It can be used in community college English courses, in writing labs for first-year university students, and in courses for high-school students who must prepare for post-secondary composition. It has also been used successfully by English upgrading teachers whose courses are individualized and self-paced.

I wish to thank my colleagues at St. Lawrence College who tested sections of the text in the class. I would also like to thank the reviewers of the manuscript, especially Nina Butska of Humber College and Susan Braley of Fanshawe College, who offered valuable suggestions for improving the text.

# WRITING
## Fundamentals

# CHAPTER ONE

# Beginning with the Foundation: Parts of Speech

All written and spoken communication depends on the sentence since only the sentence contains a complete thought. And sentences themselves are composed of words with particular functions and assigned relationships; the term "parts of speech" simply describes how words function as sentence parts. With the exception of the interjection—a word whose abrupt emotional message is obvious (Help! Oh! Wow!)—each part of speech performs a particular role *within* the sentence. There are seven of them: nouns, pronouns, verbs, adjectives, adverbs, prepositions, and conjunctions.

## A. NOUNS

A noun is a name; it names people, places, things, ideas, and general conditions. Some nouns, called proper, are capitalized because their names are particular.

> The *students* who graduated from *Glendale College* are invited to a *reception* hosted by *Professor Roberts*.

A noun's most important function, though, is as a subject (the doer) or an object (the receiver) in the sentence.

> **Subj.**          **Obj.**
> *Marie* passed the *examination* with ease.

>      **Subj.**                 **Obj.**
> Some *buildings* in Toronto have interesting *histories*.

## B. PRONOUNS

Pronouns are noun substitutions, and they are used to avoid repetition. So instead of saying, "Peter and Peter's friend, Harold, took Peter and Harold's parents to the graduation party where Peter and Harold and the parents of Peter and Harold

1

drank punch and ate tiny sandwiches...," you can say, "Peter and *his* friend, Harold, took *their* parents to the graduation party where *they all* drank punch and ate tiny sandwiches."

There are three obvious kinds of pronouns: *personal*, *possessive*, and *indefinite*.

| **Personal** | **Possessive** | **Indefinite** *(a partial list)* |
| --- | --- | --- |
| I, me | my, mine | anybody |
| you | your, yours | anything |
| he, him | his, hers | anyone |
| she, her | its | everybody |
| it | our, ours | everything |
| we, us | their, theirs | everyone |
| they, them | | somebody |
| | | something |
| | | someone |
| | | any |
| | | some |
| | | few |
| | | each |
| | | many |
| | | all |

In the following sentences all three types are used:

If *anybody* wishes to volunteer for *our* heart-fund drive, will *he* or *she* please step forward.

Has *anyone* seen *my* textbook? *I* left *it* on *somebody's* desk.

Note that some indefinite pronouns are made possessive with an apostrophe and an *s*. See pp. 120-122.

Then there are the *interrogative pronouns* that ask questions: who, which, whom, whose, what.

"*What* was the colour of the book and to *whom* did it belong?"

There are also *relative pronouns* that link clauses to their antecedents: who, which, that, whom, whose.

"The *student* (*who* left the new textbook on the *desk*) (*that* is located in our school) is still looking for it."

And finally, there are *demonstrative pronouns* that point out or demonstrate something: these, those, this, that.

*Those* who leave their books on desks in unfamiliar classrooms will surely lose them—and *that* is the truth!

Note: The demonstrative pronouns also function as adjectives when they appear immediately before nouns: *these* cars, *that* house, *this* theory, *those* students.

## C. VERBS

The verb is the heart of the sentence. It makes the sentence move and infuses it with vitality. In fact, you cannot write a sentence without a verb. Nor do you have to know what a word means to identify it as a verb, since it serves as the vital connecting link between the subject and the object.

> James *scrabbled* the test.
>
> The test *was scrabbled* by James.

Because the verb performs or receives an action or reflects a condition or an event, it provides the spark that lets a group of words project ideas.

> The flaming meteor *ploughed* into the field, *tore* through the tree line, and *crashed* against the mountain.
>
> The table lamp *was knocked* over by our cat while he *was playing* with the cord.

## D. ADJECTIVES

An adjective is a word that modifies (describes, restricts, relates to) a noun or a pronoun and that answers the questions *which*, *how many*, and *what kind*. Other adjectives, called articles—a, an, the—answer the question *which one*. Adjectives usually, but not always, precede nouns and pronouns.

> The *morning* sun crept over the *blackened* rooftops and sent *cautious* probes of *pale* light into the *gutted* buildings.
>
> The *weary* traveller, *lonely* and *forlorn*, approached the outskirts of the *deserted* city.

## E. ADVERBS

Adverbs are more flexible than adjectives. They can modify verbs, adjectives, and other adverbs, and can appear almost anywhere in the sentence. They normally answer the questions *where*, *when*, *how* and *how much*. Adverbs not only determine the precise meaning of adjectives and other adverbs, but also provide substance and glitter to verbs.

*extremely* unhappy; *inconspicuously* clever; *fairly* mild; *quite* strong; *predictably* late (modifying adjectives and adverbs)

While several sea birds wheeled *gracefully* over the undulating waves, others searched *casually* for discarded food along the beach. (modifying verbs)

## F. PREPOSITIONS

Prepositions are important in sentences because they join with nouns and pronouns to form phrases that serve as modifiers of subjects, verbs, and objects. Here are some common prepositions: at, by, for, from, in, of, on, to, with, between, over, under, through, and within. They can start some very interesting things happening in sentences.

(With simple dignity), (on the bed where he was born), he died (in silence).

Prepositional phrases are especially important in poetry, for they are often used to construct sensuous and powerful images.

We sat grown quiet (at the name of love);
We saw the last embers (of daylight) die,
And (in the trembling blue-green of the sky)
A moon, worn as if it had been a shell
Washed (by time's waters) as they rose and fell
(About the stars) and broke (in days and years).
　　　　*"Adam's Curse,"* *William Butler Yeats.*

## G. CONJUNCTIONS

Conjunctions are essential because they join similar sentence elements and thereby provide the sentence with balance and cohesion. There are four kinds of conjunctions: coordinate, correlative, subordinate, and the conjunctive adverb.

1. **Coordinate** These conjunctions are the most frequently used and are therefore the most familiar. There are seven of them: and, but, or, nor, for, yet, and so. They connect grammatically equal sentence parts such as words, phrases and clauses.

|  |  |
|---|---|
| WORDS: | Bill *and* Frank; hit *and* run; tea *or* coffee. |
| PHRASES: | (Around the corner) *and* (over the hill). |
| DEPENDENT CLAUSES: | No one knew (who he was) *or* (what he did). |
| INDEPENDENT CLAUSES: | (The director told me the actor's name), *but* (I have forgotten it). |

2. **Correlative** These conjunctions always come in pairs, and they are most often used for balance and emphasis. There are four important ones:

either . . . or; neither . . . nor; not only . . . but/but also; both . . . and. (See discussion of sentence coordination, p. 28 and 72.)

> She is *not only* a portrait painter *but also* a concert pianist.
>
> Peter is *either* going to the University of Montreal *or* to an art college in Nova Scotia.
>
> *Neither* gambling *nor* drinking is permitted in this establishment.
>
> *Both* my father *and* my uncle are volunteer firemen.

**3. Subordinate**   These conjunctions connect dependent and independent clauses, and their use is determined by the principles of subordination (see p. 29). Some of the most common subordinate conjunctions are *that*, *who*, *when*, *which*, *until*, *while*, *as* and *if*.

> He discarded his life jacket, *which* was a dangerous thing to do.
>
> I always wear goggles *when* skiing downhill.
>
> *If* you volunteer, I shall support your efforts.

**4. The Conjunctive Adverb**   Conjunctive adverbs connect related independent clauses, and they are used in sentences to sequence, qualify, and conclude. They allow the writer added flexibility in conveying ideas and information. Some common conjunctive adverbs are *therefore*, *moreover*, *however*, *nevertheless*, and *consequently* (see p. 106 for a more complete list).

> He has not answered our summons; *therefore* we shall proceed without him.
>
> Jane cannot babysit tonight; *however*, her brother has volunteered to take her place.
>
> Although the earthquake destroyed most of the town, people do, *nevertheless*, still manage to live there.

What is important to remember about parts of speech is how they join together to convey meaning. The correct positioning of verbs, pronouns, adjectives, etc., will permit you to be not only coherent and precise but also original and emphatic.

Writing effective sentences is a constant challenge, but the rewards are worth the effort; for when the proper words are used in the proper places, they can reveal the brilliance of the English language, in sentences like these:

> Still falls the Rain—
> Dark as the world òf man, black as our loss—
> Blind as the nineteen hundred and forty nails
> Upon the Cross.
>
>     *"Still Falls the Rain," Edith Sitwell*

And we are here as on a darkling plain
Swept with confused alarms of struggle and flight,
Where ignorant armies clash by night.

*"Dover Beach," Matthew Arnold*

Our birth is but a sleep and a forgetting...

*"Intimations of Immortality,"*
*William Wordsworth*

Let us go then, you and I,
When the evening is spread out against the sky
Like a patient etherized upon a table.

*"The Love Song of J. Alfred Prufrock,"*
*T.S. Eliot*

Like flies to wanton boys are we to the Gods;
They kill us for their sport.

*King Lear, Act IV, Scene I,*
*William Shakespeare*

The beauty of the world has two edges, one of laughter,
one of anguish, cutting the heart asunder.

*A Room of One's Own, Virginia Woolf*

Before we can hope to write sentences like these, however, we must first understand how they are made and patterned; these skills are examined in the following chapters.

## Exercise 1.1: Distinguishing Parts of Speech

In each of the following sentences identify the italicized words by their numbers in the blank at the right:

1. Noun    2. Pronoun    3. Adjective    4. Adverb    5. Preposition
6. Conjunction    7. Verb

EXAMPLE:    Several *blind* mice ran *under* the stairwell.        3        4

1. The footbridge hangs *between* large cliffs which are studded with *caves*.        5        1

2. *Follow* that car *down* the yellow brick road.        7        4

3. The Christmas tree was decorated by two *young* boys who lived across the street from *us*.        3        2

4. Ted *and* Carol both *won* prizes for their paintings at the art show.        6        7

5. *We* will visit Vermont in the fall *when* the leaves change colour.    2    4

6. *Try* to be *on* time tomorrow.    7    5

7. *When* shall *we* meet?    4    2

8. Toronto is the *largest* city in *Ontario*.    3    1

9. Michael *plays* hockey, *but* Brenden prefers soccer.    7    6

10. *My* father's sailboat *capsized* yesterday.    2    7

11. Please remain *in* the classroom until the *bell* rings.    5    1

12. *Which* subject do *you* prefer? English or French?    3    2

13. I know *where* the *best* restaurants are located in our city.    4    3

14. *Dr. Thomson* was only thirty years old when he was appointed a *full* professor at our university.    1    3

15. All of the rooms were booked, *so* we had to move to another *hotel*.    6    1

16. The toy *was broken* when we opened the *damaged* parcel.    7    3

17. I don't know *when* we will visit *our* friend, Helen.    4    2

18. Our hockey team won *its* first game; *however* our basketball team was beaten very soundly.    2    4

19. Please *read* the next chapter in the text *for* tomorrow.    7    5

20. My brother sold his stereo set *after* he lost *all* of his money gambling.    4    2.

# CHAPTER TWO

---

# Organizing Your Sentence

## A. WHAT IS A SENTENCE?

A sentence is a group of related words containing a complete thought. It has both a subject and a verb, and can stand alone as an independent statement. The subject is the person, place, thing or idea that the sentence is about, and the verb is the statement made about the subject. A sentence may consist of a simple verbal command without a stated subject—Follow me. Sit down. Turn to the right.—or it may have more than one subject and more than one verb as in the following examples.

> **Mary and Lisa** are enrolled in the same course. (compound subject)
>
> The spectators *clapped and cheered* when the home team ran onto the field. (compound verb)
>
> **Students and faculty** *repaired and painted* the old classroom desks. (compound subject and verb)

The complete subject of a sentence includes the subject term and its modifiers—words and phrases that describe or limit—and the complete verb includes the verb statement and the modifiers that complete its meaning.

| Complete Subject | Complete Verb |
|---|---|
| The **actor** who portrayed Count Dracula | *received* a standing ovation. |
| The **kind of music** I most enjoy | *is* dance music from the big-band era. |
| The small red and white **car** | *crashed* into a lamppost. |

But always remember that, however numerous the subject and verb modifiers, the statement cannot stand alone without a simple subject and a simple verb.

> (After being ignored time and time again,) **Mr. Roberts** *decided* (to remain silent during class discussions).

8

Without the two words, *Mr. Roberts* (simple subject) and *decided* (simple verb), the example above would not be a complete sentence.

## B. THE COMPLETE VERB

**1.** The complete verb may have one or more helping words that reflect time or fix emphasis.

> It *must have been* he who wrote the letter.
>
> She *will have gone* by the time we arrive.
>
> I *should play* tomorrow.

**2.** It may have a direct object that completes the action and that answers the questions *who* or *what*.

> Tom wrote his *term paper* yesterday. (Wrote what?)
>
> Squirrels eat *nuts*. (Eat what?)
>
> Jack drove *Carol* home last night. (Drove whom?)

**3.** It may have an indirect object that receives the action.

> He gave *me* (to me) his notebook to study.
>
> Steve told *me* (to me) a story about football.
>
> Her sister gave *her* (to her) new ski poles for Christmas.

## C. FINDING THE SIMPLE SUBJECT AND VERB

If you remember that the subject is the focus of the sentence and the verb the statements made about the subject, the order in which they appear should pose no problem. First locate the simple verb, which is the word or group of words that states something; then ask who or what is the statement about. Consider the following examples.

**1.** Although the subject usually precedes the verb, the order may be reversed.

> s
> The *runner* is exhausted. (Who is exhausted?)
>
> s
> Is the *runner* exhausted? (Who is exhausted?)
>
> s
> There is the exhausted *runner*. (Who is there?)
>
> s
> From the runner came a *sigh* of exhaustion. (What came?)

**2.** In *There is (are)* and *Here is (are)* sentences, the verb always precedes the subject.

> V       S
> There *is* only one *car* in the showroom.
>
> V       S
> There *are* more *cars* in the parking lot.
>
> V         S
> Here *is* the most expensive *car* on the market.
>
> V         S
> Here *are* the most fuel-efficient *cars* that money can buy.

Note: *here* and *there* are never the subjects of sentences; they introduce the subject term but do not participate in its activity.

**3.** Sentences that issue orders, make strong requests, or give directions take *you* (meaning the reader or listener) as the implied subject.

> (You) Go to sleep.
>
> (You) Please find the correct file.
>
> (You) Write your name and the date in your test booklet.

## Exercise 2.1 – Locating the Subject and Verb

In the following sentences locate the simple subject and verb and then write them in the blanks at the right or on a separate sheet of paper.

EXAMPLE:    Jack Reynolds, the star athlete, has won a scholarship for academic excellence.

|  | S | V |
|---|---|---|
|  | Jack Reynolds | has won |
| 1. Into the classroom walked the students. | _____ | _____ |
| 2. One of my mother's pies is missing. | _____ | _____ |
| 3. Call the team together for a meeting. | _____ | _____ |
| 4. Where is Winnipeg in relation to Calgary? | _____ | _____ |
| 5. The fertilizer was spread on the garden yesterday. | _____ | _____ |
| 6. Telling lies is a disgusting habit. | _____ | _____ |
| 7. Some of our tomatoes were picked too early. | _____ | _____ |
| 8. There are not enough textbooks in the bookstore. | _____ | _____ |

9. My sister's birthday falls on Tuesday this year. _____ _____

10. Who was here yesterday? _____ _____

11. Near the schoolyard were several tennis courts. _____ _____

12. Skiing and ice skating are my favourite winter activities. _____ _____

13. Several of our teachers are at a remedial reading conference in Toronto. _____ _____

14. Here is the winning number. _____ _____

15. Diane, fighting to stay in contention, sank a thirty foot putt on the eighteenth green. _____ _____

16. Some of the trees we planted are now infested with budworm. _____ _____

17. On the roof of our house there is a robin's nest. _____ _____

18. Failing to answer the test questions in the allotted time, James flunked his final math quiz. _____ _____

19. Please follow the dotted line. _____ _____

20. When did this happen? _____ _____

21. How many chairs are there in the room? _____ _____

22. Who fired the first shot? _____ _____

23. More than two volunteers are needed for next week's project. _____ _____

24. There are not enough tables in the cafeteria. _____ _____

25. The cause of the accident is still under investigation. _____ _____

26. Inside the barn, the fire spread rapidly. _____ _____

27. Many of our former students have won scholarships. _____ _____

28. Jogging keeps me in good physical shape all year round. _____ _____

29. Struggling to free himself from the clinging vines, Roger hacked desperately with his machete as the pursuing cannibals gained on him. _____ _____

30. Outside the cabin, the snowstorm intensified. _____ _____

# D. ENLARGING THROUGH PHRASES

The subject-verb structure, the basic unit of thought that comprises a sentence, can be expanded by attaching to it related word groups called phrases and clauses. These word groups permit us to add variety and depth to our statements.

A phrase may be defined as a group of related words without a subject and a verb and used as a single part of speech. The most common phrases are prepositional, participial, gerund, and infinitive.

**1. Phrases Introduced by Prepositions**   The prepositional phrase is introduced by a preposition—*across* the hall, *in* the house, *after* the game, *for* my sister—and is most often used as an adjective or an adverb.

> The manager *of our branch office* submitted her request *for a leave of absence*.

The italicized phrases are used as adjectives because they modify the nouns *manager* and *request*.

> All final examinations are given *in the spring at the main campus*.

The italicized phrases are used as adverbs because they modify the verb *are given* and answer the questions *when* and *where*. Other adverbial phrases will answer the questions *why*, *how*, *to what extent*, and *under what conditions*.

**2. Phrases Beginning with -ing and -ed Verbs**   The participial phrase begins with a verb form ending in *ing* in the present and *ed* or *t* in the past. Participial phrases always function as adjectives.

> *Having treated the patient*, the doctor closed her bag and left the room. (participial phrase modifying *doctor*)
>
> *Penned in by his thoughtless owners*, the dog became extremely vicious. (participial phrase modifying *dog*)
>
> The threatening letter *sent by the accused* was used as evidence in the murder trial. (participial phrase modifying *letter*)

Sometimes the participial phrase begins with a verb form that has a vowel change.

> *Drunk with power*, the General issued an ultimatum. (participial phrase modifying *General*)

Note: When participles appear with *helping words* like is, was, were and have, has, had, they function as *integral* parts of the verb:

> Father *is coming* home.
>
> The apartment *was rented* yesterday.
>
> I *have spent* my last dime on you.

**3. Phrases Beginning with -ing Words as Nouns**   The gerund phrase, like the present participle, begins with a verb form ending in *ing*; but unlike the participle, it is *always* used as a noun. Therefore the gerund phrase may serve as either the subject or the object of a sentence.

> *Skiing on ice* is very dangerous. (gerund phrase used as a subject, answering the question "What is dangerous?")

> The teacher dislikes *listening to lame excuses*. (gerund phrase used as an object, answering the question "dislikes what"?)

Remember, words ending in *ing* and answering the questions *who* or *what* are gerunds functioning as subjects or objects of sentences.

**4. Phrases with Infinitives**   The infinitive phrase begins with an infinitive—a verb preceded by the word *to*—and functions as a noun, an adjective, or an adverb.

> *To please everyone in the room* would be an impossible task. (infinitive phrase functioning as the subject)

> We were gathered together *to hear the election results*. (infinitive phrase used as an adverb answering the question *why*)

> He gave us permission *to begin our work*. (infinitive phrase used as an adjective modifying *permission*)

> We planned *to leave as soon as possible*. (infinitive phrase used as a direct object)

## Exercise 2.2 — Recognizing Phrases

In the following sentences identify the type of phrase in italics by using the following initials in the blank (or on a separate sheet):

| | |
|---|---|
| *prep.* for prepositional | *ger.* for gerund |
| *part.* for participial | *inf.* for infinitive |

EXAMPLE:   I hate *standing in line*.       Ger.

The house *on the left* has been sold.       Prep.

**1.** Bob wants *to tour Europe next year*.       *in fin*

**2.** I enjoy ice skating *on the frozen canal in Ottawa*.       *prep.*

**3.** *Before the math quiz*, we reviewed our notes in the library.       *prep.*

**4.** The woman *wearing the blue skirt* is my sister.       *part.*

**5.** *Running five miles every day* is quite an achievement.       *ger.*

**6.** *To eliminate acid rain* will cost hundreds of millions of dollars.  *infin.*

**7.** Betty's greatest thrill was *piloting a jet plane*.  *ger*

**8.** The dinner rolls, *purchased yesterday*, are already stale.  *part.*

**9.** *Writing well* is always a difficult task.  *ger*

**10.** My classmates eat their lunch *before noon every day*.  *prep*

**11.** *Surprised by the expensive gift*, Sheila was at a loss for words.  *part.*

**12.** *Taking music lessons* was not what Carl had in mind.

**13.** The warehouse *near the railroad tracks* burned down last night  *prep.*

**14.** *Worn by a world famous model*, the designer jeans were an instant success.

**15.** We enjoyed *skiing with Pat and Frank*.

**16.** The man *sitting by the exit sign* is my stepfather.

**17.** Our cat ran *after a field mouse yesterday*.

**18.** Pete certainly enjoys *swimming in his backyard pool*.

**19.** The workers decided *to join the local craft union*.

**20.** *After staying awake all night with a raging toothache*, Claudia was completely exhausted.

**21.** *To win at chess* one must concentrate intensely.

**22.** *Sought by the police in two provinces*, the criminal left the country.

**23.** *Baking award-winning pies* was Martha's claim to fame.

**24.** Susan studied all summer *to compete for the French language scholarship*.

**25.** *Frustrated by his slow start*, Don quit the race after only three laps.

**26.** The large house *near the lake* was sold yesterday.

**27.** *Learning computer programming* was Sylvia's year-long project.

**28.** *To start his own business* remains my brother's burning amibition.

**29.** The hockey puck rolled *into the net*.

**30.** The city of Quebec decided *to host the winter games*.

# E. EXPANDING WITH CLAUSES

Like phrases, clauses are groups of related words, and some function as a single part of speech; but unlike phrases, they have both a subject and a verb. There are two kinds of clauses: independent (or main) and dependent (or subordinate). An independent clause contains a complete thought and therefore stands alone. It may consist of simply a subject and a verb—*Students study*—or it may contain modifiers—Some *students study* very hard. An independent clause, then, is just another way of defining a simple sentence.

A dependent clause, on the other hand, does not stand alone. Although containing a subject and a verb, it begins with a relative pronoun (*whom, who, which, that*) or a subordinate conjunction (*if, as, since, because, while, when,* etc.) that makes it dependent upon the main clause.

> Jack fought a battle *that he couldn't win*.
>
> Martha, *who just celebrated her sixty-fifth birthday*, is now jogging around the block.
>
> *Since Peter is arriving late*, we shall start dinner without him.

Because dependent clauses function as single parts of speech, they can be divided into adjective, adverbial, and noun clauses.

**1. Clauses as Adjectives**   An adjective clause, like an adjective, modifies a noun or pronoun, and is usually introduced by a relative pronoun.

> Jim is the student *who has been nominated for an academic award*. (adjective clause modifying *student*)
>
> Mr. Flynn, *who has just been appointed Principal*, was one of my former teachers. (adjective clause modifying *Mr. Flynn*)
>
> The new car *that is parked in my driveway* belongs to my brother. (adjective clause modifying *car*)

**2. Clauses as Adverbs**   An adverb clause can modify a verb, an adjective, or another adverb, and it is usually introduced by a subordinate conjunction. An adverb clause will answer the questions *when, where, why, how, to what extent*, and *under what conditions*.

> He has not eaten anything *since his dog was killed by a car*. (adverb clause answering the question *when*)
>
> Marianne cannot take us to dinner *because she spent all her money*. (adverb clause answering the question *why*)
>
> The injured basketball player looked *as if she were going to faint*. (adverb clause answering the question *how did she look*)

3. **Clauses as Nouns**   A noun clause functions like a noun or pronoun, and can therefore be the subject, object, or subject-complement of a sentence. The major difference between noun clauses and other dependent clauses is that, in most cases, you cannot remove the noun clause and still have an intelligible sentence.

> *That he could play any position on the field* was obvious. (noun clause functioning as the subject)

> We suggested *that he write his final essay*. (noun clause functioning as the object)

> The indisputable fact is *that we lost money last year*. (noun clause functioning as a subject complement)

Note: A subject complement always relates back to the subject and usually follows linking verbs such as *is, was, were, seem, become* and *appear*.

> I will invest in *whatever company I think will make money*. (noun clause functioning as an object of a preposition)

Observe that in each case the noun clause is indispensable for the complete meaning of the sentence.

## Exercise 2.3 − Identifying Clauses

Identify the italicized dependent clauses below by writing their functions in the blanks at the right (or on a separate sheet of paper): *N* for Noun Clause, *Adj.* for Adjective Clause, and *Adv.* for Adverb Clause.

EXAMPLE:   I saw John enter the building *as I turned the corner.* _____Adv._____

> *That she will win the final match* is beyond question. _____N_____

1. *After I finished the test*, I went to the student lounge. _adv._

2. The mechanic *who repaired my car* was a former student. _adv._

3. We think *that nuclear war is suicide*. _N._

4. *What we accomplished* is beyond belief. _____

5. *Before you start your car*, be sure to fasten your seatbelt. _adj_

6. The carpenter *who repaired our coffee table* is a first-rate tennis player. _adj._

7. Mr. Zuccarelli bought the truck *that we traded in last year*. _adj_

8. *When our basketball team scored in the last two seconds of the game*, the fans went wild. _adv._

**9.** Tony Woo, *who is our computer programmer*, has won another science award.

*adj*

**10.** *If our company cannot meet the deadline*, we will surely lose the contract.

*adv*

**11.** I believe *that it is your serve*.

**12.** We will repair your television set *as soon as the parts arrive*.

**13.** *That our City Council will meet its civic responsibilities* is beyond question.

**14.** We are not interested in *what her religious beliefs are at the moment*.

**15.** Our school ordered ten dozen arborite tables *that were made in Poland*.

**16.** *When Michael entered the room*, everyone stood at attention.

**17.** *If you do not participate in class discussions*, you will be given a written examination.

**18.** I am certain *that we are scheduled for our field trip tomorrow*.

**19.** Lift the crystal punch bowl off the table *as gently as you can*.

**20.** The red and white convertible *that was in the major accident* is still being driven.

**21.** We are certain *that Helen can still win the academic prize*.

**22.** I arrived at the committee meeting *as soon as I could*.

**23.** Jack White, *who owns the corner grocery store*, was robbed last night.

**24.** Who knows *what his position will be on this issue*?

**25.** Victoria, B.C. is one city *that I want to revisit*.

**26.** The fire started *after we left the room*.

**27.** *That he will win the mathematics scholarship* is almost guaranteed.

**28.** Fred Vandergriffe, *who has recently joined our faculty*, is a former chess champion.

**29.** *Whoever is responsible for our delay* should be disciplined.

**30.** We did not attend the company picnic *because our supervisor made us work over the weekend*.

## Exercise 2.4 — Developing the Subject-Verb Structure

In each of the following sentences, expand the subject-verb structure by adding appropriate phrases and clauses. Use as many kinds of phrases and clauses as you can, but be sure the meaning is clear and logical.

EXAMPLES:   John faced the jury.
(*To hear the verdict*, John faced the jury.)

Michelle left the room.
(Michelle, *having finished her lunch*, left the room.)

He is sure.
(He is sure *that he knows who caused the accident*.)

The boat has already been sold.
(The boat *that Jim wanted to purchase* has already been sold.)

1. Nuclear war will destroy the planet.

2. Baseball is my favourite sport.

3. I feel wonderful.

4. Please review my notes.

5. Michelle finally sold her painting.

6. I forgot to lock the car door.

7. Our cities have high teenage unemployment.

8. We visited Nova Scotia last summer.

9. Sam forgot his lunch.

10. The game finally began.

11. Acid rain is killing our lakes.

12. Wait until the fire alarm stops ringing.

13. Our Trivial Pursuit game lasted three hours.

14. The auction sale was disappointing.

15. Write legibly.

16. Don't sell your stocks and bonds.

17. Our hockey team is unmotivated.

18. Frank sold his truck.

19. Toronto is now my home.

20. Our college renovated its library.

21. Stay away from hazardous waste.

22. Use the proper tools.

**23.** Carol went sailing with Peter.

**24.** My golf game has improved.

**25.** Everyone must pay his or her own way.

**26.** You may walk on the grass.

**27.** Fred finally took guitar lessons.

**28.** Alice flunked her sociology examination.

**29.** Our reading conference was held in Montreal.

**30.** Be ready when I call.

## F. TROUBLE-SHOOTING SENTENCES

Fragmentary and run-together sentences are caused by the improper use of clauses and phrases. These sentences are written when we do not quite know what we want to say or how we want to say it. Thus our sentences contain illogical and rambling statements that lead nowhere. However, by thinking before we write, and by paying proper attention to the subject-verb structure that expresses action and thought, we can avoid these awkward construction errors.

1. **Mending Fragments**    Fragments, as the name implies, are incomplete units of thought that cannot logically stand alone. Grammatically, they may be defined as dependent clauses and phrases (usually verbal phrases) that are expressed as if they were complete thoughts, and written as if they were complete sentences. There are two common types of fragments:

   (a) Dependent-Clause Fragments

   I stayed home from work yesterday. *Because I was sick.*

   Tom's new car was given to him by his uncle. *Who, I understand, is very rich.*

   Susan learned to play the piano. *When she was very young.*

   (b) Verbal-Phrase Fragment

   He was left without any money. *Having spent his last dime on a new guitar.*

   Karen was a potential heart-attack victim. *Being constantly frustrated and frequently overworked.*

   *Knowing how to win at cards.* He became a professional gambler.

Remember, a fragment cannot stand alone because it has no verb. Therefore, when proofreading, make sure you can identify the subject-verb construction that carries the meaning of each sentence.

Remember, too, that *ing* words, like *being, coming, having, doing, going,* etc., cannot stand alone as verbs without being supported by a form of the verb to be: *is, are, am, was, were*.

**2. Mending Run-Together Sentences**   Run-together sentences occur when two or more independent clauses are joined together without proper coordination or punctuation. The result is that two complete thoughts improperly overlap. The most obvious run-together mistake is the fused sentence containing two independent clauses without any punctuation.

> Jack lost his textbook/ that is why he failed the test.
>
> Our history teacher enjoys tennis/ her husband enjoys golf.

The run-together sentence, however, is most often written as a comma splice, in which two independent clauses are incorrectly separated by a comma.

> Jack lost his textbook, that is why he failed the test.
>
> Our history teacher enjoys tennis, her husband enjoys golf.

Run-together sentences are corrected in one of four ways, depending upon the relationship between the independent clauses.

(a) With a period when each clause is sufficiently independent from the other:

> My father works for a tool company. The tools he makes are of the highest quality.

(b) With a semi-colon when there is an implied connection between the independent statements:

> Mike hits baseballs with power; Jack hits them with ease.

(c) With a conjunctive adverb when you want to emphasize the specific nature of the relationship:

> Jane has to work overtime; therefore, she will be late for dinner.

Note: The conjunctive adverb is still preceded by a semi-colon to properly separate the independent statements.

(d) With a coordinate conjunction when the relationship between the two clauses is close, obvious, and logical:

> My uncle is a doctor, and my nephew is a pharmacist.

Note: The coordinate conjunction must be preceded by a comma when it connects two independent clauses.

Remember, however, that when an independent clause can more logically be subordinated, write the sentence with one dependent clause.

*Because my uncle was a doctor*, my nephew became a pharmacist.

## Exercise 2.5 − Detecting Fragments

Identify the fragments in each sentence below by writing *F* in the blank to the right or on a separate sheet of paper. If the sentence is complete write *C*.

**1.** Writing to express ourselves is an important activity. ⎯⎯⎯⎯⎯

**2.** Because it allows us to personalize knowledge. ⎯⎯⎯⎯⎯

**3.** It may also develop our critical faculties. ⎯⎯⎯⎯⎯

**4.** By allowing us to explore new ideas and areas of speculation. ⎯⎯⎯⎯⎯

**5.** Writing to explore, then, can be an important part of self-expression. ⎯⎯⎯⎯⎯

**6.** It may even be an essential step in our intellectual development. ⎯⎯⎯⎯⎯

**7.** Writing this way obliges us to put new ideas into our own words. ⎯⎯⎯⎯⎯

**8.** Which are added to and combined with our existing body of knowledge. ⎯⎯⎯⎯⎯

**9.** We are then able to discover what we know. ⎯⎯⎯⎯⎯

**10.** And more importantly, what we don't know. ⎯⎯⎯⎯⎯

**11.** This knowledge eventually leads to self-realization. ⎯⎯⎯⎯⎯

**12.** Making us more aware of our relationship to the world around us. ⎯⎯⎯⎯⎯

**13.** Finally, we develop our potential to become independent learners. ⎯⎯⎯⎯⎯

**14.** And creative problem solvers. ⎯⎯⎯⎯⎯

●　●　●

**1.** Teaching report writing can be simple and effective. ⎯⎯⎯⎯⎯

**2.** If an example-oriented approach is used. ⎯⎯⎯⎯⎯

**3.** In this approach, students are given laboratory reports with varying degrees of completeness. ⎯⎯⎯⎯⎯

**4.** The degree of completeness decreases with each successive experiment. ⎯⎯⎯⎯⎯

5. With each report serving as an example for the completion of the next laboratory report. _____

6. Thus the student is asked to complete a portion of his next report. _____

7. Using the first report as his model. _____

8. This process continues until the last few reports are reached. _____

9. At which time the student is asked to complete these reports completely on his own. _____

10. This approach ensures that the student learns by example. _____

11. Rather than being told by an instructor what he has done wrong. _____

12. Time is saved not only for the instructor but also for the student. _____

13. Furthermore, educational objectives are not sacrificed. _____


## Exercise 2.6 – Correcting Run-Together Sentences

Indicate which of the sentences below are run-together by writing *R*. Then correct the sentence by adding the proper punctuation or conjunction. If the sentence is correct, write *C*.

EXAMPLE: The men and women were working in the fields, and the children were picking strawberries. _____R_____

Every minute is important; every hour is crucial. _____R_____

She made the appointment, but she forgot to tell me. _____C_____

1. Here comes the store manager, she will tell us where to cash our cheque. _____

2. Sam drove the pick-up truck, and Phil followed him in our family car. _____

3. Our city applied for a Wintario grant, however its application was denied. _____

4. History is an important subject, I find it fascinating. _____

5. We searched long and hard for qualified computer programmers, but we couldn't find any. _____

6. We have a swimming pool on our property we also have tennis courts. _____

7. Please turn off the television set, there is nothing on that is worth watching. _____

8. The bank teller made a mistake she gave me too much money. _____

9. Our living quarters were extremely cramped; nevertheless we stayed for two nights. _____

10. When I saw the storm approaching I ran for shelter; however, I was too slow and was caught in the downpour. _____

11. The Prime Minister of Canada is leaving for England next week, he will meet the British Prime Minister. _____

12. Please turn in your reports this Friday, I intend to mark them over the weekend. _____

13. That gray automobile is not mine, nor is it Susan's, it must be Lorraine's. _____

14. George bought an electric guitar, but his mother made him sell it. _____

15. Our corn crop is small this year, perhaps we haven't had enough spring rain. _____

16. She could never succeed at tennis, however hard she tried. _____

17. The team does not need a new locker room it needs a better coach. _____

18. While reviewing last year's budget, Harold discovered a serious error that bordered on criminal negligence. _____

19. The men brought the food the women brought the eating utensils. _____

20. I cannot drive more than three hours at a time, for some reason my left leg develops a cramp. _____

21. The library closes at 9:00 p.m., however, it opens again at 8:00 a.m. _____

22. Seven students failed the final examinations, they will have to repeat the course. _____

23. Nathalie received a traffic ticket because her car's left turn signal was not working. _____

24. Chalk and erasers are not needed, we will use an overhead projector and a flip chart. _____

25. What do you think of our plan should we alter it in any way? _____

26. Alice reported in sick, therefore we shall continue without her. _____

**27.** Wanting to get more studying done, Jim locked himself in his room for three hours.  _____

**28.** Joy's Meat Market is now located near the river, the owner moved his store last week.  _____

**29.** The city was devastated by an earthquake, but its citizens are determined to rebuild it from the rubble.  _____

**30.** You help the children, I'll call the fire department.  _____

## Exercise 2.7 – Revising Sentences in the Paragraph

Rewrite the following paragraphs by correcting the sentence fragments and run-together errors. Be prepared to add or subtract punctuation and coordinating conjunctions.

Education is generally regarded as an experience that happens at a specified time in someone's life—and then recedes. It is too often considered an institutional process. Providing us with certain definable skills that are directly associated with a specific occupation or a certain social status. Thus, for many of us, education becomes an outside activity. With measurable benefits and rewards.

However, education's true nature is quite different, it is, in fact, an internal human function. One that implies intellectual and emotional growth. If we can think of it as an expansive process that allows us to deal thoughtfully with our culture and society. We will appreciate its dynamism. For if education means anything, it means change. It means a continuous interaction—a creative interaction—between man and his global environment. Therefore, in this context, we must not think of ourselves (educated people) as merely adapting to a patterned society. As if our culture were fixed and rigid—as if it were perfect, instead of perfectable.

What, then, are the real qualities and consequences of education? Well, for one, it is uncomfortable, for it never settles down. It calls up a seemingly infinite number of questions that do not have simple, quantifiable answers, it almost never provides but always demands. It suspects certainty, rejects equivocation, and resists conformity it is, at best, disquieting and, at worst, frustrating and annoying.

In view of these qualities, it follows that educated people are never really satisfied. They are never, finally, at peace within their surroundings. Because they are constantly changing. Through the absorption of new and diverse ideas and perceptions, they seek meaningful relationships between different branches of knowledge. They are not interested in simply acquiring bits of information, but in testing ideas, nor are they content with adapting to a specific societal value system, but with developing their own values. Consistent with the larger reality of the global human family.

From this brief overview of the qualities of education, it can be seen that the phrase "getting an education" can never be transitional or confined to a certain period of time "education" is a word for all seasons and for all the ages of humanity.

# G. VARIETY IN SENTENCE PATTERNS

Different combinations of dependent and independent clauses make up four basic sentence patterns: the simple, the compound, the complex, and the compound-complex. Learning when to use these different sentences will make your writing more flexible and emphatic. Depending upon what you want to say and how you want to say it, you will use each pattern for different reasons.

**1. Simple Sentence**  A simple sentence is the clearest, most direct self-supporting statement that one can make. It consists of only one independent clause, which may be long or short, and which may contain more than one subject and more than one verb. But however long, it must have only one subject-verb combination and make only one statement in order to be classified as a simple sentence.

> **Birds** *fly*.
>
> Many **birds** *fly* south in the winter.
>
> **Jack** and **Dan** study together. (compound subject)
>
> Steve *washes* and *dries* the dishes. (compound verb)
>
> **Yvette** and **Renée** *live* and **work** together. (compound subject and verb)

All of the above sentences are simple because they contain one idea. Do not be misled by a sentence with many modifiers; if it has a single subject-verb combination and says only one thing, it must be simple.

> After our long and arduous journey, **we** finally *found* the ancient city, shining in all its glory.

**2. Compound Sentence**  A compound sentence consists of a grouping of two or more independent clauses usually joined by a coordinate conjunction (and, or, nor, for, so, but) or a conjunctive adverb (however, therefore, moreover, etc.—see p. 106 for a complete list of conjunctive adverbs). Each clause must bear equal weight in order for the sentence to be properly balanced.

> (Bob won the bronze medal in the track meet), but (Jim won the silver).
>
> (Linda won the bronze medal); however, (Catherine won the silver).

Note: A comma precedes the coordinate conjunction, and a semi-colon precedes the conjunctive adverb (see pp. 87 and 106).

When two independent clauses are closely related, a semi-colon may be used to separate them.

> (Bob took notes); (Tom outlined the chapter).
>
> (Mike made the beds); (his wife did the laundry).

Remember, compound sentences must contain at least two subject-verb combinations that can be broken into simple sentences when the connectives are removed.

(He wanted to be a salesman), but (he became an accountant).

(Students may drop one subject); however, (they must inform the Registrar).

**3. Complex Sentence**  A complex sentence consists of one independent clause and one or more dependent clauses. Unlike compound sentences, complex sentences not only group statements but also indicate their order of importance. They inform the reader which statement carries more weight.

(When Deborah arrived), *Mario took the roast out of the oven.* (The second statement contains the action; the first statement merely introduces it.)

*The caretaker* (who found the diamond ring) *was given a generous reward,* (which he immediately spent). (The statements within the parentheses merely modify the words *caretaker* and *reward* in the independent clause.)

**4. Compound-Complex Sentence**  As its name implies, a compound-complex sentence has at least two independent clauses and one dependent clause. This type of sentence provides you with the greatest flexibility. It allows you not only to express ideas of equal significance but also to include other subordinate relationships within the structure of the sentence.

(Unless we improve the quality of our acting), *the director will hire new actors and actresses, or the producer will withdraw his money from the show.*

*The pub opened on time,* and *the waiters were at their stations*; however, *the customers refused to enter* (when they saw the pickets parading outside).

## Exercise 2.8 – Recognizing Sentence Patterns

Identify each of the following sentences by writing one of the following abbreviations in the blank at the right or on a separate sheet:

S—Simple                                    Cx—Complex
Cd—Compound                          Cd-Cx—Compound-Complex

EXAMPLE:   During the music recital my sister became ill
                    and had to leave.                                                          S

**1.** We found the lost camera, but we could not find
    its expensive attachments.                                                    Cd

**2.** Don Hall works as a reporter for our local newspaper.    S

**3.** We finally relaxed after the election.                               S

4. Sheila will have to work long hours if she expects to earn a company bonus.

*Cx*

5. The football game ended, but the excited fans refused to leave the stadium.

*Cd*

6. Paula was surprised when she was elected to the student council.

*Scx*

7. The intense snowstorm delayed our flight, but we managed to check into a motel that was just one mile from the airport.

*Cd-Cx*

8. John Trask and Peter Soames cleaned and polished their new sports cars.

*S*

9. Turn left at the next traffic light; our office building is located on the corner.

*SCd-Cx*

10. Before you decide to buy a new car, please read the latest consumer reports; you may save yourself a great deal of time and trouble.

*Cd-Cx*
*S*

11. After the film we had dinner at an expensive restaurant.

*S*

12. We do not want special favours; we want only what is fair and equitable.

*Cd-Cx*

13. Tom is intellectually astute, but emotionally immature.

*Cd*

14. Please refrain from smoking in the restaurant.

*S*

15. Phil found an urgent message when he returned home last night.

*Cx*

16. When the janitor saw the smoke pouring from the basement window, he phoned the fire department; however, the firefighters arrived too late to save the building.

17. I don't care who wrote the letter; it is too long and ungrammatical.

18. Don't forget to feed our pet canary.

19. Last Saturday Steven mowed the lawn, trimmed the hedge, and washed the car.

20. Our school has a good academic reputation but a mediocre sports program.

21. If we cannot settle our differences without violence, then our so-called civilized society will not survive.

22. Our athletic club is now accepting new members; however, you have only one week to apply.

23. Tina's new car, which she purchased only last week, has faulty brakes and a leaky exhaust system.

**24.** My brother has just graduated from university; he earned an "A" average, which pleased my parents very much. _____

**25.** The motorcycle skidded on the gravel, knocked over a lawn chair, and tore up our flower garden. _____

**26.** Stan Wojek, to his credit, never overcharges his customers; that is why he has such a successful plumbing contracting business. _____

**27.** Chris and Don both swim and jog, but they do not enjoy team sports. _____

**28.** Calvin, who weighs only 95 pounds, is trying out for our football team. _____

**29.** Listening to classical music can be restful, if there are no distractions. _____

**30.** Our farm is losing money; therefore my father is selling it. _____

# H. COMBINING INTO PATTERNS

In order to use sentence patterns correctly, you must understand the logic of coordination and subordination. When you coordinate ideas or statements, you place them in equal relationship, and when you subordinate them, you assign one idea more significance than the other.

**1. Joining through Coordination**   Coordination is the skill of joining together similar ideas with coordinating conjunctions (and, or, but, etc.) or with correlative conjunctions (either—or; neither—nor; not only—but also; both—and).

Proper coordination eliminates choppy sentence structure and reveals the precise relationship between similar ideas.

|  |  |
|---|---|
| CHOPPY: | Bill Roberts is an athlete. He is a scholar. He is also a friend. |
| COORDINATED: | Bill Roberts is an athlete, a scholar, and a friend. |

|  |  |
|---|---|
| CHOPPY: | There are no classes held on Saturday. The school library is open until 5:00 p.m. Students may study there. |
| COORDINATED: | There are no classes held on Saturday, but the school library is open until 5:00 p.m. for students' convenience. |

Each part of the sentence that is coordinated should have the same grammatical structure: phrases with phrases, clauses with clauses, etc.

|  |  |
|---|---|
| AWKWARD: | A card-catalogue index file will not only help you find authors of books but also in finding subjects for term papers. |
| COORDINATED: | A card-catalogue index will *not only* help you find authors of books *but also* subjects for term papers. |

|  |  |
|---|---|
| AWKWARD: | He will either do as he is told or the boss will have to fire him. |
| COORDINATED: | He will *either* do as he is told *or* be fired. |

See Chapter 5D, Employing Parallel Forms, pp. 71-76, for more examples of proper coordination.

**2. Joining through Subordination**   A sentence with subordination contains one dominant idea that is modified by grammatically subordinate words, phrases and clauses. Therefore a subordinated sentence cannot have two equal parts, since it contains only one major idea.

Effective subordination eliminates wordiness and redundancy and reveals the logical relationship between unequal ideas.

|  |  |
|---|---|
| FAULTY: | Educational theory has changed in the last five years. Its change has been dramatic. |
| SUBORDINATED: | Educational theory has changed *dramatically* in the last five years. |
| FAULTY: | Our university is famous for its medical school. It has recently added a new school of International Relations. |
| SUBORDINATED: | Our university, *which is famous for its medical school*, has recently added a new school of International Relations. |

Effective subordination permits the reader to focus on the main idea of the sentence; it ensures him that the lesser ideas will be placed in dependent clauses or phrases.

|  |  |
|---|---|
| FAULTY: | When our new office building was completed, it was January, 1978. |
| SUBORDINATED: | Our new office building was completed in January, 1978. |
| FAULTY: | Threatening to call the police after the pickets locked the factory gates, the plant manager avoided a major crisis. |
| SUBORDINATED: | The plant manager avoided a major crisis when he threatened to call the police after the pickets locked the factory gates. |

The correct use of coordination or subordination is, finally, a matter of logic. If we think through our sentences carefully, we should know when to use two equal thoughts or one equal and one unequal thought; we should know which statements can be developed by dependent clauses and which cannot. And we should know how to place emphasis by using a series of independent clauses or a combination of dependent and independent clauses. In short, we should know how to project significance by recognizing the implicit logic of English sentence structure.

## Exercise 2.9 – Coordination

Correct the following sentences by eliminating unnecessary words or by using one of the following connectives: a coordinating conjunction, a correlative conjunction, or a conjunctive adverb.

EXAMPLE: English literature is my favourite subject. European history fascinates me.

CORRECTION: English literature is my favourite subject, *but* European history fascinates me.

1. Sue might be young. She is not immature.

2. We are reading short stories and essays, and we are also reading modern drama.

3. Our school has three separate buildings. Each building has its own cafeteria. There is only one library, though.

4. Tom must be a professional athlete, or else he is a health club instructor.

5. Kathy is a writer and an actress. She does not like being referred to as a movie star.

6. Our workers dug drainage ditches and they laid cement pipe. Then they repaired the overpass, and then they ate their lunch.

7. Our city is not only clean and attractive; it is prosperous as well.

8. My nephew is a famous athlete; he is also a radio sportscaster, too.

9. I was warned not to climb alone. I did, anyway, and I fell and broke my leg.

10. Her sister is not a fashion model; she is not an actress, either. She is a clothing designer in New York City.

11. The college basketball team will either practise on Thursday evening, or it will practise on Saturday afternoon.

12. I bought a new notebook, sharpened all my pencils, and I even turned my stereo off. I still have trouble writing, though.

13. We were told that the department store would be closed for inventory, and we were told to shop by using the mail-order catalogue. It opened earlier than expected because of customers' complaints.

14. Dick is neither a university professor, and he is certainly not a high-school teacher.

15. I planted flowers, mowed the lawn, and I even trimmed the hedges. My property still needs professional landscaping, though.

16. Doris must be a good writer, or else she is a plagiarist.

17. Our home might be old. It is not poorly constructed.

18. We were told to turn in our final essays on Friday. We ignored the deadline, and we were placed on academic probation.

**19.** Peggy cooked breakfast, and she fed the baby. Then she reviewed her notes, and she wrote her newspaper article.

**20.** I am neither angry and I am certainly not upset.

## Exercise 2.10 — Subordination

Rewrite the following sentences so that the main ideas are properly emphasized.

EXAMPLE:  After he fished for hours, Tom caught a ten-pound tuna.
*Tom caught a ten-pound tuna after fishing for hours.*

**1.** It destroyed more than fifty homes before the hurricane finally diminished.

**2.** Computer technology has advanced in the last five years. Its advances have been dramatic.

**3.** The last time Montreal had a major exposition it was 1967.

**4.** Our college has a modern gymnasium. It was used for a professional basketball game last winter.

**5.** When the allies finally landed on the Normandy beaches in France, it was June 6, 1944.

**6.** Sitting by my bedroom window on Friday afternoon, I saw the bomb explode.

**7.** Our community received a Wintario grant last year. We built an indoor ice-skating rink.

**8.** When Aunt Martha visited us last week, she arrived on a skateboard.

**9.** I hitchhiked through British Columbia last summer where I observed thousands of people protesting against the nuclear arms race.

**10.** Swimming in the lake without proper supervision, the young girl nearly drowned.

**11.** The river overflowed its banks. Its flow was swift and relentless.

**12.** Located in a valley, our trailer home was swept away by the surging waters.

**13.** Standing on a hillside overlooking the town, we saw the mudslide begin.

**14.** When my family moved to Halifax, Nova Scotia, it was 1965.

**15.** Our school once employed over twenty-five teachers. It will be closed down next week.

**16.** When our hockey coach wanted to teach us a lesson on teamwork, he benched our two best players.

**17.** While attaining a speed of more than 175 miles per hour, the experimental racing car blew a gasket and began smoking.

**18.** Sally was on a theatre tour in New York City when she saw an old lady being robbed by a gang of youths.

**19.** Having bought an old painting at an auction, Michael discovered that it was a masterpiece.

**20.** We were going to Cornwall on a field trip, when our school bus was hit in the rear by a tractor-trailer.

# CHAPTER THREE

# Checking for Agreement

## A. ENSURING SUBJECT-VERB AGREEMENT

Subject-verb agreement indicates the proper relationship between the form of the verb and its subject. The verb always agrees with its subject in person (first, second, third) and number (singular, plural). Because of the various ways of organizing sentences, subjects are often camouflaged by intervening phrases and inverted word order. Therefore, to avoid using the wrong verb, we must become adept at finding the subject. The following suggestions may help.

**1.** Watch out for modifying phrases beginning with prepositions like *on*, *of* or *in* that come between the subject and the verb.

> **A box** (of nails) *was* on the workbench.
>
> **One** (of the foobball players) *is* not on the bus.
>
> Only **one person** (in five) *knows* the name of the British Prime Minister.

**2.** Watch out for inverted sentences beginning with *there* and *here*.

> WRONG: There is a great many *people* at the game.
> CORRECTED: There are a great many people at the game.
>
> WRONG: Here is the most interesting *games* of chance.
> CORRECTED: Here are the most interesting games of chance.

Remember, *there* and *here* never serve as subjects of sentences.

**3.** Do not confuse the subject with the subject complement.

> His **primary concern** *was* the sick employees.
>
> Jack's **chief interest** *was* antique automobiles.
>
> My **favourite meal** *is* meat and potatoes.

**4.** Recognize singular subjects that appear to be plural.

> **Politics** *is* a popular sport in our community.
>
> **Economics** *is* not in our school calendar this semester.
>
> **Pediatrics** *is* a branch of medicine.

Remember, collective nouns take singular verbs when referring to a group as a single unit; however, when they refer to a group as a body of individual members, they take plural verbs.

> The **committee** *is submitting* its report. (used as a single unit)
>
> The **committee** *are working* in small groups. (used as a body of individual members)
>
> The **jury** *has* not *reached* a verdict. (used as a single unit)
>
> The **jury** *are* now *sealing* their votes in the jury room. (used as a body of individual members)

Logic should tell you when the collective noun is expressed as an indivisible whole; usually the word *members* is appended to the noun to indicate plurality: jury members; committee members; team members.

**5.** Singular subjects joined by *and* take plural verbs, but if they refer to the same thing, or function as a unit, they take singular verbs.

> A **pen** and a **pencil** *are* the tools of my trade.
>
> My best **friend and confidant** *has joined* the armed forces.
>
> **Law and order** *is* the issue.

**6.** Compound subjects with *each* or *every* take singular verbs.

> Each biology student, chemistry student, and physics student *is* responsible for his or her own lab equipment.
>
> Every blond, redhead and brunette *was* judged according to her talents, not her hair style.

**7.** Compound subjects joined by either . . . or; neither . . . nor take singular verbs when both subjects are singular, and they take plural verbs when both subjects are plural. When, however, one subject is singular and the other is plural, the verb agrees with the closer subject.

> Either **John** or **Mary** *is* chairing the meeting.
>
> Neither her **pies** nor her **cakes** *were given* prizes at the country fair.
>
> Either the principal or the **students** *control* the student council's budget.
>
> Neither the actors nor the **director** *was* satisfied with the stage lighting.

**8.** Single subjects with intervening phrases like *together with*, *along with*, *in addition to*, and *as well as* take singular verbs.

> **My sister**, along with her girlfriend, *is* going on the class picnic.
>
> **Tom's stereo**, as well as his car, *was* repossessed by the finance company.
>
> **Jack's notebook**, together with his history text, *was* stolen from his locker.

Note: the commas around these phrases always separate them from the subjects of the sentences.

**9.** When the subject is used as a title, it always takes a singular verb.

> Alfred Hitchcock's **The Birds** *is* coming to our local theatre next week.
>
> **The Russians** *was* an excellent television documentary.
>
> **Cats** *has been* one of the most successful Broadway musicals in the last 5 years.

## Exercise 3.1 — Making Subject and Verb Agree

Select the correct verb in each of the following sentences and write it in the blank at the right or on a separate sheet.

**1.** Neither of Paula's brothers (is/are) coming with us this evening.     *are*

**2.** The student counsellor, as well as the school principal, (was/were) given the award for excellence during our convocation.     *was*

**3.** Neither the nurses nor the doctor (is/are) responsible for hospital routine.     *are*

**4.** Each student, teacher, and administrator (favours/favour) the construction of a fully equipped gymnasium.     *favour*

**5.** There (was/were) discovered in the reading laboratory two comic books and a motorcycle maintenance manual.     *were*

**6.** In the center of the shopping plaza (is/are) a water fountain and a newspaper stand.     *is*

**7.** There certainly (is/are) more than one way to skin a cat.     *is*

**8.** The store's refrigerators, as well as its stoves, (come/comes) in a harvest-gold colour.     *come*

**9.** (Is/Are) *Julius Caesar* or *Antony and Cleopatra* scheduled for production this year?     *Are*

**10.** In our Canadian Literature course, Alice Munro, as well as Mordecai Richler, (is/are) on our reading list.     *are*

**11.** None of the students (was/were) sufficiently prepared for the examination.

*were*

**12.** The number of automobile accidents (has been/have been) increasing the last five years.

*has been*

**13.** Everyone who attended our school dance (was/were), I am certain, impressed by the rock band.

*was*

**14.** Sandra and I are among the few who (takes/take) studying seriously.

*take*

**15.** Anyone who thinks he or she (deserves/deserve) special consideration had better think again.

*deserves*

**16.** Participating in the essay contest (were/was) one of the members of the basketball team.

*were*

**17.** Neither my textbook nor my class notes (was/were) permitted in the test room.

*were*

**18.** *The Thorn Birds* (is/are) on my summer reading list.

*is*

**19.** Only one athlete in ten (require/requires) more than eight hours sleep.

*requires*

**20.** Bruno, together with his sister Frieda, (have/has) enrolled in the computer literacy course.

*has*

**21.** Neither Helen nor I (are/am) responsible for the broken desks in the classroom.

*are*

**22.** The Disciplinary Committee (are/is) meeting behind closed doors.

*is*

**23.** The concerns of the parents for traffic safety (reflect/reflects) our City Council's concerns.

*reflect*

**24.** Phil's patience, as well as his determination, (enable/enables) him to be a first-class chess player.

*enables*

**25.** Every man, woman, and child (has been/have been) given explicit instructions.

*has been*

**26.** We were told that either the Ottawa Rough Riders or the Hamilton Tiger Cats (was/were) scheduled to play in our stadium this Sunday.

*were*

**27.** Susan, together with her friend Leslie, (have/has) finally completed nursing training at our local community college.

*have*

**28.** Neither the convicts nor the prison administration (want/wants) additional security measures.

*want*

**29.** After a full day of minding little children, peace and quiet (is/are) all that Martha desires.

*are*

**30.** Anybody who anticipated an easy essay question on the test (were/was) certainly disappointed, to say the least.

*was*

# B. PRONOUNS AGREEING WITH NOUNS

A pronoun must agree with the word it stands for (its antecedent) in person, gender, and number.

**1. Person: Watch *You*** Agreement in person errors almost always occur with the incorrect use of the pronoun *you* or its possessive, *your*.

> INCORRECT:   If anyone has to leave the room *you* had better leave now.
> CORRECT:   If *anyone* has to leave the room, *he* or *she* had better leave now.

> INCORRECT:   When I first arrived on campus, I was told that *your* student fees helped to defray the cost of the school newspaper.
> CORRECT:   When I first arrived on campus, I was told that *my* student fees helped to defray the cost of the school newspaper.

**2. Gender: Guidelines for *He* and *She*** For the most part, establishing the correct gender for a pronoun does not present a problem to native English speakers. Since the use of masculine or feminine pronouns is properly reserved for people, you simply have to identify the person being referred to and your problems are solved.

However, a difficulty does arise when you wish to refer to any unspecified or hypothetical person. In the recent past it was considered correct to refer to such persons by the pronouns *he*, *him*, *his*. Used in this manner, these pronouns were considered to refer to both men and women.

This usage is still considered to be correct and is used by many writers. However, many other, equally careful, writers feel that the use of the masculine pronoun as a "generic" pronoun creates a sex bias in their writing. They avoid using the "generic" pronoun by using *he or she/his or her* constructions; by pluralizing the referent and using *they*, *their*, *theirs*; and by rewording sentences to avoid pronoun use altogether.

The following examples demonstrate these different responses to the problem of pronoun gender.

Each member of the class must have all of his assignments turned in before he receives a final mark.

Each member of the class must have all of his or her assignments turned in before he or she receives a final mark.

All members of class must have all of their assignments turned in before they receive their final mark.

The student who left his books in the cafeteria must claim them before he leaves school.

The student who left his or her books in the cafeteria must claim them before he or she leaves school.

A child in nursery school may not be able to feed and dress himself.

A child in nursery school may not be able to eat or get dressed without help.

**3. Number: Some Rules about Singulars and Plurals** The rules for pronoun agreement in number are basically the same as those for subject-verb agreement. Therefore, a brief review should suffice.

(a) Single antecedents take singular pronouns; plural antecedents take plural pronouns.

> A few of the workers took *their* (not *his*) grievances to the supervisor.
>
> Any student who jogs near the construction site must watch *his or her* (not *their*) step.

(b) A collective noun expressed as a single unit takes a singular pronoun; collective nouns expressed as a group of individual members take a plural pronoun.

> The committee argued for hours, but could not decide how to make *their* (not *its*) recommendations public.
>
> The basketball team won *its* (not *their*) first game last Saturday.

(c) Singular antecedents connected by *or*, *nor*, or *but* take singular pronouns; however, when one is singular and the other plural, the pronoun agrees with the closer antecedent.

> Neither John nor Peter was asked to present *his* (not *their*) report to the class.
>
> Either the supervisor or the workers will win *their* (not *his*) grievance.

(d) In formal English indefinite pronouns like either, neither, anyone, everyone, someone, each, every and somebody take singular pronouns.

> Neither of the workers earned *his* (not *their*) salary last week.
>
> Everyone in class must buy *his or her* (not *their*) own lab manual.
>
> Somebody has left *his* (not *their*) jacket in the gym.

Remember, if you are not sure whether a pronoun should be singular or plural, locate the verb; it will usually reveal the number of the pronoun.

> The team *is ready* for its first game.
>
> Someone in the auditorium *has left* his or her car lights on.
>
> Neither the teacher nor the students *have agreed* on their debating topic.

## Exercise 3.2 — Making Pronouns Agree with Nouns

Select the correct pronoun in the following sentences and write it in the blank at the right or on a separate sheet. Where possible, reword the sentence to avoid the pronoun problem.

1. The technology class is trying to arrange (its/their) field trip next week.  _____

2. Anyone who wants to attend the concert this Saturday should purchase (his/their) own ticket.  _____

3. The young camper was told that (you/he) had to get up at 6:00 a.m. and make (his/your) own bed.  _____

4. Everyone in the lecture hall was asked to turn in (their/his or her) test booklet when leaving the room.  _____

5. Any actress not presently employed will receive (their/her) audition card tomorrow.  _____

6. Mr. Johnson, along with his fellow workers, was asked to contribute some of (their/his) free time to work on the United Fund drive.  _____

7. After debating with one another for hours, the team could not decide on (their/its) strategy for the next game.  _____

8. Anyone who does not wish to participate in the touch-football game will be asked to arrange (their/his or her) own transportation to our annual picnic.  _____

9. Everyone but Frank completed (their/his) two-mile run this morning.  _____

10. Neither of the lawyers could account for (their/her) client's whereabouts last Tuesday.  _____

11. Neither the sales agent nor the buyers could get (their/his) price for the merchandise.  _____

12. The rules covering student behaviour can be found in (its/their) entirety in the Student Handbook.  _____

13. No member of the teaching staff will be permitted to take (his or her/their) holidays in the fall.  _____

14. Our school's hockey team lost (their/its) final game.  _____

15. Both Jan and Carol received (their/her) scholastic award at the banquet last night.  _____

16. Each member of the audience must watch (their/his or her) TV monitor for the applause sign.  _____

17. Neither the department manager nor her staff members expected (their/her) budget to be slashed.  _____

18. Those who want to use our houseboat next weekend must pay (his/their) share of the rent.  _____

19. As I entered the bank, the sign directed (you/me) to follow the painted arrows on the floor.  _____

**20.** If anyone wishes to enjoy (himself/themselves/theirselves),
(he/they) should visit Banff National Park. _____

**21.** Every member of the school band received (his or her/their)
due recognition as a qualified musician. _____

**22.** Nobody would refuse if (he or she/they) were offered a
chance to attend the winter Olympic Games. _____

**23.** The *Ottawa Citizen* assigned (its/their) most experienced
journalist to the kidnapping story. _____

**24.** Either of my classmates will be happy to lend you (their/his)
biology notes. _____

**25.** When I joined the exercise program, I was told that (you/I)
had to have a gym suit and cushioned running shoes. _____

**26.** Neither the arbitrator nor the union members could submit (his/their) salary recommendations before the strike
deadline. _____

**27.** The student body will choose (its/their) next president
tomorrow. _____

**28.** The jury (have been/has been) deliberating for three days. _____

**29.** Our school principal, together with her academic chairmen,
will be submitting (her/their) budget recommendations to
the Board of Governors next week. _____

**30.** Every team member will memorize (his/their) blocking
assignments by tomorrow. _____

## Exercise 3.3 − Review of Agreement

Choose the correct verb and pronoun in each of the following sentences and write
them in the blanks at the right or on a separate sheet.

EXAMPLE:  The news of John's defection from the football team (were/was)
known by the time the team played (their/its) first game.

|  | **P** | **V** |
|---|---|---|
|  | its | was |

**1.** Someone is in the auditorium; it sounds as
if (they/he) (is/are) bouncing a basketball. _____  _____

**2.** The teacher will tutor any member of
the class who (wants/want) to improve
(their/his or her) math score. _____  _____

**3.** Our purchasing department (was/were)
working ten-hour days since (its/their)
budget was slashed twenty per cent. _____  _____

**4.** One of the weather forecasters in our meteorological section (predict/predicts) that (their/his) function will be taken over by the new weather satellite.      —————   —————

**5.** Either Lisa or Marie will sponsor the new legislation when (they/she) (returns/return) home from the West Coast.      —————   —————

**6.** A book of lottery tickets (were/was) lost in the men's locker room. (They/it) should be taken to the lost and found department.      —————   —————

**7.** Neither Peter nor Vincent (is/are) aware that (he/they) won lottery prizes.      —————   —————

**8.** Any person in our department who (exceed/exceeds) the speed limit will have (their/his or her) driver's licence revoked.      —————   —————

**9.** Both Clarence and George thought that (he/they) (were/was) refused membership in the country club because of racial discrimination.      —————   —————

**10.** Common sense, as well as decisiveness, (is/are) necessary for someone to do (his/their) job properly in our organization.      —————   —————

**11.** If either our teacher or our administrators (fail/fails) to take into account (his/their) academic responsibilities, then our class will not be prepared for the competition in the technology fair.      —————   —————

**12.** Among Kelly's favourite films (are/is) *Star Wars* and *Raiders of the Lost Ark*; she has seen (them/it) many times.      —————   —————

**13.** A string of firecrackers (was/were) found in the classroom, but none of our students was responsible for (their/its) presence.      —————   —————

**14.** Dr. Slaughter is one of those people who (enjoys/enjoy) both jazz and country music for (its/their) unique appeal to different ethnic and racial backgrounds.      —————   —————

**15.** (Was/were) there further recommendations by anyone at the meeting who wanted (their/his or her) views known to the safety committee?      —————   —————

16. Everyone must write a final examination if (they/he or she) (expect/expects) to get credit for the course.

  _____  _____

17. Joan is one employee in ten who (listens/ listen) carefully to the instructions given to (them/her) by the plant supervisor.

  _____  _____

18. The college camera club (are/is) meeting next week to discuss (its/their) budget.

  _____  _____

19. No one has experienced frustration until (they/he or she) (try/tries) to learn the sport of golf.

  _____  _____

20. Each of my nephews (live/lives) in a different Canadian city, but (he/they) will return to Ottawa for our family reunion.

  _____  _____

21. Our English teacher, along with several of her students, (are/is) decorating (her/ their) classroom for the crafts display next Monday.

  _____  _____

22. There (wasn't/weren't) anyone in the football stadium who did not receive (his or her/their) free bumper sticker.

  _____  _____

23. Our neighbour, in addition to several other residents, (belong/belongs) to the Neighbourhood Watch Committee, and each person is assigned (their/his or her) specific area.

  _____  _____

24. Neither the firefighter nor the building supervisor (was/were) aware that (he/they) did not have the correct key to the garage where the fire was located.

  _____  _____

25. Both Kim and her sister's friend, Beverly, (was/were) certain that (she/they) were going to receive athletic scholarships.

  _____  _____

26. Each doctor, nurse, and laboratory assistant (wear/wears) (their/his or her) own radiation suit when working in the nuclear medicine laboratory.

  _____  _____

27. Each of our new sales girls (performs/ perform) (their/her) job with enthusiasm and good will.

  _____  _____

**28.** Neither Bill nor I (are/am) sure that both
Denise and Jo Anne will pay for (their/
her) own lunch.

_____    _____

**29.** Every citizen in our community who (fail/
fails) to register to vote by next Tuesday
will receive a telephone call at (their/his
or her) residence by one of our volunteers.

_____    _____

**30.** The jury (are/is) in closed session and
won't announce (their/its) verdict until at
least next Monday.

_____    _____

## Exercise 3.4 – Revising the Paragraph for Agreement

Rewrite the following paragraphs by correcting the noun-pronoun/verb-subject
agreement errors.

Since the invention of the atomic bomb, control of nuclear weapons have
become not only desirable but absolutely essential. In the past, any nation at
war were able to kill their enemy without physically affecting the rest of the
world. After all, since the end of the Second World War there has been quite
a few small-scale wars around the globe, and anyone not directly affected
hardly suffered at all: their lifestyle did not radically change; their social
environment remained relatively stable; and they were able to do business as
usual. Our response to these wars—from the war in Vietnam to the Falkland
Islands—were generally revulsion and disgust at the obscenity of someone
slaughtering their fellow man. But at the same time everyone knew that so
long as these wars were restricted to conventional weapons, they were
relatively safe—that the bombs, land mines, and artillery shells, along with
the new Exocet missile, was capable of devastating only a limited geographical
area.

With the proliferation of nuclear weapons, however, the odds against a
small war being limited is lowering. Too many nations are storing nuclear
weapons. Too many nations use war as the only means of solving problems,
and almost none, it seems, value human rights over militarism. So long as
any one of these war-like countries were fighting with words and spears,
other nations were relatively safe. Now, however, fanaticism has risen to the
surface and is gaining access to nuclear technology. As a consequence, our
planet has never been more at peril.

Today our so-called civilization seem to have embraced war as a
logical—even a moral—alternative to the political process. You cannot get
through a twenty-four hour day without reading about a new international
crisis caused by military action. No nation trusts their neighbour; there is no
rational dialogue, no common sense, no moral commitment to peace, and
certainly no political leadership. So you are caught in a psychological bind
from which there do not seem to be any means of escape. But if we do not
soon find a solution to this insane nuclear arms race, our children will be the
endangered species.

CHAPTER FOUR

# Solving Special Problems with Verbs, Pronouns, Adjectives and Adverbs

## A. AVOIDING VERB TROUBLES

Using the wrong verb is one of the most frequent and obvious errors of the ill-educated. Fortunately our ears usually tell us when a verb is used incorrectly. For instance, we would probably never say:

> I *throwed* the ball thirty yards.

But if we were only vaguely familiar with verb tenses, we might well say:

> We *begun* the job yesterday.

Thus you should know that all verb tenses are formed from the principal parts of the verb: the present, the past, and the past participle. You should also know that most verbs add *d* or *ed* to the present infinitive to form the simple past and the past participle:

| Present | Past | Past Participle |
|---------|------|-----------------|
| (to) move | moved | moved |
| (to) watch | watched | watched |
| (to) fill | filled | filled |

PRESENT:  I *soak* my feet every afternoon.
PAST:  Yesterday I *soaked* my feet for two hours.
PAST PARTICIPLE:  I *have soaked* my feet every day for the past two years.

44

There are other verbs, however, which change forms completely. These verbs are called irregular, and they are the ones which give us the most trouble (a list of some irregular verbs is found on p. 47).

| Present | Past | Past Participle |
|---------|------|-----------------|
| (to) see | saw | seen |
| (to) do | did | done |
| (to) go | went | gone |

If you remember the following rules you should be able to avoid the most common errors of verb usage.

**1.** Always add *d* or *ed* to the past and past participle of regular verbs.

> I used (not use) to play football in high school.
>
> He was supposed (not suppose) to report to the counsellor's office.
>
> We finally passed (not past) our chemistry examination.

**2.** Do not use past participle forms to express the simple past.

> I saw (not seen) the show yesterday.
>
> She drank (not drunk) all of her milk.
>
> He was the one who did (not done) it.

**3.** The auxiliary form of the verbs *to be* and *to have* are used only with the past participle, not with the simple past.

> I have already seen (not saw) the television program.
>
> When the race was run (not ran) we were inside.
>
> If I had only known (not knew).
>
> You are too late; they have already gone (not went) to the rock concert.

**4.** Four irregular verbs deserve special attention because they are frequently confused.

| (to) lay | laid | laid |
|----------|------|------|
| (to) lie | lay | lain |
| (to) sit | sat | sat |
| (to) set | set | set |

Whenever you have occasion to use these verbs, try following these rules:

(a) When you mean ''placing'' or ''positioning'' something, use the verb *lay*.

> I *lay* my books on top of my locker every morning.
>
> Yesterday I *laid* my books on the table.
>
> I *have* always *laid* my books on top of my locker.

(b) When you mean to recline or to remain in a fixed position, use *lie*.

> *Lie* down before your headache gets worse.
>
> The dishes *lay* in the sink all day.
>
> He *had lain* ill for more than a week before he saw a doctor.

(c) When you mean to place something in position, use *set*.

> I always *set* my briefcase beside my desk.
>
> They *set* the coffee machine next to the water cooler.
>
> He *has set* himself the goal of becoming the vice-president of the company.

(d) When you mean to hold yourself in a sitting position, use *sit*.

> I *sit* in the same chair every day.
>
> Yesterday I *sat* in a different chair.
>
> I *have sat* in this chair ever since I can remember.

**5.** The third principal part of the verb (past participle) is used for the following reasons:

(a) To indicate an action completed at some indefinite time before the present. It uses the auxiliary words *have* or *has*, and is defined as the present-perfect tense.

> We *have completed* our tasks.
>
> She *has* already *finished* her homework.

(b) To indicate an action that was completed before another past action. It uses the auxiliary word *had* and is defined as the past-perfect tense.

> We *had completed* our tasks an hour before she arrived home. She *had completed* her homework by the time her brother returned.

# SOME COMMON IRREGULAR VERBS

| Present | Past | Past Participle |
|---------|------|-----------------|
| begin | began | begun |
| bite | bit | bitten |
| blow | blew | blown |
| break | broke | broken |
| bring | brought | brought (not brung) |
| burst | burst | burst |
| choose | chose | chosen |
| come | came | come |
| do | did (not done) | done |
| draw | drew | drawn |
| drink | drank (not drunk) | drunk |
| drive | drove | driven |
| eat | ate | eaten |
| fall | fell | fallen |
| fly | flew | flown |
| forget | forgot | forgotten |
| freeze | froze | frozen |
| give | gave | given |
| go | went | gone (not went) |
| grow | grew | grown |
| know | knew | known |
| lie | lay | lain (not layed) |
| ride | rode | ridden |
| ring | rang | rung |
| run | ran | run |
| see | saw (not seen) | seen |
| sing | sang | sung |
| sink | sank | sunk |
| speak | spoke | spoken |
| steal | stole | stolen |
| sting | stung | stung |
| swear | swore | sworn |
| swim | swam | swum |
| swing | swung (not swang) | swung |
| take | took | taken |
| tear | tore | torn |
| throw | threw | thrown |
| wear | wore | worn |
| write | wrote | written |

(c) To indicate an action to be completed before a specific time in the future. It uses the helping words *shall have* or *will have*, and is defined as the future-perfect tense.

We *shall have completed* our tasks by the time she arrives home.

She *will have completed* her homework by the time her brother returns.

6. When the verb in the main clause is in the present tense, the verb in the subordinate clause should also be in the present tense. Remember to be consistent in your use of verb tenses, for a paragraph containing sentences that shift tenses abruptly can be extremely awkward and confusing:

I believe that our school system *had been designed* (past perfect) by a computer programmer, one that *has* (present) no sense of humour. For instance, when I *asked* (past) the program coordinator if she *is able* (present) to judge a student's total performance merely on the basis of true or false questions, she *said* (past) "No, of course not; only our computer *had been able* (past perfect) to do that."

### Corrected
I believe that our school system *was* designed by a computer programmer, one that *had* no sense of humour. For instance, when I *asked* the program coordinator if she *were* able to judge a student's total performance merely on the basis of true or false questions, she *said*, "No, of course not; only our computer *is* able to do that."

## Exercise 4.1 – Choosing Verb Forms
Select the correct verb form in each of the following sentences and write it in the blank at the right or on a separate sheet.

1. Please (set/sit) the statue on the pedestal. _____

2. The police officer (lay/laid) wounded on the floor while the bank robbers cleaned out the vault. _____

3. Here is the woman who was (suppose/supposed) to carry our flag in the Canada Day parade. _____

4. George is the man who (swum/swam) across Lake Ontario last year. _____

5. When Deborah and I were university students, we (use/used) to study together. _____

6. By the time our friends returned from their fishing excursion, we had already (ate/eaten) our lunch. _____

7. My brother had never (flew/flown) on a jet airplane before today. _____

**8.** Susan has already (rang/rung) for room service. _____

**9.** There are twenty-four paintings to be (hanged/hung) before the art auction can begin. _____

**10.** Please (sit/set) the dishes in the sink after you finish your breakfast. _____

**11.** Harold's cabin cruiser (sprang/sprung) a leak when he grazed a rock while avoiding a speedboat. _____

**12.** Paul and Sarah were severely sunburned because they had (lain/laid) on the beach all afternoon. _____

**13.** Our baseball game had already (begun/began) when the thunderstorm arrived. _____

**14.** We were (suppose/supposed) to turn in our laboratory assignments yesterday. _____

**15.** The team members left their equipment (laying/lying) all over the locker-room floor. _____

**16.** After procrastinating for two weeks, I have finally (wrote/written) to my sister in Calgary. _____

**17.** The murderer was finally (hanged/hung) after his appeal was denied by the Supreme Court. _____

**18.** Just as the jury members were (rising/raising) from their seats the judge dismissed the witnesses and declared a mistrial. _____

**19.** Our student government had already (chose/chosen) a president before the school semester began. _____

**20.** The mayor of our city (don't/doesn't) cast a vote in city council deliberations, unless there is a tie. _____

**21.** I do not think that she has ever (come/came) to one of our meetings on time. _____

**22.** The athletic director has (spoke/spoken) very highly of Jane's gymnastic ability. _____

**23.** If the second baseman had (threw/thrown) the ball to the catcher, the runner would have been out at home plate. _____

**24.** We already (seen/saw) the science-fiction film, *Star Wars*. _____

**25.** The singer, during the course of the evening, (sang/sung) many protest songs of the sixties. _____

**26.** We could have all (went/gone) to the theatre together if Jack and Sue had arrived on time. _____

**27.** The majority of the people at the picnic thought they had (saw/seen) a flying saucer. _____

**28.** The sales agent (rung/rang) the bell a number of times,
but nobody answered the door. _____

**29.** If we had only (knew/known) the combination to the lock,
we could have saved a great deal of time and trouble. _____

**30.** The jury members were (swore/sworn) to secrecy before
they were allowed to enter the jury room. _____

## Exercise 4.2 − Correcting Verb Errors

Write the number of any incorrect verb form in the first blank to the right; then
write it correctly in the second blank. Write *C* if the verb is correctly used.
Alternatively, write your answers on a separate sheet.

$$1$$

EXAMPLE:   As we watch the football game, we *became* excited.

    _1_     _become_

**1**
Last summer I worked on a construction crew in _____ _____

**2**
the province of Nova Scotia. We had built _____ _____

**3**
roads and repaired bridges, and sometimes _____ _____

**4**
have worked ten hours a day. When I started _____ _____

**5**
the job, in early May, I weigh one-hundred and
eighty-five pounds, but by the end of August I _____ _____

**6**
lost twenty pounds as well as two inches around my _____ _____

**7**
waist. I earned enough money to pay for my _____ _____

**8**
university tuition, and I even have had enough
left over to buy a used motorcycle. I would
recommend construction work to any student who _____ _____

**9**
had to earn money during the summer months to
finance his or her education. I would suggest, _____ _____

**10**
however, that he or she were in excellent
physical condition; for the work, although _____ _____

**11**

financially rewarding, will be extremely strenuous          _____    _____
and exhausting.

## B. DETECTING PRONOUN CASE PROBLEMS

Case refers to the change in form (or inflection) of a noun or pronoun to indicate its function in a sentence. The three cases are *nominative* (used for subjects), *objective* (used for objects of verbs, prepositions and infinitives), and *possessive* (used to indicate possession). Since nouns do not change form in the nominative and objective cases, and since their change in the possessive is indicated by an apostrophe (see Punctuating Effectively, p. 120), they present no problem. It is the pronoun that gives us trouble. Most personal pronouns and the relative pronoun *who* change forms in all three cases.

| Nominative | Possessive | Objective |
|---|---|---|
| I | my, mine | me |
| we | our, ours | us |
| you | your, yours | you |
| he | his | him |
| she | her, hers | her |
| it | its | it |
| they | their, theirs | them |
| who | whose | whom |

The usage rules for pronoun case are fairly straightforward, but the application of these rules can be confusing.

**1.** When the pronoun functions as the subject of the verb or follows some form of the verb to be (is, am, was, were), it takes the nominative case.

> *He* broke the cup. (simple subject)
>
> It was *she* who acted on stage. (subject complement)

**2.** When the pronoun functions as the direct or indirect object, the object of a preposition, or the object of an infinitive, it takes the objective case.

> John told *him* about the class trip. (direct object)
>
> He gave *me* an assignment. (indirect object)
>
> He is coming for *me* in an hour. (object of the preposition *for*)
>
> My employer told me to meet *her* at the airport. (object of the infinitive *to meet*)

Many usage problems occur when pronouns are used in certain compound constructions, or when they align themselves too closely with nouns. These problem areas are isolated in the following examples:

1. When a pronoun functions as one part of a compound object containing a noun, read the sentence without the noun. Your ear will usually tell you which pronoun to use. You might write, "The coach had a meeting with *he* and the quarterback"; but you would probably never write, "The coach had a meeting with *he*." Therefore, the correct use of the pronoun is self-evident without the noun: "The coach had a meeting with *him* and the quarterback."

2. For pronouns preceding nouns, you may apply the same test used for compound construction; read the sentence without the noun. Again, you might write, "Us workers on the assembly line deserve a pay raise." But you would not write, "Us deserve a pay raise." Therefore, common sense and the process of elimination will ensure that you write, "We workers on the assembly line deserve a pay raise."

3. When the words *like* and *but* are used as prepositions, their pronouns take the objective case.

> Everyone but *him* (not he) came to the party.

> Your daughter looks like *her* (not she).

4. In clauses that follow the words *as* or *than*, the pronoun may function as either the subject or the object of the implied verb.

> She is older than *I* (am).

> I like Bill better than (I like) *him*.

> My brother earns more money than *he* (earns).

Note: When the verb is supplied, the form of the pronoun becomes obvious.

5. In informal English, pronouns that follow forms of the verb *to be* are often placed in the objective case; in formal English, however, the nominative case is preferred:

> It was *he* (not him) who has been given the responsibility.

> The major vote-getters were *they* (not them).

6. The case of the relative pronouns *who/whoever* and *whom/whomever* is determined by their function in the clauses. The easiest method of determining which case to use is by mentally rearranging the clause and then substituting *he* for *who* or *whoever*, and *him* for *whom* or *whomever*.

It is he whom the police want for questioning.
(The police want *him* for questioning.)

It is she who, I am told, went to Europe last summer.
(*She* went to Europe last summer.)

Please send the message to whoever is on duty.
(*He* is on duty.)

We will save the work for whomever they send to replace the supervisor.
(*They* send *him*.)

7. Compound personal pronouns—himself, herself, itself, themselves, etc.
—should only be used to emphasize information already given by a noun or
pronoun, or to direct the action of a verb back to the subject. These two uses
of the compound pronoun are called intensive and reflexive.

(a) Intensive (emphasizing a noun or pronoun):

The minister *himself* arranged the social function.

I *myself* served as the host.

The administrators *themselves* are to blame.

(b) Reflexive (directing the action to the subject):

I hurt *myself* on the exercise bicycle.

We have insured *ourselves* against fire and theft.

They found *themselves* without a leader.

Do not use a compound pronoun unless the noun or pronoun to which it refers
is used in the same sentence. Never, for example, say:

The players gave the game ball to John and *myself*.
(to John and *me*)

or

*Herself* and Mary Carson are tied for the lead.
(*She* and Mary Carson are tied)

Note also that *hisself* and *theirselves* are severely ungrammatical and should
never be used.

8. A pronoun used before a gerund (an *ing* verb form used as a noun) is always in
the possessive case.

I was surprised at his (not him) not wanting to go on the camping trip.

Your (not you) coming and going is driving me crazy.

His (not him) wanting to study medicine came as a pleasant surprise.

Do not confuse pronouns that function as direct objects with pronouns that precede gerunds.

> My mother saw him (not his) working in a construction camp.

> I noticed you (not your) running around the track.

## Exercise 4.3 — Using the Proper Pronoun Case

Select the correct pronoun in each of the following sentences and write it in the blank at the right or on a separate sheet.

1. No one asked Tom and (I/me) to try out for the swimming team. _____

2. There is no one as well qualified to lead our group as (her/she). _____

3. Just between you and (me/I), there doesn't seem to be any chalk in the classroom. _____

4. There was a great deal of support for (him/his) being named the valedictorian at our graduation ceremony. _____

5. I believe it was (him/he) who wore the orange sneakers to class. _____

6. (Whoever/Whomever) is ready to eat lunch may get his or her hamburger from the barbecue. _____

7. The scoring title was shared by Stephen and (I/me/myself). _____

8. (Us/We/Our) having to wait for the umpire to arrive was the reason our baseball game was delayed. _____

9. (Whom/Who) do you think will win the beauty contest this year? _____

10. We think that the chores should be shared equally between (he and she/him and her). _____

11. (We/Us) office workers should form a union before it is too late. _____

12. Everyone but (him/he) contributed to our auction sale. _____

13. Do you think Bikash is a better student than (I/me)? _____

14. It was (her/she) who found the silk purse. _____

15. The best runners in the history of our marathon race were (them/they). _____

**16.** Please give this enrollment sheet to (whomever/whoever) enters the room. _____

**17.** The teacher (hisself/himself) told us that class was cancelled next Friday. _____

**18.** Verna saw (him/his) copying someone else's homework. _____

**19.** The broken desk was placed between Fred and (I/me/myself). _____

**20.** The political leaders (theirselves/themselves) are contributing to our high inflation rate. _____

**21.** It was she, I believe, (whom/who) was selected to represent our school at the academic conference in Toronto. _____

**22.** Phil earned more money than (me/I/myself) over the summer. _____

**23.** Our team members are not as well coached as (them/they). _____

**24.** (Them/Their) agreeing to sell lottery tickets came as a big surprise. _____

**25.** Everything will be ready for you and (she/her) when the curtain is raised and the footlights go on. _____

**26.** We shall share our prize money with (whomever/whoever) we wish. _____

**27.** Both Jennifer and (I/me) bought the same hat. _____

**28.** Ivan as well as (I/me/myself) will serve drinks at our parents' anniversary party. _____

**29.** I think Claire is much more talented than (her/she). _____

**30.** (Them/They) and the school janitor are responsible for the security of the building. _____

## C. CONFUSING ADJECTIVES AND ADVERBS

Adjectives and adverbs are distinguished only by the words they modify. Adjectives modify nouns and pronouns; adverbs modify verbs, other adverbs and adjectives. Many adverbs are formed by adding *ly* to the adjective, but many others take the same form as adjectives: *fat*, *well*, *ill*, *much*, *far*, etc. As a matter of fact, there are so many exceptions to the *ly* rule that it is just barely a rule.

However, despite the spelling inconsistency of adverbs and adjectives, there are surprisingly few that give us trouble. Here are some rules that may help you avoid confusing them.

**1.** Adjectives modify nouns and pronouns—and nothing else!

> He is a *proper* gentleman at all times. (adjective modifying the noun *gentleman*)
>
> but
>
> My stereo does not work *properly*. (adverb modifying the verb *work*)
>
> He wears *conservative* ties. (adjective modifying the noun *ties*)
>
> but
>
> He dresses very *conservatively*. (adverb modifying the verb *dresses*)
>
> This is a *real* sealskin coat. (adjective modifying the noun *coat*)
>
> but
>
> Tom is a *really* fine swimmer. (adverb modifying the adjective *fine*)

**2.** Verb of the senses (*to smell, to hear, to feel, to taste, to look*), forms of the verb *to be* (*is, are, am, was, were*) and other linking words like *appear, become, seem* are followed by adjectives that modify the subject.

> She feels *bad* (not badly).
>
> The peaches tasted *sweet* (not sweetly).
>
> His clothes closet seemed *neat* (not neatly).

However, when these verbs denote action, they take adverbs, not adjectives.

> He looked *suspiciously* (not suspicious) at the new employee. (modifies *looked*)
>
> The alarm rang *loudly* (not loud) but no one was in the building to hear it. (modifies *rang*)
>
> The burglar felt *carefully* (not careful) around the door jamb. (modifies *felt*)

## D. USING FORMS OF COMPARISON

Adjectives and adverbs change form to show degrees of quality or quantity: these degrees are positive, comparative, and superlative. The comparative form of short modifiers is made by adding *er* to the positive form. The superlative form is made by adding *est*. The comparative and superlative forms of modifiers ending in *ly* or having two or more syllables are created by adding *more* and *most* to the positive form.

Note: Some adjectives and adverbs change forms completely in all degrees of comparison—good, better, best; bad, worse, worst, etc.

| Positive | Comparative | Superlative |
|---|---|---|
| cold | colder | coldest |
| fat | fatter | fattest |
| careful | more careful | most careful |
| quickly | more quickly | most quickly |

1. The comparative form of adverbs and adjectives is used to compare two persons, things, or ideas.

> My horse is *faster* than yours.
>
> Alice is *more joyful* than her sister.
>
> He is *more enthusiastic* than Paul.

2. The superlative form compares more than two persons, things, or ideas.

> My horse is the *fastest* on the track.
>
> Alice is the *most joyful* of her three sisters.
>
> John is the *most enthusiastic* member of the team.

3. Some adjectives are absolute in meaning, and therefore cannot logically be compared.

> My cup is empty. (not *the emptiest*)
>
> Her costume is unique. (not *the uniquest*)
>
> Jane is pregnant. (not *more pregnant than Mary*)

4. Avoid double comparisons.

> My friend is stingier (not more stingier) than your friend.
>
> He is the angriest (not the most angriest) man I ever met.
>
> She is my dearest (not most dearest) friend.

## Exercise 4.4 — Confusing Adjectives and Adverbs

Select the correct adjective or adverb in each of the following sentences and write it in the blank at the right or on a separate sheet.

1. My sister was once a (real/really) fine commercial artist.  _____

2. These pickles taste (bitter/bitterly).  _____

3. The child's birthday party certainly went very (smooth/smoothly).  _____

4. The dog appeared (vicious/viciously), so the mailman did not approach the front lawn of the house. _____

5. Our soccer team played very (well/good) last Saturday. _____

6. The team's desire to win was (real/really) intense during the second half of the football game. _____

7. The tragedies of Shakespeare (surely/sure) must be in our school library. _____

8. The teachers acted (different/differently) outside the classroom. _____

9. The lunch bell sounded (shrill/shrilly) throughout the empty hallways. _____

10. She is the (most silliest/silliest) girl I know. _____

11. We feel (joyful/joyfully) as the Christmas season approaches. _____

12. Marg and Betty felt (bad/badly) when they heard that Sam's mother was seriously ill. _____

13. If he had given directions more (accurate/accurately) we would have arrived much earlier. _____

14. Viola felt (good/well) after she received the results of her blood test. _____

15. She writes (quick/quickly) but speaks slowly. _____

16. Patricia's essays are (more neatly/neater) done that Pam's. _____

17. The quiz-show contestant looked (strange/strangely) after he won the first prize. _____

18. Our hockey coach works more (diligently/diligent) at our practice sessions than your hockey coach. _____

19. This (loose/loosely) tied bundle will not survive the trip. _____

20. The passenger train went (slow/slowly) as it approached the overpass. _____

21. Our teacher made the essay test (easier/more easy) than the multiple-choice quiz. _____

22. Wally must be one of the (most laziest/laziest) people I ever met. _____

23. This is the (worse/worst) winter we've ever had. _____

24. I feel (sick/sickly) whenever anyone mentions raw oysters. _____

25. Her banana-cream pie is (more sweet/sweeter) than her coconut-custard pie. _____

**26.** The recently polished coffee table felt (smooth/smoothly).　　——————

**27.** Our physics laboratory is certainly (more clean/cleaner)
than their chemistry laboratory.　　——————

**28.** She behaved (differently/different) from anyone in the room.　　——————

**29.** We did not realize that you felt so (strongly/strong) about
nuclear disarmament.　　——————

**30.** Bert played (awful/awfully) in the final game of our annual
bridge tournament.　　——————

## Exercise 4.5 — Revising the Paragraph to Solve Special Problems

Rewrite the following paragraphs by eliminating the pronoun case errors as well
as all the problems related to adverbs and adjectives.

When my friend Peter and myself tried out for a professional football team,
we expected to be treated no different from anyone else. We thought that if
we worked hard and wanted to make the team bad enough, we would be
given an impartial trial  like everyone else. Boy, were we mistaken. I never
knew what the term "rookie" implied until Peter and me reported to our first
training camp.

Us receiving a different colour jersey from the rest of the players was
the first indication that we would be treated different. Then we were told not
to talk to any of the more veteran players unless they spoke to us first.
Second, we were seated in the most gloomy end of the team cafeteria and
were always served last.

Also, most every day me and Peter had to help the trainers lug the
tackling dummies and the blocking sleds on and off the practice field. And
during calisthenics the veterans would often stand around and jeer at us for
being clumsy and most inept. Furthermore, sometimes them and the
coaches, whom were veteran players theirselves, would make us do extra
laps around the track because we moved too slow when carrying practice
equipment.

Peter and I were made to feel that we were outsiders whom were
trying to join a close-knit fraternity who had earned their more unique status
in combat. They had the scars of battle, and all we had was a burning desire
to play a game we loved with the best players available.

# CHAPTER FIVE

# Making Sentences Clear

To write clear, concise, and balanced sentences, you must be able to structure your statements so that the proper relationship of your ideas comes through. You must pay close attention to the important transitional links that connect your sentence parts and be aware of the logical pattern of parallel words and statements that provide your sentences with balance and cohesion. Your ability to write such sentences will depend on your avoiding errors in pronoun reference, dangling and misplaced modifiers, and parallel construction.

## A. PRONOUNS MUST REFER CLEARLY TO NOUNS

Pronouns are used in place of nouns to avoid repetition and to connect ideas. However, if you have not made clear what nouns the pronouns replace, your sentences will lack coherence, and thus create confusion in the mind of the reader. The following pronoun reference errors are the most common.

**1. The Hazards of Ambiguity**   Ambiguity occurs when a pronoun can refer grammatically to more than one antecedent.

> The teacher informed the student that he needed another test booklet. (Who needed the test booklet?)
>
> Mother told Jane that her pickles were not canned properly. (Whose pickles?)

Even though the reader may logically deduce your meaning, your sentence may appear ridiculous if the pronoun lacks a clear reference.

> Paula heard her daughter speak her first word upon returning from her tennis match. (Whose tennis match?)
>
> The Dean of the college told the student that his bicycle needed a taillight. (Whose bicycle?)

After Jack combed the horse's mane, it ran around the field. (What ran around the field, the horse or the mane?)

**2. Antecedents that are Only Implied**    Do not use a pronoun whose antecedent is only implied by the wording of a sentence. Make sure that your pronoun refers clearly to one antecedent.

> FAULTY:    In the armed services *they* can retire at an early age. (Who are "they"?)
>
> CORRECTED:    The men and women in the armed services can retire at an early age.
>
> FAULTY:    I am attending a Western university where *they* teach Petroleum Engineering. (Who teaches?)
>
> CORRECTED:    I am attending a Western university where Petroleum Engineering is taught. (Eliminating the pronoun sometimes clarifies the meaning.)
>
> FAULTY:    The English teacher tried hard, but *it* went right over our heads. (What went over our heads?)
>
> CORRECTED:    The English teacher tried hard, but the lesson went right over our heads.

**3. Imprecise References Cause Confusion**    Do not use a pronoun that refers vaguely to an entire clause or to a complete sentence. When words like *this*, *which*, or *it* refer to general statements, confusion results.

> FAULTY:    When it rained in the valley, *it* was because of a low pressure system.
>
> FAULTY:    The relationship between Canada and the United States has always been close, *which* has benefited the businessmen of both countries.

Usually, sentences like these can be easily corrected by rewriting them without the pronoun.

> REVISED:    It rained in the valley because of a low pressure system.
>
> or
>
> The valley had rain because of a low pressure system.
>
> REVISED:    The close relationship between Canada and the United States has benefited the businessmen of both countries.

## Exercise 5.1 — Improving Pronoun Reference

After each of the following sentences containing a faulty pronoun reference write F in the blank at the right or on a separate sheet. Then rewrite the sentence correctly. If the sentence is correct, write C instead of F.

EXAMPLE:   I am studying Nursing, because I want to be one
when I graduate.

F

REVISED:   I am studying Nursing because I want to be a nurse
when I graduate.

1. I spend most of my spare time on tennis lessons because it is my favourite sport.

2. Sue told Jane that her dog was in the yard without a leash.

3. My uncle gave me a stereo for my birthday, which pleased me a great deal.

4. I have not played soccer since graduating from high school, but I am still very much interested in it.

5. Because Christine's older sister is a nurse, this is the profession she wants to enter.

6. We inquired about our concert tickets at the information booth, but they couldn't tell us when they would be mailed.

7. After I parked my truck next to the limousine, I noticed that its tire was flat.

8. Whenever I telephone City Hall they put me on hold.

9. As our football team entered the crowded stadium, they rose and gave us a deafening cheer.

10. The members of the high-school band cannot go on our annual field trip, for they have to practise for the big game this Saturday.

11. My brother tried out for the school basketball team, but he was informed that he was not tall enough to play it.

12. Nothing we do ever pleases her and this makes us angry.

13. The members of our city council are voting to raise their salaries by ten per cent.

14. I never saw a real volcano, but I am certainly fascinated by them.

15. When it snowed along the seacoast, it was because of a low pressure system to the south of us.

16. Because coffee is the national beverage of Brazil, they drink it every day.

17. The flight attendant asked the passengers if it had been a comfortable flight.

**18.** The lawyer told the client that her case was coming to trial next Friday. _____

**19.** When Sheila volunteered to donate her time to the Muscular Dystrophy campaign, it was appreciated. _____

**20.** On the menu it says they have a special on roast beef. _____

**21.** Our committee could not reach a decision yesterday on the budget because it was too difficult. _____

**22.** Steven flunked his biology examination, which was the reason he enrolled in summer school. _____

**23.** I phoned the police department and told them about my car being stolen. _____

**24.** After living in an apartment for many years, I have come to dislike it. _____

**25.** In Gloria's latest magazine article, she writes about communal living. _____

**26.** Dan told Mel that his garden needed weeding. _____

**27.** After my cousin returned from Saudi Arabia, he could not stop commenting on their religious fervour. _____

**28.** Helen talked continuously during the concert recital, which disturbed the person sitting next to her. _____

**29.** When Fran was told to keep her opinions to herself, it annoyed her very much. _____

**30.** I know I am not supposed to eat this chocolate bar, but I can't stop snacking on them. _____

## Exercise 5.2 — Revising the Paragraph for Clear Pronoun Reference

Rewrite the following paragraphs by eliminating the pronoun reference errors.

1. When the circus came to our town, this was one of the most important events of the season. As a young boy I felt that they were somehow magical people, endowed with mysterious abilities. As I watched the tents being raised and the performers practising, I thought that it was one of the most exciting events I had ever seen. In the lion tamer's cage, for instance, he was holding back three ferocious lions with only a whip and a chair. And the clowns' acrobatics were something to behold; I thought surely they would break their necks jumping off those high ladders. But to me the most thrilling experience of the day occurred when they allowed me to ride an elephant. The handlers made the elephant kneel, and then they lifted me onto a huge saddle strapped on its back and told me to hang

on. They then led it around a track close to the main tent while I waved at all of the performers. After this, the formal opening of the circus was almost anti-climactic. To this day I can still recall the excitement that only a young boy of thirteen could feel who was allowed, for a time, to experience the magical world of the circus.

2. The day our school had a fire drill it was mass confusion: they led us into the hall and made us wait there until all of the other classes were assembled. By this time the hall was full of laughing and shouting students. Also the bell continued ringing, which prevented us from hearing their instructions. Even the teachers were disgusted at the way this was organized.

   When we were finally led outside—at least ten minutes after the bell had begun ringing—we were left standing in the rain while they checked to see if everyone was out of the building. This spoiled the entire afternoon, for once we were back inside the classroom, it was too late to see the film that she had started to show us before the fire drill began. I guess they learned their lesson, though, for it never happened again that semester.

# B. PUTTING MODIFIERS IN THE RIGHT PLACE

The position of a modifier usually determines the precise meaning of your sentence. If it is placed incorrectly, your statement will be illogical and confusing. To avoid this error, place your modifiers as closely as possible to the word or words they modify.

1. However, almost any modifier can be misplaced if there are two or more words in the sentence to which it could possibly attach itself. Consider the following modifier errors:

   MISPLACED:   The old man walked into the lamp post going to the optician.
   (Who has bad eyesight, the old man or the lamp post?)
   CORRECTED:   While going to the optician, the old man bumped into the lamp post.

   MISPLACED:   The performers danced while we joined hands with gusto.
   (Who is gusto?)
   CORRECTED:   The performers danced with gusto while we joined hands.

Also watch out for dependent clauses beginning with *which* or *that*; if they do not immediately follow the word they modify, you may write sentences like these:

   MISPLACED:   He crossed the stream in a canoe, which was recently stocked with fish.
   CORRECTED:   He crossed the stream, which was recently stocked with fish, in a canoe.

MISPLACED:  The football game was played in our stadium, that was full of penalties.

CORRECTED:  The football game that was full of penalties was played in our stadium.

**2.** Make sure you place words like *only*, *nearly* and *almost* immediately before the words they modify. If you do not, your sentence will be illogical, or it may even change in meaning:

ILLOGICAL:  During the summer vacation she nearly earned a thousand dollars. (You cannot nearly earn.)

LOGICAL:  During the summer vacation, she earned nearly a thousand dollars.

ILLOGICAL:  He almost ran twenty miles in the marathon race. (He did not almost run.)

LOGICAL:  He ran almost twenty miles in the marathon race.

Consider how the following sentences change their meanings when the word *only* is shifted:

He *only* drove a car until he bought a bicycle.
(He did nothing else except drive a car.)

He drove *only* a car until he bought a bicycle.
(He drove nothing else.)

*Only* he drove a car until he bought a bicycle.
(No one else drove.)

He drove a car *only* until he bought a bicycle.
(He stopped driving when he bought a bicycle.)

**3.** Do not make your modifier ambiguous by placing it in such a way that it could modify either of two parts of a sentence. This error is referred to as a "squinting modifier."

SQUINTING:  Students who study often get good grades. (Does *often* modify *study*, or does it refer to *good grades*?)

CORRECTED:  Students who often study get good grades.

or

Students who study get good grades often.

**4.** Good writers may sometimes use a split infinitive to achieve clarity or to place emphasis; but unless you know precisely what you are doing, avoid splitting infinitives, especially with phrases and clauses.

SPLIT:  We intend *to*, if our money holds out, *travel* out West during our semester break.

CORRECTED:  If our money holds out, we intend *to travel* out West during our semester break.

SPLIT:    I promise *to* faithfully and diligently *do* my work.
CORRECTED:    I promise *to do* my work faithfully and diligently.

## Exercise 5.3 – Misplaced Modifiers

After each of the sentences containing a misplaced modifier, write M in the blank at the right or on a separate sheet; then rewrite the sentence correctly. If the sentence is correct write C instead of M.

EXAMPLE:    We nearly took in three hundred dollars at the crafts show.                                                                    **M**

REVISED:    We took in nearly three hundred dollars at the crafts show.

1. The opera singer sang the aria with much enthusiasm.   _____

2. Phil told Martha on Saturday they would leave for their lakeside cottage.   _____

3. We ate seafood chowder in the new restaurant that had too much garlic in it.   _____

4. A person who sings frequently is happy.   _____

5. Please indicate if you wish us to send you our latest product directory on the back of the order form.   _____

6. Henry intends to, if the weather is pleasant, go golfing on one of the Thousand Islands.   _____

7. Betty frequently drinks wine with dinner.   _____

8. We heard the debate on waste disposal sites at our community college.   _____

9. By the end of the week I had almost earned a hundred dollars in tips.   _____

10. Our insurance agent told us on Tuesday to decide if we wanted to update our insurance policy.   _____

11. We nearly collected three thousand signatures on our petition.   _____

12. She almost collapsed from exhaustion after completing the marathon race.   _____

13. I purchased my bicycle from Canadian Tire with chrome fenders.   _____

14. The visiting hockey player stayed overnight at our house from Winnipeg.   _____

15. Sophie and Vic only finished their novels by the assigned date.   _____

**16.** I almost sing in the shower every day. _____

**17.** Never purchase a personal computer from a department store with a built-in disk drive. _____

**18.** With only a brief smile of goodbye, he left on his expedition to the Antarctic. _____

**19.** Jogging often strengthens the heart and lungs. _____

**20.** We intend to, whether or not you approve, enter the beauty contest. _____

**21.** We almost listen every evening to rock music on the radio. _____

**22.** Sandra read a novel in the school library that contained romance and adventure. _____

**23.** Mother told us on Friday to mow the lawn and trim the hedge. _____

**24.** Who was that woman who gave you the canary with purple shorts? _____

**25.** Paul nearly drove his motorbike two hundred miles to Toronto. _____

**26.** Our teacher showed us our marks with great sorrow. _____

**27.** Eating often causes obesity. _____

**28.** Last summer my girlfriend stayed at our school dormitory from Germany. _____

**29.** We finally found our motorcycle in the school parking lot with a broken windshield. _____

**30.** Tracy and Kim only were selected to audition for the new dramatic play. _____

## Exercise 5.4 − Revising the Paragraph to Correct Misplaced Modifiers

Rewrite the following paragraphs by eliminating the misplaced modifiers.

My sister almost ran twenty-four miles in the marathon race on Sunday. Her performance was remarkable when you consider that she only practised two weeks before the race and never ran more than ten miles. She intended to, if there were any more spaces, enter the twelve-mile race, but that race had a full complement of runners. Nevertheless, only she was the one of five racers over the age of thirty-five to run more than twenty miles.

Everyone in our family is extremely proud of her, and we now know that, with a little determination, on Sunday we can also aspire to what she accomplished. Most people know that jogging often strengthens one's cardio-vascular system and improves muscle tone, but not many people realize that running frequently improves one's self-image. Therefore I intend to follow, starting Monday, my sister's example by at least jogging five miles every day.

## C. DETECTING DANGLING MODIFIERS

Whenever you use a phrase or a clause that refers to a specific word, make sure you arrange the sentences so that the reader knows how the word and its modifier are attached. If you fail to relate clearly the modifier to the word modified, the reader will become confused and may lose interest in what you have to say.

A dangling modifier is a phrase or an elliptical clause (a clause without a subject or verb—or both) that is illogically separated from the word it modifies. Thus it appears awkwardly disconnected from the rest of the sentence. Here are a few examples of dangling constructions:

PARTICIPIAL PHRASE:   *Cited by the writer*, the student did not know the source of the quotation. (The quotation, not the student, was cited.)

GERUND PHRASE:   *Approaching the guard rail on Lookout Mountain*, a vast expanse of farmland could be seen. (Who— or what—approached the guardrail?)

INFINITIVE PHRASE:   *To appreciate the English language*, reading must be done. (Who must read?)

PREPOSITIONAL PHRASE:   *After four weeks at sea*, my wife was happy to see me. (Who was at sea?)

ELLIPTICAL CLAUSE:   *When on the top floor of the tall building*, the cars looked like tiny fish in a stream. (Where are the cars? Where is the speaker?)

To correct dangling modifiers, you must reword the entire sentence; unlike misplaced modifiers, the fractured syntax of dangling constructions cannot be cured by shifting one or two words around.

**1.** One method of correcting a dangling modifier is by locating its implied subject (by asking yourself who or what is responsible for the action), and then making it the stated subject of the main clause.

DANGLING:   After three hours of practice, a large mug of root beer was what the thirsty dancers wanted. (Who was practising?)

REVISED:   After practising for three hours, the thirsty *dancers* wanted a large mug of root beer.

DANGLING:   Before submitting any written work, careful proofreading must be done. (Who must submit the work?)

REVISED:   Before submitting any written work *you* must carefully proofread it.

**2.** Another method of correcting dangling construction is by expanding the dangling phrases or elliptical clause into a full dependent clause.

DANGLING: Watching the parade, my wallet was stolen.
REVISED: While I was watching the parade, my wallet was stolen.

DANGLING: Although tired and hungry, the drill sergeant would not let us rest.
REVISED: Although we were tired and hungry, the drill sergeant would not let us rest.

## Exercise 5.5 – Dangling Modifiers

After each of the following sentences containing a dangling modifier, write DM in the blank at the right or on a separate sheet. Then rewrite the sentence correctly. If the sentence is correct write C instead of DM.

EXAMPLE: When very young, my father took me to the circus.     __DM__

REVISED: When I was very young, my father took me to the circus.

**1.** Reluctant to put all his weight on the damaged ankle, the coach removed Bill from the game.     _____

**2.** While sailing on Lake Winnipeg, many beautiful boats could be seen.     _____

**3.** While skiing downhill without goggles, my eyes were stung by sleet and snow.     _____

**4.** To attain high marks in computer science, many hours of practice must be spent on the computer terminal.     _____

**5.** After sitting for two hours in his office, the doctor finally called me into the examining room.     _____

**6.** Jogging slowly through the woods, my eye was caught by a scampering woodchuck.     _____

**7.** To write well, one must habitually revise.     _____

**8.** Once out of the city, the air pollution no longer made his eyes water.     _____

**9.** Before beginning her modeling career, Stephanie wanted to be a teacher.     _____

**10.** While travelling from Halifax, Nova Scotia, to St. John, New Brunswick, many quaint farmhouses could be seen.     _____

11. After hearing her arguments for nuclear disarmament, my position on nuclear proliferation has changed. _____

12. As one of the leaders in our community, this slander must not remain unchallenged. _____

13. Afraid to eat any more pickle relish, the waiter removed the relish tray from Dorothy's table. _____

14. After finally being introduced to one of Canada's leading actors, they found nothing to talk about. _____

15. To win at poker, many risks must be taken. _____

16. After driving two hundred miles on two-lane roads, Carlos was completely exhausted. _____

17. Like many of today's students, financial security is one of Magda's highest priorities. _____

18. After reading five chapters of her latest novel, her theme is still unclear. _____

19. Finding the blackboard trays without erasers or chalk, the instructor was quite annoyed. _____

20. To become a first-class gymnast, great dedication and perseverance are necessary. _____

21. When only two years old, my family moved from a large city to a small farming community. _____

22. After installing the muffler, the tailpipe must be clamped properly. _____

23. When thoroughly risen, Mother removed the cake from the oven. _____

24. While under the influence of alcohol, one must never drive. _____

25. After dancing for twenty-four hours in the marathon, the doctor told me to soak my feet and have my head examined. _____

26. To obtain all your rights as citizens, it is necessary to know the laws of our country. _____

27. Before swimming in the ocean, make sure there are lifeguards on duty. _____

28. Examining my shopping receipts, it became obvious that I was overcharged at the clothing store. _____

29. To hit a golf ball properly, you must learn to keep your head perfectly still. _____

30. Once out of the office, the piped-in music no longer gave him a headache. _____

## Exercise 5.6 — Revising the Paragraph to Remove Dangling Modifiers

Rewrite the following paragraphs by eliminating the dangling modifiers.

The computer applications conference I attended in Toronto was certainly a worthwhile experience. Working in today's computer environment I met some very important and interesting people. While attending the seminars, which were conducted by highly trained professionals, the knowledge I gained about systems management will, I feel, be invaluable in the future. As a former computer programmer, this training experience allowed me to realize the enormous potential for computers in a modern office environment. To be successful in today's competitive marketplace, professional development must be an intrinsic part of our working lives.

Therefore, I would highly recommend that everyone in our management group attend the next conference because, like many of today's managers, knowledge of computer applications is our bread and butter. Also, attached for your convenience, my letter includes a detailed evaluation of the seminars I attended. If any questions should arise or further information be required, my office will be happy to respond.

## D. EMPLOYING PARALLEL FORMS

We signal the reader that two or more ideas have equal value by placing them in the same grammatical form; this enables us to express these ideas clearly and emphatically. However, to position parallel ideas properly, we must pay close attention to the logic of grammatical relationships.

1. **Correcting Faulty Coordination** When word groups are linked by a coordinating conjunction, they should each have the same grammatical construction. Consider the parallel structure of the following word groups:

    Our locker room is small, chilly, and dirty. (parallel adjectives)

    I enjoy playing football and hockey. (parallel nouns)

    Our dog ran across the lawn and under the hedge. (parallel phrases)

    We requested that he sing our favourite songs and that he allow us to record them. (parallel clauses)

    I want to learn English, and she wants to learn French. (parallel sentences)

Notice how awkward sentences look and sound when they contain unequal elements.

    She works diligently and at night.

    He spends a great deal of money and foolishly.

    I was told to report to the supervisor and that I should bring my tools.

Two very common types of error in coordination involve the use of *and who/and which* constructions and the use of correlative conjunctions. These errors are discussed in the following sections.

**(a) And Who/And Which Constructions**   The awkward *and who/and which* construction is one of the most common yet most serious errors made by students, for it results in an illogical link between dependent and independent clauses. To avoid this error, follow this rule: Never use *and who* or *and which* clauses unless they are preceded by *who* or *which* clauses.

> FAULTY:   Tom Clark, wise and intelligent, *and who* is our union representative, has been promoted to foreman.
> CORRECTED:   Tom Clark, *who* is wise and intelligent, *and who* is our union representative, has been promoted to foreman.

> FAULTY:   James Joyce's *Ulysses*, a long and complicated novel *and which* is on our reading list, has been banned by the school board.
> CORRECTED:   James Joyce's *Ulysses*, *which* is a long and complicated novel, *and which* is on our reading list, has been banned by the school board.

**(b) Correlative Conjunction**   Correlative conjunctions are always used in pairs: *either...or*; *neither...nor*; *not only...but also*; *both...and*. Because they are used to compare and contrast similar statements, each part of the conjunction must be followed by the same grammatical construction. The proper use of correlative conjunctions will enable you to write clear, well-balanced sentences.

> UNBALANCED:   I want either to study English Literature or study World History.
> BALANCED:   I want to study either English Literature or World History.

> UNBALANCED:   Our new car not only is more economical but also it is more comfortable than our old one.
> BALANCED:   Our new car is not only more economical but also more comfortable than our old one.

**2. Making Series Parallel**   When words or groups of words are placed in a series, they must be parallel in both meaning and structure. Observe how the proper use of parallel series tightens your sentence structure and clarifies your meaning.

> FAULTY:   When we arrived home we unpacked our suitcases, took showers, and then we went to sleep after eating our lunch.
> REVISED:   When we arrived home we unpacked our suitcases, took our showers, ate our lunch, and went to sleep.

FAULTY: Many people choose air transportation because it is fast, offers convenience, and it is not very expensive.

REVISED: Many people choose air transportation because it is fast, convenient, and inexpensive.

FAULTY: You should strive to cooperate with your colleagues to bring about change, for improving communication and professional development.

REVISED: You should strive to cooperate with your colleagues to bring about change, to improve communication, and to further professional development.

**3. Watching Incorrect Omissions**  By omitting essential words in a parallel construction, you force one word to serve the grammatical requirements of two different statements.

One of the most common omissions in student writing occurs in the *has/have . . . will/shall* constructions.

He always has and always will *compete* for the highest honours.

I always have and always shall practise diligently.

To correct this type of omission error, test the verb with each of its auxiliary words; if it appears in the wrong tense, the construction is unparallel.

CORRECTION: He always has competed (not compete) and always will compete (not competed) for the highest honours.

CORRECTION: I always have practised (not practise) diligently and always shall. (Practise is understood.)

**4. Comparisons Using Than or As**  When *than* or *as* are used to join parallel constructions, make sure that the things or ideas they compare are logically and gramatically alike.

ILLOGICAL: The students attending our school are more intelligent than your school. (compare people—students—to a thing—a building)

LOGICAL: The students attending our school are more intelligent than the students attending your school.

ILLOGICAL: His learning is as extensive as Paul. (compares an abstract quality—learning—to a proper noun—Paul)

LOGICAL: His learning is as extensive as Paul's learning. (or simply Paul's)

## Exercise 5.7 — Correcting Faulty Parallelism

After each of the following sentences containing errors in parallel construction, write P in the blank at the right or on a separate sheet. Then rewrite the sentence correctly. If the sentence contains no error, write C instead of P.

EXAMPLE:  I cannot decide whether I should remain in school
or to withdraw.                                               <u>  P  </u>

REVISED:  I cannot decide whether to remain in school or to
withdraw.                                                      <u>  C  </u>

**1.** I decided to live in this city because I wanted a better job,
for its social activities, and because of a clean environment.      <u>        </u>

**2.** My sister was a teacher, a school principal, and finally
she became a successful business executive.                         <u>        </u>

**3.** Carl wants not only to compete, but he wants also to win a
gold medal.                                                         <u>        </u>

**4.** Our next door neighbour, a shy and quiet man, and who is
a member of the local Rotary Club, was once a com-
mando in the Canadian Armed Forces.                                 <u>        </u>

**5.** She is neither young nor is she inexperienced.                 <u>        </u>

**6.** My father's car is sporty, fast, expensive, and it is also
quite comfortable.                                                  <u>        </u>

**7.** Debbie enjoys playing cards, reading novels, listening to
classical music, and going on camping trips.                        <u>        </u>

**8.** Our school's computers are more advanced than your
school.                                                            <u>        </u>

**9.** Soccer is Europe's most popular sport, and which is becoming more popular every year in North America.                       <u>        </u>

**10.** I am either going to study electrical engineering at university, or I might try studying electrical technology at our
local community college.                                            <u>        </u>

**11.** He is not only a star basketball player but also an excellent student.                                                      <u>        </u>

**12.** My parents always have and always will vote in the national
election.                                                          <u>        </u>

**13.** She contributes and works for the peace movement in
Canada.                                                            <u>        </u>

**14.** Fernando practises judo every day and strenuously.            <u>        </u>

**15.** Dominic not only works hard, he studies hard as well.         <u>        </u>

**16.** Jake helps his wife by dusting and cooking his own meals.     <u>        </u>

**17.** When we arrived at the lake we unpacked the car, fed the
dog, and aired out the cottage.                                     <u>        </u>

18. She either plays a flute or oboe in the symphony orchestra.  ―――――

19. Our city's buildings are not as modern as your city.  ―――――

20. Both our teachers as well as our students wanted the gymnasium repainted.  ―――――

21. My favourite teacher, a native of Australia, and who is also our tennis coach, is moving to another city next semester.  ―――――

22. An industrial plant with well-motivated and qualified workers and having the latest high-technology equipment will succeed in today's competitive marketplace.  ―――――

23. My sister asked for the family car and that she be allowed to stay out after twelve o'clock.  ―――――

24. If I had my choice of seeing a rock concert or opera, I would choose the opera.  ―――――

25. My teacher asked me to state my opinion of the short story and that I should talk about the main character.  ―――――

26. Susan always has promoted women's rights and always will.  ―――――

27. Sky-diving is extremely hazardous and which requires great skill and concentration.  ―――――

28. My mother studied physics, mathematics, and now she is studying world history.  ―――――

29. Maria not only collects old coins, she collects stamps as well.  ―――――

30. Hockey in Canada is more popular than the United States.  ―――――

## Exercise 5.8 — Revising the Paragraph to Improve Parallelisms

Rewrite the following paragraphs by eliminating errors in parallel structure.

1. The introduction should not only motivate readers to read the body of your report, it should contain the report's purpose, the background of the problem, the problem's limits, and the guidelines of the solution. There may be instances, however, when your introduction need only include the purpose of the report; for example, your readers may have already familiarized themselves with the general areas of your research and are conversant with the technical context of your development and proposed solution. You must be careful, though, not to give the impression that you will deal with larger problems than your report actually covers; for nothing is more frustrating to readers than being led to expect more than

they are actually given. Readers always have and always will rebel at being misled by promises in the introduction that are not developed in the body and the conclusion does not fulfill.

2. What can we do to improve the image of science and technology as something that can be understood and controlled and by ordinary men? Well, we can start by educating the public, both in school as well as outside it, in the way in which scientific discoveries affect our daily lives. We may pursue this educational process in a number of ways: in our schools we can arrange student field trips to high-technology industries so that students can see for themselves the direct application of scientific developments; by inviting speakers working in the mainstream of science and who can talk about their work in progress; and organizing more scientific forums where different students can exchange ideas. In the non-academic sector, we can devote more newspaper and magazine space to news stories that are scientifically oriented, and by sponsoring more television programs that examine, in layman's language, present and future research in science as well as in technology.

For too long now the average citizen has been suspicious and apprehensive about the methods science uses to understand nature; therefore, it is about time we opened some windows and let in some air that is fresh. Strengthening our lines of communication would be an excellent and solid beginning.

# CHAPTER SIX

# Keys to Better Spelling

Poor spelling is not an incurable disease. True, some people have better visual memories than other people, and some have great success in sounding out words phonetically. But most people, with a little concerted effort, can easily overcome their spelling handicap. Here are a few suggestions.

1. **Write with a dictionary**   If you are not sure of the spelling of a word, get into the habit of looking it up in a dictionary. If you look up the word often enough, your mere exposure to it will help you spell it correctly.

2. **Divide words into syllables**   If you are not quite sure how to spell a word, pronounce it carefully by breaking it into syllables. Although many English words are not spelled the way they are pronounced, many more are; so by pronouncing words first you will not write *atheletics* for *athletics*, or *grievious* for *grievous*, or *villian* for *villain*, or *envirment* for *environment*.

3. **Proofread everything you write**   This simple device for picking out spelling errors is too often ignored by students. Many of our errors result from simple carelessness, and are therefore easily revealed by a careful re-reading. If you have left letters out, or transposed letters, or confused one word with another because of its sound, proofreading will enable you to find virtually all of these mistakes.

4. **Make a list**   Compose a list of the words you most frequently misspell and write them correctly. As you learn to spell them more proficiently and encounter new words that give you trouble, you will continually add new words to, and subtract old words from, your list. In doing so, you will always have a running record of your rate of improvement.

5. **Read something every day**   Simply exposing yourself to words will aid your spelling when you write. Reading is the easiest and least obnoxious method of learning to spell. Memorizing the spelling of words that you rarely see in print

(because you do not read) is next to useless. You might as well try learning punctuation by watching television. So whatever else you do to improve your spelling, make sure you read—every day.

## A. THE RULES

Although English spelling has almost as many exceptions as rules, there are several useful rules that will help you to spell hundreds of words correctly.

### 1. The *ie* and the *ei* words

The *ie* rhyme is still the most effective way to learn this rule:

> Write *i* before *e* except after *c*
> or when sounded as *a*
> as in *neighbour* and *weigh*.

Examples of *i* before *e*: achieve, grief, field, piece, relief

Examples of *e* before *i*: sleigh, receipt, foreign, ceiling

Common exceptions: either, neither, weird, seize, height

### 2. Words ending in *y*

(a) Words ending in *y* preceded by a consonant change *y* to *i* before adding all suffixes except *ing*.

| EXAMPLES: | mercy/merciful | study/studying |
|---|---|---|
| | try/tried | hurry/hurrying |
| | fry/fried | worry/worrying |

(b) Words ending in *y* preceded by a vowel retain the *y* before all suffix endings.

| EXAMPLES: | stay/stayed; portray/portrayed; enjoy/enjoyed |
|---|---|
| COMMON EXCEPTIONS: | lay/laid; say/said; slay/slain |

### 3. Dropping the final *e*

(a) The final *e* is dropped before a suffix beginning with a vowel; it is retained before a suffix beginning with a consonant.

Examples of final *e* dropped: change/changing; force/forcing; desire/desirable

Examples of final *e* retained: hope/hopeless; use/useful; excite/excitement

Exceptions: argument, truly, awful, ninth, wholly

(b) The final *e* is also retained after a soft *c* or *g* if the suffix begins with *a* or *o*.

EXAMPLES: notice/noticeable; change/changeable; advantage/advantageous; courage/courageous

## 4. Doubling the final consonant

(a) Double the final consonant following a single vowel before you add a suffix beginning with a vowel when the following conditions occur:

   (i) The word has only one syllable.
   Examples: swim/swimming; trip/tripped; ship/shipped

   (ii) The word is accented on the last syllable.
   Examples: begin/beginning; compel/compelled; occur, occurred.

(b) If the accent shifts to the first syllable when a suffix beginning with a vowel is added, do not double the final consonant.

EXAMPLES:   prefer/preference; confer/conference; defer/deference

## 5. Plurals: Adding *s* or *es*.

(a) Add *s* to nouns ending in *y* preceded by a vowel.

EXAMPLES:   valleys, keys, clays, guys

(b) Add *es* to form the plurals of words ending in *ch*, *x*, , *sh* or *s*.

EXAMPLES:   axes, marshes, taxes, churches, buses

(c) Add only *s* to nouns ending in *o* preceded by a vowel.

EXAMPLES:   cameos, folios, radios, rodeos

# B. CONFUSING WORDS THAT SOUND OR LOOK ALIKE

**1.** accede/exceed
   *accede* means to comply with; *exceed* means to surpass.
**2.** accept/except
   *accept* means to take or receive; *except* means to exclude.
**3.** adapt/adopt
   *adapt* means to adjust; *adopt* means to choose or take possession of.
**4.** advice/advise
   *advice* is a noun meaning information given or recommendations made;
   *advise* is a verb meaning to give counsel.
**5.** affect/effect
   *affect* as a verb means to influence or to change; *effect* as a noun means result
   or outcome, and as a verb to fulfill or to bring about.
**6.** altar/alter
   an *altar* is a part of a church; *alter* is a verb meaning to change.

**7.** beside/besides

*beside* means by the side of; *besides* means in addition to.

**8.** born/borne

*born* means brought into life; *borne* means carried or endured.

**9.** breath/breathe

*breath* is a noun meaning respiration; *breathe* is a verb meaning the act of inhaling and exhaling, respiring.

**10.** choose/chose

*choose* means to select; *chose* is the past tense of choose.

**11.** cite/site/sight

*cite* is a verb meaning to quote; *site* is a noun meaning a place; and *sight* is a noun meaning vision or a particular view.

**12.** clothes/cloths

*clothes* means wearing apparel; *cloths* are fabrics from which clothes are made, or simply pieces of fabric.

**13.** coarse/course

*coarse* means rough or common; *course* can mean the direction taken, a plan of action, a path of movement, or a fixed plan of study (as in a school subject).

**14.** complement/compliment

*complement* is a noun meaning that which completes or fulfills; *compliment* as a verb means to praise, and as a noun means a flattering remark.

**15.** conscience/conscious

*conscience* is a noun meaning the sense of right and wrong; *conscious* is an adjective meaning aware, able to think and feel, in the normal waking state.

**16.** council/counsel

*council* is a noun meaning an assembly; *counsel* as a verb means to give advice, and as a noun means an attorney (or anyone whose advice is sought).

**17.** decent/descent

*decent* means proper or commendable; *descent* means a going down, a way to go down, a downward slope, and also ancestry.

**18.** desert/dessert

*desert* as a noun means a barren land, and as a verb means to abandon; *dessert* is the last course of a meal.

**19.** device/devise

*device* is a noun meaning a mechanical contrivance, a design; *devise* is a verb meaning to plan or scheme.

**20.** dyeing/dying

*dyeing* means changing the colour of something; *dying* means approaching death.

**21.** emigrate/immigrate

*emigrate* means to leave a country in order to live in another country; *immigrate* means to enter a country for the purpose of taking up permanent residence.

**22.** farther/further

*farther* means at a greater distance, and it refers to space; *further* means in addition to, and it refers to time, quantity or degree.

**23.** formally/formerly

*formally* means in a formal manner; *formerly* means before or preceding.

**24.** heal/heel

*heal* means to cure; *heel* as a noun means a part of the human foot, a part of a shoe or sock, and as a verb means to furnish with a heel, or to walk closely at someone's heels.

**25.** its/it's

*its* is the possessive form of it; *it's* is a contraction of it is.

**26.** later/latter

*later* means after a period of time or after a previous event; *latter* means the second in a series of two (the opposite of former).

**27.** lead/led

*lead* as a verb means to guide, and as a noun it means a type of metal; *led* is the past tense of the verb to lead.

**28.** lesson/lessen

*lesson* is a noun meaning an exercise designed to teach something; *lessen* is a verb meaning to make small.

**29.** liable/libel

*liable* means responsible; *libel* as a verb means to defame, and as a noun means a malicious misrepresentation of someone.

**30.** lightening/lightning

*lightening* means making lighter; *lightning* means an electrical discharge in the atmosphere.

**31.** lose/loose

*lose* means to suffer the loss of something; *loose* as an adjective means unbound, and as a verb means to release.

**32.** passed/past

*passed* is a tense of the verb meaning to move along or move by; *past* is a noun meaning time gone by.

**33.** peace/piece

*peace* means calmness, serenity, the absence of conflict; *piece* means a portion of something.

**34.** perfect/prefect

*perfect* means without fault; *prefect* means a type of official.

**35.** personal/personnel

*personal* means private or belonging to a certain individual; *personnel* means the staff of a company or an organization.

**36.** precede/proceed

*precede* means to go before; *proceed* means to advance or go ahead.

**37.** prescribe/proscribe

*prescribe* means to order or advise; *proscribe* means to forbid.

**38.** principle/prinicipal

*principle* means a general rule; *principal* as an adjective means the first, and as a noun means a sum of money that draws interest or a chief official of a school.

**39.** quiet/quite

*quiet* means calm, silent; *quite* means entirely, completely.

**40.** respectively/respectfully

*respectively* means in a given order; *respectfully* means in a courteous manner.

**41.** rite/right/write

*rite* means a ceremony or ritual; *right* means correct; and *write* means to inscribe.

**42.** stationary/stationery

*stationary* means fixed, unmovable; *stationery* means writing materials.

**43.** strait/straight

*strait* is a water passageway; *straight* means not crooked.

**44.** than/then

*than* is a conjunction that compares; *then* is an adverb meaning at a given time.

**45.** their/there/they're

*their* is a possessive pronoun meaning belonging to them; *there* is an adverb meaning in that place; and *they're* is a contraction of they are.

**46.** threw/through/thorough

*threw* is the past tense of throw; *through* can mean in one side and out the other, or from end to end, or it can mean by use of, or completed; and *thorough* means carried to completion, omitting nothing, painstaking.

**47.** to/two/too

*to* is a preposition meaning toward; *two* is the number 2; and *too* is an adverb meaning more than enough, more than average, or also.

**48.** vice/vise

*vice* means sin, wickedness, or an undesirable habit; *vise* means a type of clamp.

**49.** were/where

*were* is the past tense of the verb to be; *where* is an adverb meaning a place in which.

**50.** weather/whether

*weather* refers to the state of the atmosphere; *whether* means if.

**51.** whose/who's

*whose* is the possessive of who; *who's* is a contraction of who is.

**52.** your/you're

*your* is a possessive pronoun; *you're* is a contraction of you are.

## Exercise 6.1 − Spelling

Identify the misspelled words in the following sentences, and then spell them correctly in the blank at the right or on a separate sheet. If the sentence contains no spelling error, write C in the blank or beside the number of the sentence on your worksheet.

**1.** Our organization is libel for the damages if our victory party gets out of control. _____

**2.** We must adapt a new method of evaluation before proceeding. _____

**3.** His conscience would not let him dessert his helpless comrades. _____

**4.** Sally can breath under water for two minutes as long as she remains stationary. _____

**5.** Their could not be a better site for our new gymnasium. _____

**6.** The principles of mathematics are absolute. _____

**7.** This welding devise was formerly owned by the city engineering department. _____

**8.** Thelma went straight to her academic advisor for council. _____

**9.** Our house is situated in a quiet part of town, were there are no commercial buildings or apartment houses. _____

**10.** My yearly health examination was quite thorough, but I past with flying colours. _____

11. Our high-school band, led by two drum majorettes, proceeded us into the football stadium.  _____

12. Our plant personnel must be safety conscious at all times.  _____

13. When my best friend immigrated to Australia, I felt deserted.  _____

14. We do not know whether he is threw repairing the duplicating machine.  _____

15. I do not know were my English course is being held.  _____

16. Danielle could not hike any further because the heel came off her boot.  _____

17. Please tell me whose responsible for enrolling students in their proper courses. ·  _____

18. Our school principal excepted the safety award on behalf of the staff and students.  _____

19. Stella's marks were higher then Barbara's, but both their marks were lower than Olaf's.  _____

20. I asked for a leave of absense, and my supervisor assented.  _____

21. I was eighteen when my first child was borne.  _____

22. The scoutmaster led us to shelter when the lightening struck the tree, but the storm soon passed, allowing us to proceed with our hike.  _____

23. Its too bad that City Council will not pass more stringent pollution regulations.  _____

24. You must site the sources of your quotations before turning in your essays.  _____

25. Our office has quite enough stationary for our immediate needs.  _____

26. They're sure that we are not too late to register for next semester.  _____

27. We have a full compliment of workers; all we need is more work.  _____

28. Our team is liable to loose its next game if we do not permit our athletes to use the practice field this Friday.  _____

29. My reasons for resigning are personal; please do not attempt to council me any further.  _____

30. Of the two distinct procedures, the later proved more cost effective and adaptable.  _____

# Some Frequently Misspelled Words

| | | | |
|---|---|---|---|
| absence | becoming | definitely | fortunately |
| accept | believe | delinquency | forty |
| acceptable | benefited | dependent | fulfilled |
| accessible | bicycle | descend | government |
| accidentally | boundaries | describe | grammar |
| accommodate | bulletin | desirable | grateful |
| accomplish | bureau | despair | grievance |
| accumulate | business | desperate | guarantee |
| accustomed | calendar | despised | height |
| achievement | candidate | develop | heroes |
| acquaintance | careful | dining | hindrance |
| acquire | cemetery | disappeared | hoping |
| across | changeable | disappoint | humorous |
| address | chargeable | disastrous | hypocrisy |
| adequate | colonel | dissatisfied | immediately |
| adjustment | coming | effect | immigrants |
| adolescent | commission | efficiency | imminent |
| advantageous | commit | eighth | importance |
| advisable | commitment | elementary | incidentally |
| affect | committee | eligible | independent |
| aggravate | comparable | embarrass | indispensable |
| aisle | comparatively | eminent | inevitable |
| allot | compelled | emphasize | influential |
| altogether | competition | enforceable | intelligence |
| amateur | completely | entrance | interesting |
| analyze | conceivable | environment | interfere |
| anniversary | condemn | equipped | interpreted |
| answer | conquer | equivalent | interrupt |
| anxious | conscience | especially | irrelevant |
| apologizing | conscious | exaggerated | irresistible |
| apparent | consequently | except | knowledge |
| appearance | conspicuous | excitement | laboratory |
| approximate | consistent | exhausted | legitimate |
| approximately | continually | existence | leisurely |
| argument | counterfeit | explanation | library |
| arrangement | courteous | extraordinary | license |
| aroused | curiosity | familiar | lieutenant |
| athlete | deceive | fascination | loneliness |
| attendance | decent | February | maintenance |
| basically | deficiencies | foreign | marriage |

| | | | |
|---|---|---|---|
| mathematics | possess | reference | superstitious |
| miniature | possession | referred | supplement |
| mischievous | possibility | relieve | suppress |
| morale | potato | repetition | surprise |
| mortgage | practically | resemblance | surround |
| necessary | precede | resistance | syllables |
| niece | preference | restaurant | synonym |
| ninety | preferred | rhythm | temperament |
| noticeable | prejudiced | ridiculous | temporary |
| obstacle | preparation | safety | thorough |
| occasion | prevalent | satisfactorily | through |
| occurred | primitive | scarcely | tragedy |
| occurrence | privilege | schedule | transferred |
| omission | probably | scissors | truly |
| omitted | proceed | secretary | twelfth |
| opportunity | procedure | seized | typewriter |
| optimistic | professional | sensible | unanimous |
| parallel | professor | separate | undoubtedly |
| paralyzed | profitable | sergeant | unnecessary |
| parliament | prominent | serviceable | usually |
| particular | pronunciation | shining | varieties |
| peaceable | psychology | similar | vegetable |
| perceive | pursue | solemn | vengeance |
| perform | pursuing | sophomore | vigorous |
| permanent | quantity | staring | village |
| permissible | quitting | strength | villain |
| perseverance | receipt | studying | weird |
| persistent | receive | succeed | wholly |
| personnel | recipes | successful | withhold |
| phenomenon | recognize | sufficient | woman |
| piece | recommend | superintendent | writing |
| planned | recurrent | supersede | |

# CHAPTER SEVEN

# Punctuating Effectively

Punctuation marks may be understood as signposts that guide readers through our written statements, or they may be compared to the verbal inflections we employ in speech. When we pause between statements, raise or lower our voices, or adjust the pitch, we are controlling the meaning of what we say. The same thing happens in written expression. When we punctuate properly we permit readers to follow our ideas and to respond to the stress we place on those ideas.

Punctuation, then, is our directive to our readers, informing them how we want them to read our prose. They will accept our control so long as we are consistent—so long, that is, as our ideas and statements flow in a steady and logical pattern. The omission or misuse of punctuation marks short-circuits this flow of ideas and causes readers to lose confidence in our ability to convey meaning. Thus proper punctuation permits us to place emphasis, to convey mood, and to marshal ideas.

## A. MASTERING THE COMMA

Because commas serve more functions inside the sentence than any other mark of punctuation, they are the most difficult marks to master. But, when used properly, they tighten and clarify sentence structure, pace our readers through our thoughts, and substitute for the many important inflections that we employ to convey meaning in speech.

The comma's function may be divided into two general areas: (1) To separate internal sentence elements that otherwise would destroy clarity and confuse the reader, and (2) to set off parenthetical sentence elements that interrupt the flow of thought between the words, phrases, and clauses.

### 1. Commas that Separate

(a) *Separating Independent Clauses*
When two independent clauses are joined by a coordinating conjunction (and, but, or, etc.), they must be separated by a comma.

We mowed the lawn, but we failed to water the garden.

The workers went on strike, and the citizens supported their demands.

Conjunctions that do not join independent clauses do not require commas.

Depending on the weather, Mr. Robinson will *fly* or *drive* to his business meeting. (two verbs; no comma)

The ball sailed *over the goalpost* and *into the stands*. (two phrases; no comma)

We think *that he is breaking the law* and *that he will soon be caught*. (two dependent clauses; no comma)

(b) *Separating Elements in a Series*

A series consists of three or more words or word groups that have the same grammatical function in the sentence. When a coordinating conjunction joins the last two elements, a comma is placed before it.

*Peter, Henry,* and *Elizabeth* were all invited to the school dance. (a series of nouns)

My parents *shopped* in London, *dined* in Paris, and *skied* in Switzerland. (a series of verbs)

The stray dog ran *down the hall, through the laboratory*, and *into my office*. (a series of phrases)

We were told *that the test would be long, that it would be difficult*, and *that it would count towards our final mark*. (a series of dependent clauses)

"*I came, I saw, I conquered*." (a series of short, independent clauses)

Note: The comma may be omitted in a series when a conjunction is used to connect each element.

Jack *and* Tom *and* Bill all made the starting team.

Please take off your coats *and* sit down *and* listen.

For his birthday, I shall buy my younger brother a toy fire engine *or* a wind-up racing car *or* a picture puzzle.

(c) *Separating Coordinate Adjectives*

Two or more adjectives are coordinate when they equally modify the same noun or pronoun. To test whether or not adjectives are coordinate, reverse their order and place *and* between them. If they read intelligibly, separate them with commas.

The alert, energetic students passed the test.
The energetic *and* alert students passed the test.

The clear, cold mountain stream flowed near our camp.
The cold *and* clear mountain stream flowed near our camp.

Observe how the adjectives below differ from the coordinate adjectives:

She was wearing a tattered fur coat.

John became an accomplished modern dancer.

If we try to reverse their order and insert a conjunction, the sentences become nonsensical, for the last adjective is too closely related to the noun.

She was wearing a fur *and* tattered coat. (the word *tattered* modifies *fur* as well as *coat*)

John became a modern *and* accomplished dancer. (the word *accomplished* modifies *modern* as well as *dancer*)

(d) *Separating to Prevent Misunderstanding*
Some words and phrases must be separated from the rest of the sentence by a comma to avoid confusing—and sometimes amusing—the reader.

CONFUSING: Outside the crowd pressed against the police barriers.
REVISED: Outside, the crowd pressed against the police barriers.

CONFUSING: When basting Mother often covers the turkey with a cheese cloth.
REVISED: When basting, Mother often covers the turkey with a cheese cloth.

CONFUSING: At nine thirty students entered the Dean's office.
REVISED: At nine, thirty students entered the Dean's office.

# Exercise 7.1 — Commas That Separate Independent Clauses and Elements in a Series

In the following sentences insert commas where you think they are needed. If you must place one or more commas in a sentence, write W in the blank to the right; if the sentence is correctly punctuated, write C in the blank. If you are working on a separate sheet of paper, rewrite the sentences and insert commas where you think they are necessary. if the sentence is correct, simply write C.

EXAMPLE: Tom, Joe, and Jim went to the show together.     ___W___

We saw him enter the store, but we did not see him leave.     ___C___

**1.** Do you like to snack on pretzels peanuts or potato chips?     _____

2. Irving has already eaten but his brother is still waiting to be served. _____

3. Did she want both a salad and a cup of soup? _____

4. My car needs an oil change and a tune-up and a new left front tire. _____

5. We won the game but lost the match. _____

6. Initially, William resisted the pressure to have his name placed in nomination but he finally relented after realizing that he was the overwhelming choice of the nominating committee. _____

7. The bank tellers tried to form a union, but they could not muster enough votes. _____

8. Our chairperson sent us each a memorandum and then called a general meeting. _____

9. Both Alexandria and Hector are intelligent and industrious and generous. _____

10. Last summer our province was hit by a severe drought several small tornadoes and a flash flood that caused millions of dollars worth of damage. _____

11. The summer sale will begin on Thursday and end on Saturday. _____

12. Tomorrow the school cafeteria will serve either hot dogs and baked beans or fish and chips. _____

13. Our entertainment committee planned the menu rented the hall and hired the band. _____

14. My music teacher was once a famous concert pianist but now he rarely gives concerts. _____

15. All of the faculty members think that the school semester is too long that classes are too large and that the grading system is too lenient. _____

16. My father's company manufactures circuit boards computer chips and small batteries. _____

17. The school band plays in city parades and at half-time shows during the football season. _____

18. During our trip to Disney World we visited science exhibits ate in a Polynesian restaurant and went on amusement rides. _____

19. Dylan and Sean auditioned for the play but they were not chosen for any of the major roles. _____

**20.** John bought the computer and then never used it. _____

**21.** Potato salad and cold meat and hot dogs are my favourite picnic foods. _____

**22.** I entered the room closed the blinds and then went to bed. _____

**23.** The film we saw last night was too long and too violent and much too juvenile. _____

**24.** Mr. Lammons sent the package last Thursday but we never received it until this Wednesday. _____

**25.** The children ran into the school yard jumped on the swings climbed on the monkey bars and then began celebrating the beginning of their summer recess. _____

**26.** Our parents think that we should learn about the harmful effects of drugs alcohol and tobacco. _____

**27.** The severe thunderstorm blew down small trees knocked down telephone wires and short-circuited the power lines. _____

**28.** Maureen's clothes are chic and well-tailored and expensive. _____

**29.** The game began on time but half the spectators were still not seated. _____

**30.** Dr. Harrington was a famous surgeon and the first to perform a heart transplant operation in our province. _____

## Exercise 7.2 — Commas that Separate Coordinate Adjectives and Confusing Sentence Elements

Insert the necessary commas in the following sentences. When you add commas, place W in the blank to the right of the sentence. If the sentence needs no further punctuation, write C in the blank. If you are working on a separate sheet of paper, rewrite the sentences inserting the necessary commas. If the sentence is already correct, simply write C.

EXAMPLE:   The dark, chilly room was shut off from the rest of the house.    **W**

The large brown dog was pulling the small red sled.    **C**

**1.** With Michael Lisa was quite secure. _____

**2.** Hugh wore a light brown suit and a dark green tie. _____

**3.** The cold damp dreary afternoon lowered everyone's spirits. _____

**4.** High above the workers placed another girder on the skeleton of the new apartment building.   _____

**5.** They finally released the snowy white doves over the cavernous football stadium.   _____

**6.** Something must be done about our slow inefficient outdated transportation system.   _____

**7.** Inside the factory thermometer reached 35 degrees celsius.   _____

**8.** He hit a high fly ball to the speedy left fielder.   _____

**9.** The long lonely tedious hours that I spent on my meticulous historical research finally paid off with an ''A'' grade on my final term paper.   _____

**10.** By nine fifty people were lined up outside the department store.   _____

**11.** We stood on the shore and watched the swift graceful sailboats glide across the azure blue lake.   _____

**12.** Our new computer literacy course was offered in one of our largest refurbished well-lighted classrooms on the first floor.   _____

**13.** Without stopping the subway train rushed by the station platform.   _____

**14.** Hurrying to greet his family in the crowded airport lounge, Henry tripped over a small brown suitcase and broke his arm.   _____

**15.** My favourite summer drink is a long tall cold glass of lemonade.   _____

**16.** Debbie was a quiet shy introverted girl before she joined our drama club.   _____

**17.** Outside the roads were covered with ice.   _____

**18.** The placid sea and the purple sunset made our South Sea island an ideal and a picturesque retreat.   _____

**19.** The green shag rug and the dark brown chesterfield blended together very well.   _____

**20.** Surprisingly university graduates are not finding decent jobs.   _____

**21.** My favourite summer sports are sailing and water skiing.   _____

**22.** Loud tumultuous cheers greeted our strong well-conditioned athletes when they entered the crowded gymnasium.   _____

**23.** While cooking the chef was annoyed by the suffocating heat in the large kitchen. _____

**24.** Her long dull monotone speech was a major disappointment. _____

**25.** Just as Bill was punting his dog ran onto the field. _____

**26.** Wilma's light blue Chevrolet was stolen by a tall woman in bright yellow running shorts. _____

**27.** I missed too many valuable opportunities to acquire the necessary skills to earn a comfortable living. _____

**28.** His long sloppy ungrammatical essay received a well-deserved failing grade. _____

**29.** The hot humid sultry summer afternoon was not a good time of day to play tennis. _____

**30.** Far below the automobiles looked like tiny bugs. _____

**2. Commas That Set Off**   Certain parenthetical words and word groups are set apart because they interrupt the normal rhythm of the sentence. Most of these parenthetical elements occur within the sentence and are therefore set off by two commas; others, however, occur at the beginning or the end of the sentence, and are set off by only one comma. But wherever these parenthetical expressions occur, they are set off from the rest of the sentence because they interrupt the flow of ideas or contain information unessential to the meaning of the sentence.

(a) *Setting Off Nonrestrictive Modifiers*

A nonrestrictive modifier is a phrase or clause that adds non-essential information to the core of the sentence, and may be deleted without altering the meaning of the sentence.

John Williams, who wears red ties, is my best friend.

The fact that your best friend has a preference for red ties is irrelevant information; it does not restrict or qualify the basic sentence statement. Now consider this sentence:

The man who wears red ties is my best friend.

Now the modifier is restrictive because without its information the reader would not know which man is your best friend (the one with the red tie); therefore you cannot delete the modifier and still maintain the sense of the sentence. Remember, only modifying phrases or clauses with commas around them can be safely removed from the body of the sentence; those that do not have commas cannot be removed without affecting the meaning of the sentence. Thus, one is restrictive (no commas) and the other nonrestrictive (two commas). Consider the following examples.

NONRESTRICTIVE: The traffic cop, *with a whistle in his mouth*, guided the school children across the street.

RESTRICTIVE: The traffic cop with the whistle in his mouth is the one who guided the children across the street. (The modifying phrase points out which policeman.)

NONRESTRICTIVE: Cliff Jackson, *who has a bearskin rug on his floor*, is a famous Canadian trapper.

RESTRICTIVE: The man with the bearskin rug on his floor is a famous Canadian trapper. (The modifying clause identifies the man.)

NONRESTRICTIVE: The British Museum, *where Karl Marx did most of his research on economic theory*, is prized by scholars all over the world.

RESTRICTIVE: The museum where Karl Marx did most of his research on economic theory is prized by scholars from all over the world. (The modifying clause identifies the museum.)

The same distinction can be made about adverbial clauses that end sentences. If the clauses contain essential information, they are restrictive.

NONRESTRICTIVE: I plan to visit Spain, *where the weather is pleasant and the prices are low.*

RESTRICTIVE: I plan to visit Spain if the weather is pleasant and the prices are reasonable. (The weather and the prices will determine whether or not you visit Spain.)

NONRESTRICTIVE: Martin will try out for the basketball team, *although he is not even six feet tall.*

RESTRICTIVE: Martin will try out for the basketball team if he is tall enough. (His height will determine whether or not he tries out for the team.)

NONRESTRICTIVE: We are moving to Vermont in the fall, *when the leaves change colours.*

RESTRICTIVE: We are moving to Vermont when the leaves change colours. (The clause contains precise information about when you are moving.)

## (b) *Setting Off Appositives*

An appositive is a noun, along with its modifiers, that is closely related to another noun as an explanation: Mike, the student; Joe, the barber; Fred, the mailman, etc. Since an appositive can also be restrictive and nonrestrictive, it obeys the same comma rule as phrases and clauses do.

NONRESTRICTIVE: Ms. Price, *the Dean of Students*, has been promoted to Vice-President.

> Bertrand Russell, *the famous twentieth-century philoso-pher*, often demonstrated for nuclear disarmament.

Observe the difference in the appositives that contain essential explanatory information. They are more obviously restrictive, and therefore do not take commas:

> RESTRICTIVE: My sister *Peggy* is arriving by train. (explains which sister)
> The number *seven* is considered lucky by many people. (explains which number is considered lucky)

### (c) *Setting Off Sentence Modifiers*

Commas set off parenthetical words and phrases that modify whole clauses and sentences. These modifiers are used for summary, emphasis, or transition; they give direction to the writer's ideas and often reveal the precise tone he wishes to convey. A partial list of the most commonly used modifiers may be found below.

It is true, *nevertheless*, that the price of oil will increase next month.

He is, *by the way*, a straight "A" student.

*After all*, nobody is perfect.

*However*, if you do not agree, we will revise our plans.

---

**Some Sentence Modifiers**

| | | |
|---|---|---|
| accordingly | in addition | otherwise |
| after all | in fact | perhaps |
| also | in my opinion | personally |
| as a matter of fact | in other words | still |
| as a result | in short | that is |
| as a rule | indeed | therefore |
| at any rate | meanwhile | thus |
| besides | moreover | too |
| by the way | namely | well |
| consequently | naturally | without a doubt |
| finally | nevertheless | without question |
| first, second, etc. | no doubt | yes, no |
| for example | obviously | |
| for instance | of course | |
| furthermore | on the contrary | |
| hence | on the other hand | |
| however | on the whole | |

Remember, when these modifiers occur in the middle of a sentence, two commas are needed to set them off.

WRONG: We are, *on the whole* fairly well off.
CORRECTED: We are, on the whole, fairly well off.

### (d) *Setting Off Absolute Constructions*

Absolute constructions are verbal phrases that, although set apart from the rest of the sentence, cannot stand alone as complete statements. Like other sentence modifiers, they interrupt the flow of thought and modify whole clauses or sentences. Many of these phrases are idioms that are often used in speech.

*Weather permitting*, we shall arrive on time.

*Times being what they are*, we are lucky to be able to afford a vacation.

He is, *to be sure*, a first-rate scholar.

### (e) *Setting Off Contrasting Sentence Elements*

Contrasting elements are normally used for clarification, and they usually begin with the words *not*, *yet*, or *but*.

He suffered, *but survived*.

Paul is an electrical technologist, *not an electrical engineer*.

The sprinter ran swiftly, *yet gracefully*.

### (f) *Setting Off Long Introductory Phrases and Adverbial Clauses*

To ensure clarity, long introductory phrases and adverbial clauses are set off from the rest of the sentence by a comma.

*When the customers arrived at the store*, the door was locked. (introductory clause)

*As the crippled plane landed*, the firefighters sprayed foam on the runway. (introductory clause)

*After leaving the classroom*, we played basketball in the gym. (introductory phrase)

*With such an abundance of fresh fruit and vegetables*, we shall have no trouble finding customers. (introductory phrase)

Note: Short phrases and clauses are set off by commas only if the sentence may be misread without punctuation.

UNCLEAR: While I was bathing the dog jumped into the tub.
CORRECTED: While I was bathing, the dog jumped into the tub.

UNCLEAR: After running a cold shower was what I wanted.
CORRECTED: After running, a cold shower was what I wanted.

(See page 87, Commas That Separate.)

(g) *Setting Off Names in a Direct Address*
When a name or a title is used to address someone, it is set off by commas.

May we continue, *Mr. Bradley*, when you are finished talking?

We have loaded the ship, *Captain*, and now it is ready to leave the harbour.

Complete your answer sheet, *Tom*, before you turn in your test booklet.

(h) *Setting Off Speakers Directly Quoted*
The words that identify the speaker of a direct quotation are set off by a comma. When inserted in the middle of a quotation the words are set off by two commas.

The hockey coach said, "If you miss one more practice, you're off the team."

"Follow me," ordered the General.

"I think," remarked the defendant, "the sentence is too harsh."

Note: The words specifying who the speaker is are not set off if the quotation is indirect.

The defendant commented that he thought the Judge's sentence was too harsh.

The coach told me that if I miss one more practice I will be off the team.

The General ordered us to follow him.

(i) *Setting Off Echo Questions*
Echo questions are parenthetical expressions, usually occurring in speech. They may occur in the middle or at the end of a sentence.

You were elected, *weren't you*, to the local school board?

You are aware, *aren't you*, that jackets and ties must be worn to the ceremony?

You live at home, *don't you*?

(j) *Setting Off Mild Interjections*
These are expressions that, although parenthetical, are not really exclamatory, and therefore require no exclamation point.

*My word*, it certainly is a dismal afternoon.

*Heavens*, I do not have a clue to what you mean.

*My*, *my*, you certainly have grown during the past year.

*Well*, *well*, you have started the job already.

# Exercise 7.3 – Commas That Set Off Non-Restrictive Modifiers, Appositives, and Introductory Phrases and Clauses

Insert the necessary commas within the following sentences whose elements are not properly set off. Write W in the blank to the right of each sentence you correct or on a separate sheet; if the sentence requires no further punctuation, write C in the blank. Or, rewrite the sentences which require commas, inserting them where necessary.

EXAMPLE:　Farmers who purchase new tractors will be given government subsidies.　　　　C

Playing with intensity, our team rallied and finally won.　　　　W

Paul Baker, our team captain, was awarded the game ball.　　　　W

1. My father who recently retired from the fire department is lecturing on fire safety at our local high school. _____

2. The running shoes that I purchased from the sporting goods store on Main Street have ripped across the heel. _____

3. *Peter the Great* is the title of an award-winning book by Robert K. Massie. _____

4. After completing his homework assignment Teddy decided to play a computer game. _____

5. After lunch Ingrid went shopping. _____

6. Harold Baines our Vice-President is being transferred to Montreal. _____

7. Tracy Kidder's novel *The Soul of a New Machine* is a fascinating story about computer engineers. _____

8. Any student who wishes to apply for a student loan must fill out an application form at our Student Services Department. _____

9. Whatever happened to Melvin Matlock our former cost accountant? _____

10. The woman who was driving the red Ford left her grocery cart in the parking lot. _____

11. During the graduation ceremony our college president received the Citizen-of-the-Year award. _____

12. Our local radio announcer Pat Carson is retiring next month. _____

13. Students who use the library consistently will probably receive the highest grades in English Literature. _____

14. The mechanic who repaired my car's transmission did an excellent job.  _____

15. Elizabeth I the Virgin Queen was one of the most influential monarchs in English history.  _____

16. With so much work to do how can you sit and watch television for the rest of the evening?  _____

17. After class we played basketball in the schoolyard.  _____

18. The Wicked Witch of the West is a character in Walt Disney's *Snow White and the Seven Dwarfs*.  _____

19. *Joshua Then and Now* by Mordecai Richler is my favourite Canadian novel.  _____

20. My sister Peggy is arriving next Wednesday.  _____

21. Veronica Mitford the chairman of our Business Department is visiting Greece this summer.  _____

22. When we arrived home after 1:00 a.m. we found our babysitter playing Trivial Pursuit with our son.  _____

23. The boy wearing the green hat scored two goals for our hockey team last night.  _____

24. During the play the leading lady became ill.  _____

25. Abraham Lincoln the Great Emancipator is one of the most revered American presidents.  _____

26. Having won six straight hands of poker Jack decided to cash in his winnings and go home.  _____

27. The Canadian Prairies where I lived for many years is having a severe drought this summer.  _____

28. The story of John the Baptist is one of the most intriguing Bible stories that I have ever read.  _____

29. Our local community college which is located just north of the city is building a new gymnasium next to the soccer field.  _____

30. The English teacher who wears a rose in his lapel has just published a book of short stories.  _____

## Exercise 7.4 – Commas That Set Off Sentence Modifiers, Absolute Constructions and Contrasting Elements

Insert the necessary commas within the following sentences whose elements are not properly set off. Write W in the blank to the right of each sentence you correct; if the sentence requires no further punctuation, write C in the blank. Or, if you are working on a separate sheet, rewrite those sentences which need commas, inserting them in their proper places.

EXAMPLE:   On the contrary, we approve of your actions.            _____W_____

To be certain of a seat on the train, arrive at the
station at least thirty minutes early.                            _____C_____

She was a model, not a dress designer.                           _____W_____

1. Sheila is in fact a first-class soccer player.                _____

2. We are obviously late for class.                              _____

3. Times being what they are he is fortunate to get even
   a part-time job.                                              _____

4. They will probably arrive about 9:00 p.m. weather
   permitting.                                                   _____

5. The actors rehearsing without scenery or proper lighting
   had to rely on their imaginations.                           _____

6. You should have bought a magazine not a lottery ticket.       _____

7. She is indeed a famous physicist.                            _____

8. You are certainly not eating much tonight.                   _____

9. As a rule my organization never sponsors organized sports.   _____

10. They were tired but happy after their courageous win in
    the Olympic trials.                                          _____

11. However difficult the assignment it must be turned in on time. _____

12. On the contrary Frankie is a first-rate student as well as
    a remarkable athlete.                                        _____

13. The young girl swimming without supervision almost
    drowned in the pool.                                         _____

14. All of us I am certain were terrified of flying for the first time. _____

15. The racing turtles took a long time but finally reached
    their destination.                                           _____

16. Recommended highly her latest novel was a major literary
    disappointment.                                              _____

17. Adolph is without question a first-class brewmaster.        _____

18. We will resume our tennis match when the weather clears.     _____

19. Our teacher although a severe disciplinarian was always
    willing to work with the slower students.                    _____

**20.** The clouds were thick and grey yet somehow peaceful
and benign.     _____

**21.** To be sure you're on time set your watch five minutes ahead.     _____

**22.** Tony is a Virgo not a Capricorn.     _____

**23.** Our auction sale was not as successful as we had hoped,
but we are nevertheless still planning our historical field
trip to Quebec City.     _____

**24.** All things being equal our debating team did a
respectable job.     _____

**25.** We are naturally worried about our upcoming examinations.     _____

**26.** Whatever the cost we shall prevail.     _____

**27.** Julia having nowhere to go decided to return home
to her parents.     _____

**28.** Our coach was loud and gruff yet fair and understanding.     _____

**29.** It seems that we bought everything at the auction
but the Brooklyn Bridge.     _____

**30.** Our university in my opinion has the best library
in Eastern Canada.     _____

## Exercise 7.5 — Commas That Set Off Names, Speakers, Echo Questions, and Mild Interjections

Insert the necessary commas within the following sentences whose elements are
not properly set off. Write W in the blank to the right of each sentence you correct
or on a separate sheet. If the sentence requires no further puctuation, write C in
the blank. Or, if you are working on a separate sheet, rewrite those sentences
which need commas, inserting them in their proper places.

EXAMPLE:   "Pay attention, John, or you will miss important
information."    __W__

"I haven't decided what dress to purchase," replied
Jane.    __W__

Tom made the team, didn't he?    __C__

**1.** Tell me Fred why did you refuse to cooperate?     _____

**2.** "Of course" replied the police officer "we will do
everything possible to apprehend the criminal."     _____

**3.** I almost flunked English didn't I?     _____

**4.** John told me that he was through with teaching.     _____

**5.** No Father I haven't had the car washed yet.                                          _____

**6.** "The trousers look too tight" stated the tailor.                                     _____

**7.** We are not yet ready to attack General.                                              _____

**8.** I spoke to Leslie just the way I am speaking to you.                                 _____

**9.** There there you shouldn't get so upset.                                              _____

**10.** She told him to mind his own business.                                              _____

**11.** No no don't turn on the power until the green light goes on.                        _____

**12.** Mr. Wallace will hand out our marks on Monday, won't he?                            _____

**13.** May we count on your support Reverend for our
Cancer Fund drive?                                                                          _____

**14.** Well well you have finally arrived.                                                 _____

**15.** The president of our student body asked the school
administrators if they would keep the library open
on Sundays.                                                                                _____

**16.** "The men did their best sir but the river is still rising."                         _____

**17.** Jonathan said "Whenever I exercise too long, my legs ache."                         _____

**18.** Dr. Motluk told us not to worry about our grades.                                   _____

**19.** We are sorry Mrs. Donaldson but we cannot extend
your credit.                                                                               _____

**20.** Gee your performance was certainly exciting to watch.                               _____

**21.** Our group leader asked us if we wanted to end our therapy
session early.                                                                             _____

**22.** "Not unless you do" we replied.                                                     _____

**23.** "The plane leaves in ten minutes" announced the flight
steward "so please have your boarding passes ready."                                       _____

**24.** Our instructor is aware isn't he that next Friday is a
civic holiday?                                                                             _____

**25.** Doesn't Alice know that the show starts at eight o'clock?                           _____

**26.** You have already booked our hotel room haven't you?                                 _____

**27.** Good gracious this is a lively party.                                               _____

**28.** The old gentleman said, "My my you are certainly in a
hurry aren't you?"                                                                          _____

**29.** Mr. Simpson told us that he was going into hospital for a
serious operation.                                                                         _____

**30.** "If we lose this game" said the coach "we're out of the
playoffs."                                                                                 _____

## Exercise 7.6 — Comma Review Exercise

Insert the necessary commas in the following sentences whose elements are not properly separated or set off; then write W in the blank to the right of each sentence you correct. If the sentence needs no further punctuation, write C in the blank. Or, if you are working on a separate sheet rewrite sentences which require additional commas, inserting them where necessary.

EXAMPLE: May we sample your fudge, Helen, before we
begin our diet.                                              W

I practised diligently but failed to qualify for the
team.                                                       C

Tom Bennett, who wears loud ties, has just
purchased a pink suit.                                       W

1. We have sold our stocks and bonds but we are still
very much in debt.                                          _____

2. To succeed in college you must attend all classes do all
your home assignments and study for all your tests.        _____

3. My mother and father vacationed in California and Hawaii,
but they did not have time to see the surfboard races in
Honolulu or the Olympic Games in Los Angeles.              _____

4. The brisk refreshing invigorating swim in the ocean
was just what I needed.                                     _____

5. Unfortunately hard liquor was served at our graduation party.  _____

6. Just after ten thirty men showed up to apply for the
part-time job that was advertised in the newspaper.        _____

7. My uncle who was once a stage actor is directing
our high-school play.                                      _____

8. Charlie Silverman our Vice-President of Manufacturing
has purchased a computer for his office.                   _____

9. The truck that skidded off the icy road is being examined
by our local police.                                       _____

10. Since I last saw her on stage in Vancouver she has aged
considerably.                                              _____

11. She is as a matter of fact in danger of losing her scholarship.  _____

12. No Mr. Sopinka you may not leave the room.              _____

13. Marge is frequently late for rehearsals.                _____

14. Well well what have we here? Is it human animal or
vegetable?                                                 _____

15. My father is a mechanical engineer not an electrical engineer.  _____

16. We have advertised for used cars but they seem to be rare commodities in our small city.  _____

17. ''You have a lovely home'' replied Sandra.  _____

18. Goodness I didn't think our shopping trip would take this long.  _____

19. That kitten is certainly playful isn't she?  _____

20. Watch out for the train Juan; it is not slowing down.  _____

21. We all attended the meeting and then met for lunch.  _____

22. ''I am not giving out grades today'' announced the teacher ''and that is final.''  _____

23. Our city is without doubt located in one of the most scenic areas of Canada.  _____

24. Mr. Chasen told his supervisor that the welding machine was unsafe.  _____

25. I drove to the supermarket picked up my groceries and then went on a picnic.  _____

26. No George the test will not be given on Friday.  _____

27. My guidance counsellor who was once a professional hockey player is now working on his Ph.D. degree.  _____

28. Down below the basement of the apartment building was rapidly filling with water.  _____

29. Since her last appearance on stage she has gained weight.  _____

30. Carol Hoffman my favourite singer is retiring next year.  _____

31. After dinner we intend to play scrabble.  _____

32. The school bus on which our son rides was in a minor accident last Tuesday.  _____

33. The baseball game should start on time weather permitting.  _____

34. Our order will arrive next week won't it?  _____

35. The cups and saucers and dishes were all broken after the minor earthquake.  _____

36. Our company is located in Quebec not New Brunswick.  _____

37. All things being equal I believe our gymnastic team will win a gold medal.  _____

38. After the last shift of coal miners returned to the surface they decided to strike for better working conditions.  _____

**39.** We have increased our sales but not our profits. _____

**40.** ''You may not practise your saxophone'' replied Brenda
''until your father awakens.'' _____


# B. EMPLOYING THE SEMICOLON

The semicolon may be thought of as a small period because it tells the reader to stop briefly before proceeding. It balances as well as separates. It balances related independent clauses, and it separates a series of complicated word groups that contain commas.

**1.** Semicolons are used between structurally related independent clauses *not* joined by a coordinate conjunction.

> John plays hockey for pleasure; his brother plays hockey for money.
>
> We will not meet this afternoon; we will meet tomorrow morning.

Make sure both clauses are independent before you place a semicolon between them. Semicolons are never used to separate dependent from independent clauses.

> WRONG: After the doctor delivered Jane's baby; he smoked a cigar with her husband.
>
> CORRECT: After the doctor delivered Jane's baby, he smoked a cigar with her husband.

**2.** Use a semicolon before a conjunctive adverb that connects two independent clauses.

> I did not study for Friday's test; therefore, I shall probably fail.
>
> She was ill when the skating competition took place; nevertheless she came in second.

The comma after the conjunctive adverb is now optional. If you wish to emphasize the adverb, use a comma; otherwise you may leave it out.

Note: Be certain that the conjunctive adverb does, in fact, connect two independent clauses before you place a semicolon before it. If it is used parenthetically within the sentence, it must be set off by commas.

> WRONG: We are still optimistic, but we are; nevertheless, prepared for the worst.
>
> CORRECT: We are still optimistic, but we are, nevertheless, prepared for the worst.

WRONG:   Our guests are due to arrive at noon; we should; therefore, light the barbecue.

CORRECT:   Our guests are due to arrive at noon; we should therefore light the barbecue.

---

### Commonly Used Conjunctive Adverbs

| | | |
|---|---|---|
| accordingly | instead | nonetheless |
| besides | indeed | otherwise |
| consequently | likewise | then |
| furthermore | meanwhile | therefore |
| hence | moreover | thus |
| however | nevertheless | |

---

**3.** Use a semicolon between independent clauses connected by a coordinate conjunction when the clauses are long and contain internal punctuation.

> The financial section of the daily newspaper, where the stock quotations are located, is read diligently by my employer; but I prefer the sports section, since my son is a minor league baseball player.

> When I first went away to college, my father gave me an electric typewriter; but my sister, knowing my communication difficulty, presented me with an Oxford dictionary.

**4.** Use a semicolon to separate items in a series when each item contains two or more pieces of information set off by commas.

> My second-semester instructors are Mr. Boyle, English; Dr. Carpenter, Physics; Ms. Paulson, Mathematics; and Dr. Priestly, Psychology.

> I was interviewed for my job by Elizabeth Gray, Vice-President, Marketing; Jim Barber, Vice-President, Manufacturing; and by Jack Payne, Sales Manager.

**5.** Use semicolons before independent clauses introduced by the expressions *namely*, *that is (i.e.)*, *for example*, or *for instance*.

> You must be alert at all times; that is, when an opportunity arises, grab it.

> We think that he is highly qualified for the chairman's position; for example, he has more than ten years' teaching experience.

## Exercise 7.7 — The Semicolon

Supply semicolons wherever required in the following sentences. Write W in the blank to the right of each sentence that needs a semicolon. If the sentence is properly punctuated, write C in the blank. Alternatively write out the corrected sentences on a separate sheet.

EXAMPLE:   Our camping equipment did not arrive on time;
therefore, we must delay our trip.                          \_\_\_\_W\_\_\_\_

The Director of Marketing, the Vice-President of
Finance, and the Chairman of the Board are now
meeting in the President's office.                          \_\_\_\_C\_\_\_\_

1. Many students eat sandwiches for lunch, some, however,
   prefer hot meals.                                        _____

2. I find it difficult taking notes in class, I cannot tell what is
   important and what isn't.                                _____

3. My sister is blind in one eye, nevertheless she is still
   a voracious reader.                                      _____

4. During the play Katherine misplaced her glasses, but she
   found them under her seat during the intermission.       _____

5. She thinks that everyone is against her, perhaps she is right.   _____

6. Phil Hancock, Vice-President, Sally Renke, Treasurer,
   and Daphne Gleeson, Executive Secretary, are responsible
   for organizing our budget meeting.                       _____

7. Thomas Klein was not asked to direct our play, although
   he is an experienced stage director.                     _____

8. I am perfectly fine, I don't need help from anyone.       _____

9. Irma was late for class every day last week; she is therefore
   being disciplined.                                       _____

10. After our long, hot, exhausting volleyball game, we all
    wanted to drive to the ocean for a swim, but Jim refused
    to lend us his car.                                     _____

11. He firmly believes that his company is financially healthy,
    he is therefore going ahead with the business merger.   _____

12. Keep your mind on your work, for example turn off
    the radio while you are studying.                       _____

13. The troops are ready, sir, they are waiting for inspection.   _____

14. We are determined to finish our hike, however difficult
    the terrain.                                            _____

15. Castor, Inc., Montreal, Thomson Engineering Ltd.,
    Toronto, and Delphin Products, Calgary, are all hiring
    students for the summer.                                _____

16. Our company is presently overextended, that is, we have
    no cash flow.                                           _____

17. During the concert Marie fell asleep, but she awoke
    before the final song.                                  _____

18. Our college offers technology and business courses,
your college, however, concentrates on applied arts.  _____

19. Morris Friedman, Howard Brubaker, and Leslie Sanders are
being transferred to our store in Victoria, B.C. next month.  _____

20. The jungle is dangerous and the natives are unfriendly,
nevertheless we shall continue our journey.  _____

21. Everyone in our small town was terrified—you wouldn't
believe how terrified—because the killer was still at large,
for he had promised, when he returned, to wreak vengeance
on the townspeople.

22. He vowed to climb the mountain, however long it took.  _____

23. Try being careful with your money, for example,
don't charge your meals when you eat out in restaurants.  _____

24. My car is almost paid for now I am going to buy a boat.  _____

25. We must reduce our inventory now, or we will have
to declare bankruptcy.  _____

26. Marg tried to get to the bank before it closed, however,
she was too late.  _____

27. Mark Boudreau, the producer, Trish Cassidy, the actress,
and Harold Wood, the director were eating together
at the new French restaurant.  _____

28. We will have to ask for donations, we don't have
enough money yet for our baseball uniforms.  _____

29. I never expected to be nominated, therefore, I must decline.  _____

30. George is needed on the other side of the construction site.
We had therefore better give him his messages now.  _____

## C. USING THE COLON AND THE DASH PROPERLY

The colon and the dash are alike in that they both introduce explanations and items in series, but they are unlike in that one is more formal and the other more emphatic.

1. **The Colon** Do not confuse the colon with a period or semicolon. It separates sentence elements but does not complete a thought. Rather, it has an introductory function, informing the reader that a piece of sequential information or an explanatory statement will follow.

   (a) Use a colon to introduce a long statement that summarizes, amplifies, or explains a previous statement.

      The Registrar told us everything we needed to know: he informed us of classroom locations, test schedules, and library hours.

The job was not up to my expectations: the salary was too low and the working conditions were sub-standard.

(b) Use a colon to introduce an extended or a formal quotation.

Professor Matthews was outraged when he made the following declaration: "I am not now, never have been, nor never will be a Communist."

One of the most significant statements on human love was made by Erich Fromm: "The love for my own self is inseparably connected with love for any other human being."

(c) Use a colon to introduce a series of words, phrases, or clauses.

I was told to purchase the following items: a hammer, a wrench, a saw, and a pair of pliers.

The requests she made were these: she wanted her lunch delivered, her mail opened, and her office reorganized.

Note: Be sure that an introductory antecedent such as *the following*, *these*, or *as follows* precedes the colon. Do not place a colon immediately after a verb or preposition.

WRONG:   The meal consisted of: bread, cheese, meat, and tea.

The workers demanded: more money, better pension benefits, and extended health care.

To correct these sentences you must either include an antecedent or remove the colon.

The meal consisted of bread, cheese, meat, and tea.

The workers made the following demands: more money, better pension benefits, and extended health care.

(d) Use a colon after formal salutations in business letters and between figures separating minutes and hours:

Dear Sir:       Gentlemen:        10:15 − 1:05

**2. The Dash**   The dash is one of the least understood—and therefore one of the most abused—marks of punctuation. Unskilled writers tend to use it indiscriminately as a substitute for other marks of punctuation. The dash has two general characteristics: it is informal and emphatic. It can substitute for a colon when a less formal introductory break is required, and it can substitute for a comma when a greater stress is needed to set off a parenthetical element. However, for other reasons than these two, the dash is not a proper replacement for a colon or a comma.

(a) Use dashes to set off a parenthetical series that already contains commas.

My favourite meal—roast beef, corn-on-the-cob, and home-fried potatoes —is being prepared right now.

Snow, sleet and rain—that is what we drove through last night.

(b) Use dashes to indicate a break in thought too abrupt and severe to be set off by commas.

He said that he would meet us near the ticket counter—or was it the news-stand?

The antique car—it was in mint condition—sold for almost twenty thousand dollars.

Jim already paid for our tickets—at least I hope he did!

(c) Use a dash to make single words more emphatic.

Money—that is all he thinks about.

Our citizens ask for only one thing—freedom!

(d) Use a dash in place of a colon when you wish to present an informal series or explanation.

Our arrangement is simple—he handles sales, and I oversee production.

He had an amazing variety of clutter on his desk—old pencils, worn erasers, bent paper clips, and elastic bands of different sizes.

## Exercise 7.8 — The Colon and the Dash

Each of the following sentences requires either a colon or a dash. Insert the correct punctuation mark within the parenthesis; then, in the blank to the right, indicate your choice by writing CN for colon and DS for dash. Alternatively rewrite the corrected sentence on a separate sheet and write either CN or DS beside it.

EXAMPLE:  Dan wanted the following items from the
stationery store (:) envelopes, writing paper,
memo pads, and ink erasers.                                        CN

Ellen's new dog (−) a black and white terrier (−)
made friends with us almost immediately.                          DS

**1.** I think we have brought all of our tools ( ) we have
hammers, saws, nails, pliers, and screwdrivers.                   _____

**2.** She ended her talk with this statement ( ) "If you can't
stand the heat, get out of the kitchen."                          _____

**3.** Skiing, curling, ice skating ( ) these are my favourite winter sports.                                              _____

**4.** Yesterday there was an automobile accident on King Street ( ) or was it Park Street ( ) and the damage is estimated to be in excess of five thousand dollars.                                              _____

**5.** I thought I made myself clear ( ) I do not accept late assignments.                                              _____

**6.** Last Saturday ( ) or was it Sunday ( ) our next-door neighbours moved to Vancouver.                                              _____

**7.** We need only one thing to make our barbecue a success ( ) good weather.                                              _____

**8.** We spent the entire day preparing for our auction sale ( ) we collected the promised donations, made the bidding cards, and set up the tables to hold the merchandise.                                              _____

**9.** What famous historical personage made the following statement ( ) ''Let them eat cake''?                                              _____

**10.** My favourite tree ( ) it is a blue spruce ( ) is being cut down by the city next week.                                              _____

**11.** Global pollution ( ) especially water pollution ( ) is endangering the health of millions of people.                                              _____

**12.** The circus is coming to town next week ( ) or is it the following week.                                              _____

**13.** Girls and rock music ( ) that's all my sons ever think about!                                              _____

**14.** The principal speaker made her point very well ( ) she said fiscal responsibility must be shared by everyone.                                              _____

**15.** Most of our office furniture ( ) chairs, desks, file cabinets, and bookcases ( ) arrived last week.                                              _____

**16.** My dentist always gives out this piece of advice ( ) ''Preventive maintenance costs less than extraction.''                                              _____

**17.** Drug addiction ( ) this problem is a major blight on our society.                                              _____

**18.** Stephanie has three brothers ( ) Kevin, Mark, and Sean ( ) who are outstanding scholars.                                              _____

**19.** Mr. Kozol finally settled his financial problems ( ) he sold his dry-cleaning business.                                              _____

**20.** Our store has an interesting collection of pottery ( ) there are flower pots, mixing bowls, ashtrays, and assorted cups and saucers.                                              _____

21. Three Canadian writers ( ) Margaret Atwood,
    Alice Munro, and Robertson Davies ( ) will be studied
    in our English course next semester.                    _____

22. Sports ( ) that is all he talks about!                   _____

23. Which teacher made the following statement ( ) "Cigarette
    smoking is one of the least intelligent habits that students
    can acquire"?                                           _____

24. His solution was drastic ( ) he fired half his employees.  _____

25. I have only one thing to say before I leave ( ) stay alert.  _____

26. Our recommendations were as follows ( ) expand the
    library, cut class size, hire more qualified teachers,
    and reduce your support services.                       _____

27. There were four limousines ( ) or was it five ( )
    parked outside the luxury hotel.                        _____

28. Don't be concerned about Melanie ( ) worry about Sophie.  _____

29. The following items were ordered by our hospital
    administrators ( ) surgical equipment, hospital beds,
    two dozen thermometers, and three wheelchairs.          _____

30. There are only three subjects that I am enjoying this
    semester ( ) mathematics, computer science, and English.  _____

## D. WHEN TO USE QUOTATION MARKS

1. Quotation marks are used to enclose direct quotations—the precise words that
   someone else has spoken or written.

   > "I am not yet ready to step down," said the vice-president.

   > "Yes, I expect to be elected," said the candidate, "and by a wide margin."

   > During convocation the main speaker told us to "...improve that which we
   > find lacking and to promote that which we find ignored."

2. Do not use quotation marks to set off indirect quotations—someone else's
   statements paraphrased in your own words.

   > The vice-president said that she was not yet ready to step down.

   > The candidate said he expected to be elected by a wide margin.

   > At our convocation the main speaker told us to go out into the world and
   > make our marks.

Note: Commas and periods are placed inside the final quotation marks;
colons and semicolons are placed outside them. All other punctuation marks
are placed outside unless they are part of the quotation.

He said, "I am leaving now, and I shall not return."

The football player said that he enjoys the game of football because "I love the physical contact"; however, in his private life he insisted he was "as gentle as a lamb."

The man shouted, "Help! Help! I'm drowning!"; unfortunately, no one was near enough to save him.

**3.** Use quotation marks to enclose words and phrases with special or restricted meanings, such as technical or colloquial terms, names out of context, or humorous expressions.

When I questioned the test schedules, the student agreed by saying, "right on."

I could tell that he must have watched many Hollywood gangster movies when he called his pistol a "heater."

In organized crime, a man who murders for money is called "a hit man."

His major "architectural" accomplishment was building a fence around his property.

Note: Do not use quotation marks to apologize for slang expessions or inappropriate language. If you have to excuse an expression, you probably should not have used it in the first place.

WRONG: He is "lousy" with money.
She is a "witch," and that's all there is to it!

**4.** Quotation marks are used to enclose the titles of short published material such as articles in magazines and newspapers, short poems and short stories, chapters from books, and essays in a collection.

The article, "A Program to Feed the Hungry," was written by Charles Gordon in the October issue of *The Atlantic* magazine.

"For Esme with Love and Squalor" is the title of a short story by J.D. Salinger.

The first chapter of the novel I am reading is entitled "The Way I See It."

**5.** Use *single quotation marks* to enclose a quotation within a quotation.

On the first day of class our instructor said, "Before I became a teacher my best friend, who used to be a teacher, told me, 'Do not try to mould students to fit one pattern; they are individuals, not faceless products.' I try to remember that advice at the beginning of every semester."

The article in *Time* quoted the major as saying, "When I arrived in Vietnam, I was told by my superior, 'If you can't save the town, destroy it!' "

# E. WHEN TO USE ITALICS

In printed material italics are a special slanted typeface. In typing or handwriting, italics are indicated by underlining.

**1.** Italicize the titles of published materials of a considerable length: books, magazines, newspapers, pamphlets, and long poems.

> The *New York Times* gave a favourable review to John Fowles' latest novel, *Daniel Martin*.
>
> *Harper's* is one magazine I read every month.
>
> *Paradise Lost*, by John Milton, is considered to be England's greatest epic poem.

**2.** Italicize names of motion pictures, television programs, plays, and works of art.

> My sister has seen *Gone With the Wind* seven times.
>
> I think *A Long Day's Journey into Night* is Eugene O'Neill's finest play.
>
> Picasso's *Guernica* is a painting about death and destruction.

**3.** Italicize the names of ships, trains, airplanes, and (now) spacecraft.

> The *Queen Mary* sailed from New York on Friday.
>
> *Apollo Nine* was placed in orbit exactly on schedule.

**4.** Italicize foreign words and phrases that have not yet become an accepted part of the English language.

> He committed an incredible *faux pas*.
>
> Spaghetti is at its best when it is cooked *al dente*.

Note: Some foreign words and expressions are now considered a part of the English language; for instance, "a la carte," "vice versa," and "status quo" no longer require italics. If you are in doubt as to what expressions to italicize, consult your dictionary.

**5.** Italicize words, letters and figures used specifically as words, letters and figures.

> When writing contracts, you should cross all your *t*'s.
>
> You must not confuse the word *perfect* with the word *prefect*.
>
> His *5*'s look like *3*'s, and his *1*'s look like *7*'s.

# Exercise 7.9 — Quotations and Italics

Supply quotation marks or italics (underscoring) wherever required in the following sentences. Then write W in the blank to the right of each sentence you correct. If the sentence needs no further punctuation, write C in the blank. Alternatively, write out the corrected sentences on a separate sheet.

EXAMPLE:   Jane Austen's <u>Pride and Prejudice</u> is one of the
most well-constructed novels ever written.                  ___C___

The expression "crow's feet" is used to describe
the wrinkles at the corners of someone's eyes.              ___W___

She said that she would protect the children.               ___C___

**1.** The title of the short story I am reading is Henry's Cat.   _____

**2.** Sorry, she said, I didn't know you were busy.   _____

**3.** Just before the examination began one of our class members
asked if she could go to the bathroom.   _____

**4.** Our local theatre group is performing The Odd Couple
next month.   _____

**5.** The editorial in yesterday's newspaper was entitled
Can We Afford Foreign Aid?   _____

**6.** Which Romantic poet wrote Ode on a Grecian Urn?   _____

**7.** When I asked Marcel how he enjoyed his camping trip,
he said it was a bummer.   _____

**8.** Cecilia is the name of our new sailboat.   _____

**9.** Hill Street Blues is my favourite television drama.   _____

**10.** His dull, maudlin, monotone speech went on ad infinitum.   _____

**11.** When can we expect to receive our order? asked the
purchasing agent.   _____

**12.** What famous Shakespearian tragedy contains these lines:
The slings and arrows of outrageous fortune?   _____

**13.** The store manager told the clerk that she was rude to one of
the store's best customers.   _____

**14.** Leonardo DaVinci's famous painting, The Mona Lisa,
is on loan to our national museum.   _____

**15.** Sans Souci is the name of our newest French restaurant.   _____

**16.** How many o's are in the word meaning to select?   _____

**17.** When I expressed my concern about his misfortune,
he simply replied, C'est la vie.   _____

**18.** No, I haven't visited Montreal for two years, said Nancy,
but I intend to shop there next week.   _____

19. Once More to the Lake is one of E.B. White's finest stories.　————————

20. Don't use the word adapt when you mean to take possession of.　————————

21. I read both the New York Times and the Globe and Mail every day.　————————

22. In James Thurber's collection of short stories entitled Thurber Country, one of my favourites is Teacher's Pet.　————————

23. What famous Canadian novelist wrote The Stone Angel?　————————

24. His major engineering achievement was digging a drainage ditch.　————————

25. The word love in tennis has a completely different meaning from its conventional usage.　————————

26. The film, Joshua Then and Now, is being released very soon.　————————

27. The Nuclear Winter was the lead article in this month's Maclean's magazine.　————————

28. The space shuttle Enterprise has already been on two missions.　————————

29. My grandfather still refers to a cigar as a stogie.　————————

30. The Thousand Islands is my favourite vacation area.　————————

## F. WHAT SHOULD BE CAPITALIZED?

Your decision to capitalize will be determined, to a great extent, by your need to be specific, for only proper nouns, which give specific names to people, places, and things take capitals.

> PEOPLE:　Aunt Sally, Jack Horner, Mrs. McDonnell, Professor Stuart, Captain Smith.
>
> PLACES:　Asia, Germany, Quebec, Montreal, California, Los Angeles, Dry Gulch.
>
> THINGS:　The National Arts Center, Delta High School, Twinkles Cup Cakes.

Other words and abbreviations require capitals simply because of English-usage conventions and can best be learned through simple exposure—by reading. There are specific capitalization rules, though, and here are some that may help.

1. Capitalize the first word in every sentence and in every direct quotation.

> *We* lived in Winnipeg for five years.
>
> *As* the doctor was leaving, he said, "*Call* me if there is any change in the patient's condition."

**2.** Capitalize the names of cities, provinces, states, countries, and specific avenues, streets and highways.

Our children live in *Vancouver*, *British Columbia*, but our parents live in *Tampa*, *Florida*, in the southern part of the *United States*.

We moved from *Maple Avenue* to *Regent Street*, two blocks from the *Mackenzie Throughway*.

**3.** Capitalize names of buildings, ships, mountains, bodies of water, parks, or geographical locations.

The *CN Tower* is the highest free-standing structure in the world.

We sailed from *Halifax*, *Nova Scotia*, to *Hamburg*, *Germany*, on *The Bremen*.

*Mount Madison*, near *Heron Lake*, is where the light plane crashed last weekend.

*Banff National Park* in the *Canadian West* is one of the most scenic parks I have ever visited.

**4.** Capitalize major words in titles of publications, except for articles (a, an, the), prepositions (at, in, on, of, with, etc.), and minor connectives (and, as, but, or, etc.).

I have just finished reading Edgar Allan Poe's *The Fall of the House of Usher*.

Our teacher assigned us *A Jest of God* to report on in class.

**5.** Capitalize branches of government, political parties, religious groups, and names of organizations and nationalities.

*The Department of Labour* is staffed by members of *The Conservative Party*.

*The Knights of Columbus* is a *Catholic* organization.

The city of Kitchener, Ontario, has a large *German* community.

**6.** Capitalize names of schools and businesses.

Carol transferred from *Bruce Secretarial School* to *Packenham Community College*, but her girlfriend decided to remain at the *University of Ottawa*.

The *A.J. Peterson Company* is the major supplier of our drill bits.

**7.** Capitalize formal titles and terms of family relationships when they are used as parts of proper names or as substitutes for proper names.

*Professor Daniels* cancelled her classes on the advice of her physician, *Dr. Allison*.

*Uncle Pat* and *Aunt Ruth* have just returned from their Mexican holidays.

*Father* and *Mother* are flying to Europe next week.

**8.** Capitalize abbreviations of titles and academic degrees used after proper names.

Thomas Nelson, *Ph.D.*, Peter Reynolds, *M.D.*, and David Phelps, *P.Eng.*, are all former members of our fraternity.

**9.** Capitalize days of the week, and months of the year, but not names of seasons.

The first *Monday* in *April* is when the lottery draw will take place.

The fall season usually ends in *October*, and then winter sets in.

**10.** Capitalize names of civic holidays and names having historic or religious significance.

*Christmas* and *Thanksgiving* are my favourite holidays; but *Remembrance Day* has a special meaning for my parents, for my uncle was a casualty of *World War II*.

The feast of *The Nativity* is celebrated by Christians throughout the world.

Knowing when not to capitalize is just as important as knowing when to capitalize, for if your use of capital letters appears arbitrary and haphazard to your reader, he may very well lose interest in what you have to say. You will avoid misplacing capitals if you remember the following rules.

**1.** Do not capitalize the name of a subject in school unless it is the name of a language or a part of a course with a designated title.

Helen is studying *physics*, *chemistry*, *math*, and *English*, but Paul has concentrated his studies in the ***Romance*** languages of *French*, *Italian*, and *Spanish*.

*Sociology* 110 and *Psychology* 212 are being offered in the spring semester.

**2.** Do not capitalize general geographical locations used as points on the compass unless they designate a specific geographical region.

To find our cottage you must drive *north* for twenty miles, then *east* for three miles; we are located just *south* of Bear Mountain.

The ***Far East*** is no longer a mysterious part of the world.

**3.** Do not capitalize the second part of a hyphenated word unless it is used as a proper name.

We walked all the way from Thirty-*second* Avenue to Forty-*fifth* Street.

Last semester we studied the *Franco-Prussian War*; and this semester we will be assigned term papers on the *Pan-American* Peace Conference.

**4.** Do not capitalize general terms of family relationships, titles that are not used as proper names, and the word *the* when it is not a specific part of a proper name or title.

It is obvious that *the* United States was instrumental in organizing *the* North Atlantic Treaty Organization.

I believe that my *father* and your *uncle* are related.

Our family *doctor* and her husband are visiting their son who is a *captain* in the army.

**5.** Never capitalize for emphasis.

I want you to do it *now*. (not ''I want you to do it *Now*.'')

Jack told Ed to ''*cool it*.'' (not ''Jack told Ed to *Cool It*.'')

## Exercise 7.10 — Capitalizing Correctly

In each of the sentences below, find the capitalization mistake and write it correctly in the blank space at the right or on a separate sheet.

**1.** My father was just hired by samson and sons, a consulting firm.  _____

**2.** Our holidays start on the first tuesday in june.  _____

**3.** My Mother is doing volunteer work at the Johnsville Civic Hospital.  _____

**4.** Harold went to Law School at the University of Toronto.  _____

**5.** My doctor said contentedly, ''you are in perfect health.''  _____

**6.** My best friend is moving to Calgary, Alberta, in the Spring.  _____

**7.** Last summer I visited epcot center, which is located near disney world in Florida.  _____

**8.** The new east indian restaurant opened last night.  _____

**9.** This year I am enrolled in Geometry, History, and French.  _____

**10.** Our family dentist teaches oral hygiene at the Community College.  _____

**11.** Jack's Brother and Ruth's Cousin both attend The Taylor Institute of Electronics.  _____

**12.** The road to Jackson's pond is full of potholes.  _____

**13.** We want Justice—not anarchy.  _____

**14.** There is a small polish community near our industrial park. _____

**15.** La Paz is a city in what south American country? _____

**16.** Professor Erskine said that the Canadian north is rich in minerals. _____

**17.** Easter service is being held at 5:00 a.m. in our Church. _____

**18.** Forty-Second Street and Broadway is Manhattan's busiest thoroughfare. _____

**19.** Our High School is undergoing extensive structural repairs. _____

**20.** Psychology 102, Sociology 103, and spanish are the only electives offered this semester. _____

**21.** Borden crescent is being repaved this summer. _____

**22.** The local Golf Club is honouring its founder, Ian McShane, next Tuesday. _____

**23.** I believe that father will run in the next election. _____

**24.** My university professor does not have a ph.d., but he is an expert on Shakespeare's poetry. _____

**25.** Is Canada a member of The North Atlantic Treaty Organization? _____

**26.** When we informed Craig of our intention to bicycle through the Rockies, he just yawned and said, "don't include me in your plans." _____

**27.** The airplane landed safely at Hanover air field after it was struck by lightning. _____

**28.** Our College has the best civil technology program in the East. _____

**29.** I passed Chemistry, but I could not achieve a passing grade in English. _____

**30.** Is Peterborough North of Toronto? _____

## G. THE FUNCTIONS OF THE APOSTROPHE

Apostrophes have three major uses: (1) they form the possessive case of nouns and indefinite pronouns; (2) they indicate the omission of letters in contractions; and (3) they form plurals of letters and numbers, and of words that do not normally take the plural form. These three uses are detailed below.

### 1. To Show Possession

    (a) Add both an apostrophe and an *s* to nouns that do not end in *s*.

Tom's hat is still on the rack. (the hat of Tom)

The car's windshield was cracked. (the windshield of the car)

Where is the men's locker room? (the locker room of the men)

(b) Add both an apostrophe and an *s* or an apostrophe only to singular nouns that already end in *s*. As a general rule, if the extra *s* makes pronunciation awkward, the apostrophe alone is sufficient.

The Tomkins' (or Tomkins's) garage is on fire.

The Jones' (or Jones's) party was a huge success.

Jesus' (but not Jesus's) Sermon on the Mount is preserved in The New Testament.

(c) Add only an apostrophe to plural nouns already ending in *s*.

The room is cluttered with the boys' gym equipment.

Ladies' purses were selling for half price.

Our parents' car would not start.

(d) Add both an apostrophe and an *s* to indefinite pronouns.

Everyone's name is on the guest list. (the name of everyone)

Somebody's headlights are still on. (the headlights of somebody)

Note: Personal and relative pronouns in the possessive case never take apostrophes: its, hers, his, ours, yours, theirs and whose.

The flower is losing its (not *it's*) petals.

Whose (not *who's*) sweater is on the table?

**2. To Indicate Omission**   Apostrophes are used in contractions to indicate the omission of letters or numbers.

We don't (do not) have our textbooks yet.

It's (it is) almost time to get ready, for the race begins at ten o'clock (of the clock).

She's (she is) a member of the class of '63 (1963).

Note: Be sure to place the apostrophe where the omission occurs.

They're (not Theyr'e) the best of friends. (they are)

Isn't (not Is'nt) it time for the game to start? (is not)

**3. To Form Plurals**  Add both an apostrophe and an *s* to form the plural of letters, numbers and words.

> Your *t's* look like *r's* and your *v's* look like *u's*.
>
> You write your *7's* much differently than I do.
>
> There are too many *and's* in your sentences.

## Exercise 7.11 — The Apostrophe

Find the word with the apostrophe error in each of the sentences below, and write it correctly in the blank to the right or on a separate sheet. If the sentence contains no error, write C.

**1.** Whose going to buy lunch this time?                                   _____

**2.** Our new car lost its hubcap on the country road.                      _____

**3.** The mens' room is right next to the ladies' room.                     _____

**4.** If Soames believes that we will pay for his theatre tickets, he's very much mistaken.                                           _____

**5.** Whose bike is that in our driveway?                                   _____

**6.** Someones purse was left on the seat of Hank's boat.                   _____

**7.** Theyre not going to the Jones' party, are they?                       _____

**8.** I have trouble reading you're writing because your *t's* look like *r's* and your *n's* look like *m's*.                        _____

**9.** Shakespeare's *Coriolanus* is one of my favourite Elizabethan tragedies.                                                        _____

**10.** The Ryans roses won first prize at the flower show.                  _____

**11.** Joe's '51 Oldsmobile was bought by an antique collectors' wife.                                                              _____

**12.** There's no reason why Marie's parents' can't win the sailboat race this Saturday.                                    _____

**13.** Who's the student who's going to attend the awards ceremony on our behalf?                                        _____

**14.** Our teams lack of motivation is not the coach's fault.              _____

**15.** The Bennetts have just redecorated they're house.                   _____

**16.** Tom Smiths' luggage was lost by the airline's baggage handlers.                                                            _____

**17.** Its a shame that he's not allowed to participate in the school's drug rehabilitation program.                         _____

**18.** The churches' bells' were all ringing at once.                      _____

**19.** My parents' mortgage will be paid off in June of 86. ——————

**20.** The childrens' bicycles were laying all over our lawn. ——————

**21.** Since Michael's brothers started working, they have become more responsible and less impulsive. ——————

**22.** Lets attend the jazz concert at the Arts Center tommorrow. ——————

**23.** Now's the time to get they're attention before they leave the union hall. ——————

**24.** Our cats food was eaten by our two cocker spaniels. ——————

**25.** Thats the truck my sister's boyfriend owns. ——————

**26.** She's very impressed by his new cars' interior. ——————

**27.** Tourists spend a great deal of money in southern Ontario's vacation resorts. ——————

**28.** A joggers' exercise program has just been initiated at our local YM/YWCA. ——————

**29.** Her sister's sons wont participate in winter sports. ——————

**30.** The Sylvesters farm has not made any money since '79. ——————

# H. THE DISTINCT USES OF PARENTHESES AND BRACKETS

Both of these marks of punctuation have a very restricted use, and therefore should be used sparingly. There are few occasions in formal writing when you will be required to use parentheses or brackets, but when you do use them be sure that you know the precise function they serve.

## 1. Parentheses

Parentheses are employed only to set off non-essential and independent elements. The material enclosed within parentheses usually contains explanatory or clarifying information outside the main idea (thought) of the sentence. Remember, parentheses de-emphasize. Thus if you want to stress a parenthetical sentence element, use dashes—not parentheses.

(a) Parentheses are used to enclose explanations or clarifications that are separate from, and irrelevant to, the essential meaning of the sentence.

We are alarmed at the high addiction rate (75%) of the new tranquillizing drug.

Our instructor told us that the results of our English examination were very promising (our test scores were among the highest in the province) and that he expects us to do better next time.

The city failed to live up to its agreemeent with the sanitary engineers (formerly known as garbage collectors), and now they are threatening to strike.

(b) Parentheses are used to enclose numbers or letters that enumerate items in a series.

We asked for the following benefits in our contract negotiations: (1) flexible working hours, (2) a company dental plan, and (3) two more vacation days a year.

When the new recruits arrived, they were told (a) to get their flu shots, (b) to report to the testing room, and (c) to turn in their civilian clothes.

(c) Parentheses are used to enclose dates of birth and death, and of significant historical events:

William Shakespeare (1554-1616) is considered by many to be the greatest dramatist of any age.

The American Revolution (1776) marked the beginning of a unique political vision of human freedom.

Note: All the punctuation normally required for the sentence is placed outside the closing parenthesis.

As soon as I arrived (late in the afternoon), I called a meeting of all the executives.

I came as quickly as I could (I broke all speed limits); however, I was not in time to prevent the company takeover.

## 2. Brackets

Do not confuse brackets with parentheses. Brackets have only *one* use: they enclose editorial insertions.

(a) Brackets are used in quoted material to enclose editorial comments or corrections:

"Our citizens can no longer tolerate a 10% unemployment rate. [The annual unemployment figures were 8.5%.] We must create jobs in the public sector of our economy."

"We entered the city of Toledo [Spain] from the south."

Note: In quoting you may sometimes find it necessary to use *sic* (meaning *thus*) to inform the reader that a factual or a spelling error belongs to the quotation, and not to you.

"On December 8, 1941 [sic] Pearl Harbor was attacked by the Japanese."

"There are no heroines or villians [sic] in our play."

## Exercise 7.12 — Parentheses and Brackets

In the following sentences place either parentheses or brackets around the italicized expressions. Then, in the blank to the right, indicate your selection by writing PR for parentheses and BR for brackets.

EXAMPLE: The anniversary of the dropping of the atomic bomb
on Hiroshima (*August 6, 1945*) is still marked
by the Japanese.                                                PR

"We will never surrender; we will fight to the very
last man!" [*The author surrendered to the enemy
two days after this statement was written.*]                    BR

1. Margaret Tillotson *now Mrs. J. Feeney* was a famous
name in women's golf in the 1950's.                             _____

2. The widow of Tom Warden *1906-1953*, the founder of
our club, is being honoured at our annual banquet.             _____

3. Dr. Felix Shepherd *he is an ex-Olympian swimmer*
will lecture next Tuesday on the cardio-vascular benefits
of jogging.                                                     _____

4. "Shakespeare's greatest tragedy *Hamlet* depicted a young
man with a fine mind and a delicate sensitivity on the
brink of madness."                                             _____

5. "The Prime Minister of Canada resides in Ottawa, the city
with the highest free-standing structure in the world—the
CN Tower." *The author has mistaken Ottawa for Toronto.*       _____

6. "The Bermuda Rectangle *sic* has been blamed for a number
of airplane crashes during the past ten years."               _____

7. This rapidly accelerating rate of inflation *12% last year* must
be stopped, or our country will experience financial ruin.    _____

8. "John Steinbeck's great novel of the Depression era
*The Grapes of Wrath* is a perfect example of the novel
as social commentary."                                        _____

9. The announcer informed us of two clear signs of an
impending heart attack: *1* a tightening of the chest and
*2* difficulty breathing.                                     _____

10. Our instructions were issued in point form: *a* assemble as
a class in the hallway opposite our classroom, *b* walk calmly
to the nearest exit, *c* assemble on the lawn to the rear of the
building, and *d* wait for the fire bell to stop ringing before
re-entering the building.                                     _____

**11.** Jonathan Swift *1667-1745* and Alexander Pope *1688-1744* are my favourite eighteenth-century poets. _____

**12.** As we entered the old, decrepit building *it was built in 1786*, the floor creaked and a pigeon flew through a hole in the roof. _____

**13.** "This incredibly brilliant preface *Dr. Samuel Johnson's Preface to Shakespeare*, published before his edition of Shakespeare's plays, is the finest monument to genius that I have ever read." _____

**14.** "The assassination of Archduke Francis Ferdinand *June 28, 1914* was purported to precipitate World War I." _____

**15.** "Margaret Lawrence *sic* is my favourite Canadian novelist." _____

**16.** "This great naval base, full of hallowed memories, *Pearl Harbor* will never be abandoned." _____

**17.** Arthur Gottleib *the movie mogul* is being wed for the fifth time at a small, private ceremony in his Hollywood mansion. _____

**18.** Before we were considered for the physical fitness award, we had to accomplish three things: *1* we had to jog five miles without stopping, *2* do sixty consecutive push-ups, and *3* swim five laps in three minutes. _____

**19.** "Because of the new advances in medicine, our infant mortality rate is below two per cent." *The figure is actually 1.05%.* _____

**20.** The last T-34 jet trainer *affectionately known as the Pussycat* was taken out of service yesterday. _____

# I. END PUNCTUATION – THE PERIOD, QUESTION MARK, AND EXCLAMATION POINT

## 1. Period

(a) Periods are most commonly used to mark the end of a sentence that makes a statement or issues a command.

I purchased my notebook in the bookstore.

Don't trip over the step.

(b) Periods are used to mark the end of an elliptical element that functions as a transitional expression or as a short answer to a question.

Now, *to get down to business.*

"You are going, aren't you?" "*Of course.*"

"Do you want to rest?" "*Yes.*"

(c) Periods are used to mark the end of polite commands and requests that are phrased as questions.

May we hear from you in the near future.

Would you mail this letter for me after lunch.

May I request your attention.

(d) Periods are used after most abbreviations.

Mr.   Dr.   Ph.D.   a.m.   f.o.b.   mfg.

Note: Many abbreviations composed of capitals and representing single initials or organizations do not require periods.

RCA   UAW   CIA   TWA   NATO   CBC   RCAF

(e) Three periods are used within quotations to indicate the omission of words; four periods are used to indicate word omissions at the end of a sentence either within the quotation or at the end of the quotation (the last of the four periods is treated as the end punctuation of the sentence).

She replied, "Our last quarter's financial statement...reflects a loss of revenue over the previous quarter." (The omitted passage: "prepared by our accounting department....")

"We have not yet found the money...." (Omitted passage: "that was lost yesterday.")

"Events followed one after the other.... We were always kept busy." (Omitted passage: "with amazing frequency.")

Note: These series of periods, known as ellipsis marks, take one typewriter space between each period.

## 2. The Question Mark

(a) Question marks are used after all direct questions.

What do you mean?

The judge asked, "Are you ready to present your case?"

(b) Question marks are used after elliptical words and phrases (see p. 126) expressed as questions.

Where shall we meet you? *In front of the bank?*

You managed to complete all the work. *How?*

You want me to get you a wrench. *What for?*

## 3. The Exclamation Point

(a) Exclamation points should be used only to express strong feelings or surprise.

Fire!   Help me!   Run for your life!   How did he do it!

Note: Do not overuse exclamation points. When they are used too frequently for emphasis they lose their effectiveness.

WRONG:   Well! Well! You finally arrived!
CORRECT:   Well, well, you've finally arrived.

WRONG:   Oh! I didn't expect you!
CORRECT:   Oh, I didn't expect you.

Your common sense will usually tell you how much emphasis an expression requires.

# Exercise 7.13 — Periods, Question Marks and Exclamation Points

Supply periods, question marks, and exclamation points wherever required in the following sentences. Then write W in the blank to the right of each sentence you correct. If the sentence is properly punctuated, write C in the blank. Alternatively, rewrite corrected sentences on a separate sheet.

| | | |
|---|---|---|
| EXAMPLE: | Will you please stop that noise? | W |
| | Look out for the falling rock! | W |
| | Why haven't you stopped smoking? | C |

1. Wipe your feet before entering the house!   _____

2. Will you please step to the rear of the elevator?   _____

3. Find the guilty party and then punish him.   _____

4. You asked me if I know the time? I don't have a watch.   _____

5. May I have your undivided attention now?   _____

6. At 9:00 p.m. Mr. Samuels is giving out the door prizes.   _____

7. He works at the RCA plant on Fredrick Street.   _____

8. When do you finish work? At five o'clock.   _____

9. Susan asked her mother if she could attend our graduation party?   _____

10. Watch your step when you leave the store!   _____

11. Dr Tracy is operating at 10:00 a.m.   _____

12. What did you make for supper. Baked ham?   _____

**13.** Nelson Associates is buying Craymore Inc next month. _____

**14.** We always listen to CBC stereo every Tuesday evening. _____

**15.** The scaffold is falling. Watch out. _____

**16.** Now, to get down to business! _____

**17.** Will someone please answer the telephone? _____

**18.** Well! Well! She finally paid her debts. _____

**19.** When is our English test scheduled. Next week. _____

**20.** Stuart has a Ph.D. in chemistry, and Sharon has an MA in history. _____

**21.** Mrs Sherwood works for the RCMP. _____

**22.** Oh my, she certainly has a large appetite! _____

**23.** Why haven't you told your supervisor about the defective ball bearing. _____

**24.** Please take your seats and open your textbooks! _____

**25.** You managed to escape from jail. How. _____

**26.** Stand up straight when I am speaking to you! _____

**27.** Watch out for the fire engine. It's heading right for us. _____

**28.** Don't slam the door when you leave! _____

**29.** Dr. McCrory asked Mrs Thomson if she had a YWCA card. _____

**30.** When does the show start. After the commercial? _____

## Exercise 7.14 — Punctuation Review Exercise

Supply all necessary punctuation in the following sentences. Then write W in the blank to the right of each sentence you correct. (There are no comma errors, so do not add or subtract commas.) If the sentence needs no further punctuation, write C in the blank. Alternatively, rewrite corrected sentences on a separate sheet.

EXAMPLE: My supervisor told me to purchase the following items: safety shoes, canvas gloves, and welding goggles. ___C___

"No, Tom," said Helen, "I cannot help you with your work; you must do it yourself." ___W___

**1.** Find the correct file copy then send it to the supervisor of the Personnel Department. _____

**2.** When Frank first started pitching for our team he was only sixteen years old at the time we never dreamed that he would someday be a star in the major leagues. _____

3. Please tell me the source of the following statement "We have nothing to fear but fear itself." ——————

4. Sheila cannot learn to play the saxophone, however hard she tries. ——————

5. Three RCMP officers Clarke, Dixon, and Hannick are being awarded medals for bravery this afternoon. ——————

6. Soap operas that's all she watches on TV. ——————

7. Without your moral support, announced the mayor, I could never have solved our financial problems. ——————

8. Some convicts refer to prison as the joint. ——————

9. Fun Tomorrow is the title of the biography of John Morgan Gray, a revered Canadian publisher. ——————

10. Nell asked us where we were holding our next nuclear disarmament meeting We told her in the church basement. ——————

11. The Displaced Person is the title of a short story by Flannery O'Connor. ——————

12. Travis, Inc and Sterling Mfg have just signed contracts to supply the CP Hotel chain. ——————

13. She said that we must leave. ——————

14. I read about our budding Canadian film industry in Saturday Night magazine. ——————

15. Tyrone Welland, Vice-President Joanne Bickel, Treasurer and Harry Jerome, Sales Manager are holding a meeting in the board room at 10:00 a.m. ——————

16. Would you mind moving out of my way ——————

17. The space shuttle Discovery has just achieved orbit. ——————

18. When is the train due to arrive? asked Jane. ——————

19. Jerry is mature, dependable, honest, and industrious that is, he can handle responsibility. ——————

20. She collected our reports last Friday or was it Thursday? ——————

21. Don't try to lift the cartons yourself wait until you have help. ——————

22. We ordered the following garden supplies fertilizer, grass seed, shears, and rakes. ——————

23. The Daisy is the name of my father's new sailboat. ——————

24. Its not a question of time; its a question of money. ——————

25. Watch out The rock is falling. ——————

**26.** "*Wonderland*, the amusement park, is located just north of Ottawa, Ont." It is actually located north of Toronto.  _____

**27.** The assassination of Robert F. Kennedy 1926-1968 shocked everyone in North America.  _____

**28.** When shall we arrange our holiday? In the Spring or Fall?  _____

**29.** The term stonewall was popularized during the Nixon presidency.  _____

**30.** Sam Donat the guy who owns *Sam's Garage* has just won ten thousand dollars in the lottery.  _____

**31.** We must carry on, whatever the consequences.  _____

**32.** Please stop eating your peas with a fork!  _____

**33.** My favourite television program, The Avengers, has not been renewed by the sponsors.  _____

**34.** Physics, spanish, and chemistry are all being taught in the new wing of our high school.  _____

**35.** "Pierre Burton, sic I believe, is the author of *The Last Spike*."  _____

**36.** Please make sure that we are provided with blankets, warm boots, earmuffs, and plenty of hot coffee.  _____

**37.** When military men refer to weapons that kill and maim people, they use the term ordinance.  _____

**38.** Three surgeons Dr. Barnett, Dr. Kravitz, and Dr. Matteo are performing the delicate transplant operation.  _____

**39.** Please follow this procedure: 1 make sure the transmission is in neutral; 2 pull the emergency brake; 3 turn the wheels toward the curb, and 4 lock the car doors before you leave.  _____

**40.** What would you like for dinner roast beef  _____

**41.** Whenever Carlos finishes talking on the telephone, he signs off by saying ciao.  _____

**42.** Roberta Peterson has a Ph D in French literature and David Samuelson has an M Ed from Queens University.  _____

**43.** We studied Shakespeare's *Macbeth* last september.  _____

**44.** Your writing is awkward because your i's look like e's and your w's look like u's.  _____

**45.** Sailing to Byzantium is one of William Butler Yeats' most famous poems.  _____

**46.** Would everyone please walk slowly toward the fire exits         _____

**47.** The Gleasons party was a huge success.         _____

**48.** The play, Long Day's Journey into Night, is my favourite modern tragedy.         _____

**49.** We toured the Statue of Liberty when we visited New York last September.         _____

**50.** My pay cheque was delayed in the mail therefore I shall have to borrow lunch money.         _____

# CHAPTER EIGHT

# Choosing the Right Words

To write clear, precise prose we must use the English language efficiently. That means our words and phrases should be properly positioned and should clearly denote our intended meaning. When we fail to write with precision, words lose their flavour, sentences fail to couch ideas, and the vitality of our thoughts dissipates into verbiage; invariably our written messages become boring, trite, pretentious, and even unintelligible.

*Faulty Diction* is the term we use to describe language that is both inflated and inappropriate. Although many of our diction errors overlap, all faulty diction is either wordy or imprecise or both. Also, there are certain stock words and expressions that we tend to overuse. These problems can be discussed under the following headings: *Clichés*, *Jargon*, *Wordiness*, and *Redundancy*. A number of common usage mistakes, including grammatically incorrect words and phrases, are collected in a glossary of usage and diction on pages 141-154.

## A. KEEPING YOUR LANGUAGE FRESH: CLICHÉS TO AVOID

Clichés, also referred to as trite or hackneyed expressions, are catch phrases that have lost their vitality from overuse. Some are dull litanies of dubious wisdom that substitute for fresher, more precise expressions, but all are excuses for originality that prevent us from expanding our vocabulary and refining our thinking. Think of a deflated balloon and you will understand how flaccid clichés appear to a literate reader. Unfortunately, they seem to be increasing each year. Here are some of the most awkward clichés; there are, of course, many more:

| | | |
|---|---|---|
| **1.** all things being equal | **5.** busy as a bee | **9.** diamond in the rough |
| **2.** any shape or form | **6.** call a spade a spade | **10.** doomed to failure |
| **3.** better late than never | **7.** clear as night and day | **11.** easier said than done |
| **4.** bring to a head | **8.** cool as a cucumber | **12.** few and far between |

13. fly off the handle
14. gentle as a lamb
15. happy as a lark
16. hit the nail on the head
17. if and when
18. in the nick of time
19. it goes without saying
20. last but not least

21. long arm of the law
22. nipped in the bud
23. par for the course
24. perfectly clear
25. ripe old age
26. see the light
27. ships that pass in the night
28. slowly but surely

29. strike while the iron is hot
30. tale of woe
31. this day and age
32. time is money
33. to make a long story short
34. to the bitter end
35. vicious circle

## Exercise 8.1 – Detecting Clichés

Correct the following sentences by replacing the clichés with more precise and vigorous expressions of your own.

EXAMPLE:   It is as *clear as night and day* that we must *bring our deliberations to a head*.

CORRECTION:   It is obvious that we must conclude our deliberations.

1. We will not agree to his proposals in any shape or form.

2. If and when we decide to invest in the stock market, we will make sure that we will strike while the iron is hot.

3. I suppose Denise's contribution was better late than never.

4. We discovered the hydraulic system failure in the nick of time.

5. Thelma told us a tale of woe when we enquired about her health.

6. Our scoring opportunities were few and far between; nevertheless, we fought to the bitter end.

7. I want to make myself perfectly clear when I tell you that I intend to call a spade a spade.

8. In this day and age it is difficult to save money.

9. It goes without saying that our company must increase its cash flow, or it will be doomed to failure.

10. We are slowly but surely losing our freedom; therefore we must bring our divisive debate to a head before our union movement is nipped in the bud.

11. Making money in a tight money market is easier said than done.

12. His position on disarmament is as clear as night and day, but we must make him see the light when it comes to his taxation policy.

13. Even though Shirley was bitterly attacked for her opinions on women's rights, she remained cool as a cucumber.

14. Robert found a diamond in the rough when he married Claudia.

15. In our organization time is money, so you are expected to remain busy as bees.

## Exercise 8.2 — Changing Clichés to Fresh Expressions

Fill in the blanks with ten more clichés from the media or from your daily conversations; then correct them by writing ten sentences with fresher, more original expressions. Alternatively, write your list of clichés and your improved sentences on a separate sheet.

1. _____    6. _____

2. _____    7. _____

3. _____    8. _____

4. _____    9. _____

5. _____   10. _____


1. _____

2. _____

3. _____

4. _____

5. _____

6. _____

7. _____

8. _____

9. _____

10. _____


## B. MAKING YOUR WRITING PRECISE: WATCH JARGON

We use clichés when we rely on time-worn expressions to convey our meaning, but we use jargon when we turn to unusual or technical language to impress or mislead. In the most literal sense, jargon is private language, usually developed within particular institutions, disciplines, or professions. Many jargon expressions have legitimate meanings within a restricted context. For instance, a computer "run" adequately describes a computational process within the computer industry, and the term "bottom line" may be a serviceable expression in an accounting office; but when these terms and others like them are used in everyday language, they lose their legitimacy and become awkward and overbearing:

> Would you *run* through your explanation once again so that we can come to the *bottom line* of your proposal.

In common English this sentence would look something like this:

> Please repeat your explanation so that we can understand the point of your proposal.

In short, when used outside their proper context, jargon expressions are occasionally wordy, often pretentious, and always imprecise. Here are some common jargon words and phrases we should try to avoid. (See the Glossary of Usage and Diction for others.)

1. address the issue
2. ball park figures
3. cognizant of
4. consciousness raising
5. contact (to mean *speak* or *meet with*)
6. dialogue (as a verb)
7. effective and efficient
8. effectuate
9. expertise
10. feedback
11. field (to mean profession: *teaching field, engineering field*)
12. guesstimate
13. impact (as a verb)
14. identify with
15. in the picture
16. input
17. interface
18. liaise (as a verb)
19. low profile
20. meaningful relationship
21. on stream
22. posture
23. predisposed to
24. relate to (to mean *understand*)
25. scenario
26. share with
27. substantial number
28. thrust
29. time frame
30. upcoming
31. -wise (as a suffix attached to a noun: *timewise, weatherwise*)

## Exercise 8.3 − Replacing Jargon

Correct the following sentences by replacing the jargon expressions with your own words and phrases.

EXAMPLE: Bill did not have enough *expertise* to fill the new management position.

CORRECTION: Bill did not have enough knowledge and experience to fill the new management position.

1. Before we put our competitors in the picture let's rethink our posture on long-term investments.

2. Our company must become more effective and efficient or the funding cutbacks will impact negatively on our organization.

3. I need her financial input before I can guesstimate our expenditures next fall.

4. If he approves our budget, perhaps then we can liaise with our marketing people next week.

5. In the upcoming semester we will hire someone in the engineering field to teach a construction course.

6. If we do not soon address the issue of wages, we will have a strike on our hands.

7. I can relate to your position, but can you identify with my special circumstances?

8. When we put George in the picture, how long will it take him to effectuate a change in his department?

9. What time frame do you have in mind when you refer to a cutback in production?

10. We must interface our two marketing strategies.

11. Our estimates, at this time, are only ball park figures.

12. The thrust of her proposal was meant to help you achieve a meaningful relationship with your staff.

13. If you contact our representative in Montreal, he will dialogue with our advertising agency next week.

14. What kind of feedback did you get from your workshop on communications?

15. Ladies and gentlemen, I know you are cognizant of the importance of the new office complex to our image, so let me share with you an artist's sketch of the proposed building.

## Exercise 8.4 − Alternatives to Jargon

Fill in the blanks with ten more jargon words and phrases; then correct them by writing sentences with clearer, more precise expressions. Alternatively, write out your jargon words and sentences on a separate page.

1. _____   6. _____

2. _____   7. _____

3. _____   8. _____

4. _____   9. _____

5. _____   10. _____

1. _____

**2.** _____

**3.** _____

**4.** _____

**5.** _____

**6.** _____

**7.** _____

**8.** _____

**9.** _____

**10.** _____

## C. WRITING CONCISELY: AVOIDING WORDINESS

Because effective writing is always economical, there is a direct correlation between the number of words we use and the clarity of our message. Wordiness is a sure sign that we have failed to plan our sentences or to think through our ideas. The more we rely on certain inflated expressions, the more insensitive we become to the exact connotations of words and the more we ignore the principles of balance, coherence, and directness in constructing sentences. Consequently we write, "I am not in a position to pay your tuition expenses due to the fact that I am presently financially embarrassed...," instead of "I cannot pay your tuition fees because I have no money." The following are some of the most commonly used inflated expressions; there are others in the glossary.

1. a small number of
2. absolutely nothing
3. afford an opportunity
4. at a later date
5. at an early date
6. by means of
7. come to the conclusion
8. despite the fact that
9. for the purpose of
10. for the reason that
11. in a position to
12. inasmuch as
13. in receipt of
14. in the nature of
15. in the near future
16. in the vicinity of
17. in view of the fact that
18. meet with your approval
19. not in a position to
20. on the occasion of
21. on the part of
22. owing to the fact that
23. seldom ever
24. subsequent to
25. the month of March, June, September, etc.
26. until such time as
27. with a view to
28. without fail
29. without further delay
30. with reference to

## Exercise 8.5 — Making Sentences Concise

Correct the following sentences by replacing the wordy expression with clearer, more concise words and phrases.

EXAMPLE: Did my sister's home-made pie meet with your approval?

CORRECTION: Did you enjoy my sister's home-made pie?

1. Our delivery date was delayed for the reason that our production line was shut down for two days.

2. We finally found our lost dog in the vicinity of the old churchyard.

3. They opened their broken safe by means of a welding torch.

4. For the purpose of clarity, we shall give each of you a translation of our business memoranda.

5. Our company adopted a new order-processing system with a view to increasing our sales.

6. Marg seldom ever eats fatty foods.

7. If I am afforded an opportunity, I shall participate in the student exchange program.

8. With reference to your request for maternity leave, we will process it immediately.

9. The decision on the part of our company to diversify was, in my opinion, a big mistake.

10. We have absolutely nothing to contribute to the conversation.

11. They will inform us at a later date about our request for a salary advance.

12. Despite the fact that Herman won the race, he is still not considered a significant athlete.

13. We are in receipt of your letter and intend to follow your recommendations.

14. I cannot respond to your proposal until such time as I have all the pertinent information.

15. On the occasion of our twentieth wedding anniversary, we went on an ocean cruise.

# D. ONLY WHAT IS NECESSARY: AVOIDING REDUNDANCIES

A redundant expression is one which contains two or more words that convey the same idea. Thus it is both wordy and repetitious. Correcting redundancies is usually a matter of eliminating one or two words or of substituting one precise word for an entire expression.

We seem to write redundant phrases when attempting to emphasize a noun with an adjective which duplicates the idea—*exact* replica, *end* result, *new* innovation—or when using two similar words in a compound expression—first and foremost, each and every, fear and dread.

Basically, we write redundancies for the same reason we use wordy expressions: a failure to strive for precision and economy in constructing sentences and an insensitivity to the meaning of words. Here are some of the most obvious redundancies; there are more in the glossary.

| | |
|---|---|
| 1. actual fact | 17. mental attitude |
| 2. adequate enough | 18. my personal opinion |
| 3. agreeable and satisfactory | 19. necessary requirements |
| 4. collect together | 20. new beginner |
| 5. common, ordinary | 21. new innovation |
| 6. complete and total | 22. red in colour |
| 7. connect up | 23. same, identical |
| 8. disappear from view | 24. serious crisis |
| 9. end result | 25. sincere and earnest |
| 10. entirely eliminated | 26. small in size |
| 11. erode away | 27. strict accuracy |
| 12. exact replica | 28. surround on all sides |
| 13. fear and dread | 29. utter impossibility |
| 14. first and foremost | 30. very unique |
| 15. free gift | 31. visible to the eye |
| 16. hope and trust | |

## Exercise 8.6 — Removing Redundancies

Correct the redundancies in the following sentences by placing a parenthesis around unnecessary words and, if necessary, by changing the articles to suit the alteration (e.g. *a* to *an*). Alternatively, rewrite the following sentences, eliminating redundancies.

EXAMPLE:   From where we were standing, the space shuttle was barely visible (to the eye) as it approached the California coast.

1. The drug store was giving out free gifts of disposable razors as part of its promotion campaign.

2. There was a complete and total blackout last night that lasted for two hours.

3. My son always disappears from view when it is time for supper.

4. Martha's collection of antique jewellery is very unique.

5. We must maintain strict accuracy when we announce our budget for next year.

6. If we collect together enough household donations we can have a successful garage sale.

7. After our students connected up the high speed printer to the terminal outlet, we all breathed a sigh of relief.

8. The end result of his deliberations was the abolition of our advertising department.

**9.** My sister and I bought the same, identical dress in different stores.

**10.** Ted's new car is red in colour.

**11.** Our golf course was much too difficult for the new beginner.

**12.** We had a serious crisis at school yesterday when our chemistry laboratory caught fire.

**13.** The used-car dealer seemed sincere and earnest when he told us that one of his cars was never driven in the winter.

**14.** Our new car may be small in size, but it is certainly comfortable.

**15.** If you want my personal opinion about her sudden promotion, just ask me when there is no one around.

## E. PROPER USAGE

Usage mistakes result from spelling errors, words out of place, double negatives, and colloquial expressions that may not be used in formal English. We make usage mistakes because our bad habits in speech spill into our writing. Certain awkward and ungrammatical expressions take hold and are reinforced by our sometimes semi-literate environment. Thus it is difficult to stop writing "Between you and I" when you hear so many people using this expression in daily speech, or when your ear tells you to write *use to* instead of *used to*.

Habitual reading and familiarity with a dictionary will usually solve these usage problems. But if you read only sporadically and fail to confirm proper word use with a dictionary, your usage mistakes will be a constant source of irritation—both to you and to your readers. While people may overlook your occasional trite or wordy expression, they will not tolerate incorrect and illogical usage. Some of the most common—and most serious—usage errors may be found in the glossary.

### Glossary of Usage and Diction

**1. ability/capacity** Ability means the power to or quality of being able to accomplish something; in formal writing capacity means the power or ability to hold or receive something, but it may be used informally as a synonym for ability.

She has the *ability* to be a first-rate tennis player.

Our holding tanks have a five-hundred gallon *capacity*.

**2. aggravate** To aggravate means to make worse; it should not be used in formal writing to mean to *annoy* or *irritate*.

The football player *aggravated* his knee injury.

His hostile questions *annoyed* (not "aggravated") the speaker.

**3. agree to/agree with**  To agree to means to consent to something; to agree with means to be in accord with someone or something.

We *agree to* the conditions in the contract.

I completely *agree with* your proposal for increasing production.

**4. all-around**  A misspelling of *all-round*.

He is an *all-round* (not "all-around") athlete.

**5. allusion/illusion**  Allusion means an indirect reference; illusion means a false idea or belief, a false perception.

The education study made an *allusion* to our poor library facilities.

Helen is under the *illusion* that she will not have to take mathematics next semester.

**6. along the line of**  A wordy and awkward substitution for *like* or *similar to*.

We need a tool *similar to* (not "along the line of") a socket wrench.

**7. alot**  a misspelling of *a lot*.

There are *a lot* (not "alot") of unfinished reports on my desk.

Note: A lot is an overused expression; substitute expressions like *a great deal*, *very many*, or *a large amount* whenever you can.

We have *a great deal* (not "a lot") to learn.

**8. already/all ready**  Already means previously or before this time; all ready means completely prepared.

The company has *already* met their financial demands.

Our team is *all ready* for the big game.

**9. alright**  A misspelling of *all right*.

I had a headache last night, but I feel *all right* (not "alright") today.

**10. altogether/all together**  Altogether means entirely or completely; all together means gathered in a group.

They are *altogether* (entirely) too inexperienced to compete for this contract.

The class of '62 were *all together* for the first time this year.

**11. am/are of the opinion**   A wordy expression meaning *believe* or *think*.

I *believe* (not "am of the opinion") that our office is understaffed.

**12. among/between**   Among is used in connection with more than two persons or things; between is used in connection with only two persons or things.

The prize money will be divided *between* Ralph and Dorothy.

There are quite a few people from Western Canada *among* the convention delegates.

Note: *Between* may be used with more than two persons or things when they are considered as pairs within a listing.

There are many cultural differences *between* the United States, Canada, and Mexico.

**13. amoral/immoral**   Amoral means indifferent to moral standards; immoral means contrary to moral standards.

The relentless pursuit of money and fame seems to be an *amoral* force in our society.

Denying shelter to homeless refugees is *immoral*.

**14. anyone/any one**   Anyone is used to refer to any member of a group; any one is used to refer to a specific person or thing within a group.

*Anyone* could pass this test.

*Any one* of us workers could be fired tomorrow.

*Any one* of these ball-point pens will be sufficient.

**15. anywheres/nowheres/somewheres**   Awkward misspellings of *anywhere*, *nowhere* and *somewhere*.

You may sit *anywhere* (not "anywheres").

They were *nowhere* (not "nowheres") to be found.

I left my notebook *somewhere* (not "somewheres") near the water fountain.

**16. around**   An inappropriate synonym for *nearly* or *approximately*; the word *about* is preferred in formal writing.

We are *about* (not "around") half way through our work.

**17. argue with/argue against**   You argue with someone, but you argue against something.

> I intend to *argue with* the chairman about his committee's report.
>
> I intend to *argue against* the committee's report.

**18. as**   *As* is inappropriate when used in place of words like *because*, *since*, *that*, *if*, *whether* or *for*.

> I cannot attend class tomorrow *because* (not "as") I have a dental appointment.
>
> We are not certain *whether/that/if* (not "as") we can meet your sales deadline.

**19. as to whether**   An awkward and wordy substitute for *whether*.

> *Whether* (not "as to whether") we will change our present policy remains to be seen.

**20. as yet**   A colloquial substitute for *yet*.

> We have not *yet* (not "as yet") finished counting our receipts.

**21. at the present time**   A wordy expression meaning *now*.

> We are not accepting any more job applications *now* (not "at the present time").

**22. awfully**   An awkward intensive when used in place of words like *very*, *greatly*, *extremely*, *immensely*, etc.

> The house was *very* (not "awfully") quiet.
>
> She is *extremely* (not "awfully") shy.

**23. basic fundamentals**   A severely redundant phrase for *basics* or *fundamentals*.

> The *basics* (not "basic fundamentals") of electricity are taught by Professor Stevens.

**24. be sure and**   Colloquial expression for *be sure to*.

> *Be sure to* (not "be sure and") mail the letter on your way to work.

**25. being as/being as how/being that**   Colloquial substitutes for *because* or *since*.

> *Since* (not "being as" or "being that") you haven't had your lunch yet, we shall dine together.

I am still not satisfied with your performance *because* (not "being as how")
you have not proven your determination to succeed.

**26. between you and I**  A commonly misused expression for *between you and me*.

Just *between you and me* (not "between you and I"), I think our company
will be awarded the contract.

**27. bring/take**  To bring means to carry toward (from the point of view of the speaker or writer); to take means to carry away from.

Please *take* these slippers to your father.

Will you *bring* my reading glasses when you return?

**28. but that/but what**  Awkward and non-standard expressions for *that*.

I do not doubt for a moment *that* (not "but that/what") the thief will be caught.

**29. cancel out**  The *out* is redundant after cancel.

I am afraid I will have to *cancel* (not "cancel out") our dinner engagement.

**30. can't hardly/can't scarcely**  These expressions are ungrammatical double negatives for *can hardly* and *can scarcely*.

I *can hardly* (not "can't hardly/scarcely") believe he is sixty years old.

**31. compare to/compare with**  To compare to means to seek similarity; to compare with means to seek both similarities and differences.

I often *compare* my grandfather *to* one of the Old Testament patriarchs.

When I *compare* my lab results *with* Jim's, we shall know the most efficient
method of approaching the problem.

**32. consensus of opinion**  A redundant expression for *consensus*.

The *consensus* (not "consensus of opinion") of the delegates was that the
resolution should be adopted at once.

**33. continual/continuous**  Continual means occurring at frequent intervals, repeated often; continuous means occurring without interruption.

There were *continual* interruptions throughout the rock concert.

There was a *continuous* flow of water through the sluice gates.

**34. continue on**   The *on* is redundant after *continue*.

Please *continue* (not "continue on") with your report.

**35. correspond to/correspond with**   To correspond to means to be similar or equal to; to correspond with means to communicate by letter.

This item in the manual of instructions *corresponds to* the part I need to repair my automobile.

I often *correspond with* my uncle who is living in Europe.

**36. could of**   A colloquial expression for the contraction *could've* (could have).

We *could've* (not "could of") won first prize if we had bought a ticket.

**37. couple of**   A colloquial experssion for *a few* or *several*.

We had *a few* or *several* (not "a couple of") friends over for dinner.

Note:   When referring specifically to two persons or things, do not use *couple of*.

We each had *two* (not "a couple of") hot dogs while watching the baseball game.

**38. differ from/differ with**   Differ from indicates that two things are not alike; differ with indicates a disagreement between two people or two groups of people.

Our test results *differ from* yours.

I *differ with* you over the interpretation of the test results.

**39. different than**   In formal writing the preposition *from* is preferred after different.

Canadian football is not too *different from* (not "different than") American football.

**40. disinterested/uninterested**   Disinterested means impartial or unbiased; uninterested means indifferent to.

A judge must keep an open mind so that he can remain *disinterested* during the trial.

His students remained *uninterested* in the library assignment.

**41. due to the fact that**   A wordy substitute for *because* or *since*.

We were late for work *because* (not "due to the fact that") the commuter train was delayed by the snowstorm.

**42. each and every**   A redundant expression for *each* or *every*.

*Each* (not "each and every") rose on the bush was in bloom.

*Every* (not "each and every") person in the room should contribute to the cancer drive.

**43. feature**   A colloquialism when used to mean *to place emphasis on* or *to give prominence to*.

Helen will be *given a prominent role* (not "featured") in our new play.

Note:   Feature should never be used as a substitute for *appreciate* or *imagine*.

I do not *appreciate* (not "feature") ballet dancing.

Can you *imagine* (not "feature") his taking flying lessons?

**44. fewer/less**   Fewer means a smaller number of countable objects; less means smaller in amount, proportion, or degree.

Mike used *fewer* words than Tom to express the same idea.

We had *less* snow this week than last week.

**45. fix**   To fix means to fasten in place, or to mend. It should not be used to mean *a difficult situation* or *to take revenge on*.

When our car ran off the road in the middle of the night, we found ourselves *in a difficult situation* (not "in a fix").

The next time he kicks sand in my face I will *take my revenge* (not "fix him").

**46. free of**   A colloquialism for *free from*.

We are finally *free from* (not "free of") debt.

**47. get**   An incorrect synonym for *understand* or *irritate*.

I explained the process carefully, but he did not *understand* (not "get") it.

His constant arguing *irritates* (not "gets to") me.

**48. got**   an incorrect synonym for *purchase*, *own* or *must*.

My sister just *purchased* (not "got") a new car.

John and Peter each *own* (not "have got") a stereo.

I *must* (not "I've got to") return my library books.

**49. hadn't ought to**   A colloquial expression for *should not*.

James *should not* (not "hadn't ought to") have purchased so many expensive clothes.

**50. half of a/a half a**   Both are non-standard for *a half* or *half a*.

Please purchase *a half* pound (not "a half a pound" or "half of a pound") of butter when you go to the market.

**51. hanged/hung**   Hanged is used for people; hung is used for objects.

We have just *hung* several paintings this morning.

This morning the murderer was sentenced to be *hanged*.

**52. have got to**   A colloquial expression for *must* or *have to*.

We *must* (not "have got to") prepare dinner before our guests arrive.

**53. healthy/healthful**   Healthy means having good health; healthful means causing good health.

We diet and exercise to remain *healthy*.

Fresh air and exercise are *healthful*.

**54. hopefully**   An overworked adverb incorrectly used to mean *let us hope*.

*Let us hope* (not "hopefully") all of our financial problems will be solved by tomorrow.

**55. identical with**   Colloquial for *identical to*.

My coat is *identical to* (not "identical with") the one that was on sale last week.

**56. imply/infer**   To imply means to suggest; to infer means to conclude from evidence.

He *implied* that the meeting would be cancelled.

I have *inferred* from his comments that the meeting will no longer be necessary.

**57. in back of**   A colloquial expression for *behind*.

My golf ball is *behind* (not ''in back of'') the tree.

**58. in regards to**   A colloquial substitute for *regarding* or *in regard to*.

We shall take no further action *regarding* (not ''in regards to'') your memo of August 28th.

**59. in terms of**   A wordy and meaningless expression for the preposition *about* or *of*.

I was thinking *of* (not ''in terms of'') baseball when I used the term ''line drive.''

**60. in the event that**   A wordy substitute for *if*.

*If* (not ''in the event that'') he doesn't agree to our plan, we will proceed without him.

**61. in the last analysis**   A wordy and trite expression incorrectly used to mean *ultimately* or *conclusively*.

We will *ultimately* (not ''in the last analysis'') agree to their terms.

I have decided *conclusively* (not ''in the last analysis'') to abandon the project.

**62. initiate/instigate**   To initiate means to begin or originate; to instigate means to incite or urge on.

We *initiated* our new program last week.

Emma was responsible for *instigating* the workers' rebellion.

**63. inside of**   A redundant phrase for *inside*.

Please place the parcel *inside* (not ''inside of'') the container.

Note:   *Inside of* should never be used as a synonym for *within* when referring to time.

John will arrive *within* (not ''inside of'') a week.

**64. irregardless**   Colloquial for *regardless*.

We shall carry on *regardless* (not ''irregardless'') of the consequences.

**65. is when/is where**   Clauses beginning with *when* or *where* never follow the verb *to be* when an action is implied.

In golf a par *occurs when* (not "is where") a player puts the ball in the hole in the required number of strokes.

A comma splice *happens* (not "is when") when a comma is substituted for a period or a semi-colon between two independent clauses.

**66. it stands to reason**   A wordy cliché used vaguely to mean *obvious* or *apparent*.

It is *obvious* (not "it stands to reason") that quality control is our highest priority.

**67. -ize**   A perfectly legitimate English suffix that has been relentlessly abused by jargon makers who create verbs like maximize, finalize, priorize, utilize, formalize, and other such gobbledygook words.

Make your maximum effort (not "*maximize* your effort").

Our plans will be made final (not "*finalized*").

Make your presentation prior to the meeting (not "*priorize* your presentation").

Make use of your athletic ability (not "*utilize* your athletic ability").

Please write your remarks in a formal manner (not "*formalize* your remarks").

**68. kind of a/sort of a**   The *a* in both expressions is superfluous.

A certain *kind of* (not "kind of a") lubricant should be used.

Note:   *Sort of* or *Kind of* should never be used to mean *rather* or *somewhat*.

It was *rather* (not "sort of") pleasant sitting in the rocking chair on the back porch.

**69. lay/lie**   Lay is a transitive verb (taking an object) meaning to put; lie is an intransitive verb (taking no object) meaning to recline or remain.

Please *lay* my briefcase on my desk.

I think I will *lie* down until my headache goes away.

**70. learn/teach**   Learn means to acquire knowledge; teach means to impart knowledge.

I shall *teach* him all I know.

Unfortunately, he *learns* very slowly.

**71. lend/loan**   In formal writing *loan* is preferred as a noun, *lend* as a verb.

> I haven't any money to *lend* you.
>
> You will have to apply for a *loan* at the bank.

**72. let/leave**   Let means to allow to; leave means to depart.

> Would you please *let* the cat out before you come to bed?
>
> We shall *leave* in an hour.

**73. like**   Like is incorrectly used in place of *as* or *as if* in making comparisons or contrasts.

> The machinery performed *as* (not "like") we expected.
>
> He behaved *as if* (not "like") he were already president of the company.

**74. likely/liable**   Likely suggests probability; liable suggests an undesirable risk, the probablity of something unpleasant taking place.

> We are *likely* to be promoted this year.
>
> If Kathy is not careful she is *liable* to hurt herself on that swing.

**75. maybe/may be**   Maybe means perhaps; may be is an expression of possibility.

> *Maybe* we should study for our test tomorrow.
>
> There *may be* an increase in our taxes next year.

**76. might of**   A colloquial expression for *might have*.

> She *might have* (not "might of") won the race if she had trained harder.

**77. most/almost**   Most means greatest in amount, quality, or degree; almost means very nearly.

> She is the *most* unselfish person I ever met.
>
> Tom ate *almost* a pound of chocolate.

**78. nowheres near**   A colloquial expresion for *not nearly.*

> He is *not nearly* (not "nowheres near") as talented as his sister.

**79. off of**   The *of* after *off* is redundant.

> Take the casserole *off* (not "off of") the stove.

**80. on account of**   An undesirable and awkward substitute for *because*.

Mara missed her finance class *because* (not "on account of") her car had a flat tire.

**81. on condition that**   A wordy expression meaning *if*.

I will accept the prize money *if* (not "on condition that") I can share it with my teammates.

**82. outside of**   The *of* after *outside* is redundant.

Please place the lawnmower *outside* (not "outside of") the tool shed.

Note:   *Outside of* should never be used as a substitute for *except for* or *beside*.

*Except for* (not "outside of") his tendency to be slow, Paul is a dependable worker.

**83. over with**   A colloquial expression for *finally* or *completely finished*.

I am relieved that our examinations are *finally finished* (not "over with").

**84. plan on**   Colloquial for *plan to*.

All of us *plan to attend* (not "plan on attending") a rock concert this Friday.

**85. practical/practicable**   Practical means useful or sensible; practicable means feasible or able to be put into practice.

His observations were *practical* and to the point.

Your suggestions for redesigning the assembly line are simply not *practicable*.

**86. prior than**   Incorrect for *prior to*.

Please submit your term essay *prior to* (not "prior than") the final examination date.

**87. rarely ever**   The word *ever* is redundant.

We *rarely* (not "rarely ever") eat dinner before seven o'clock.

**88. reason is because**   An undesirable substitute for *the reason is that*.

I cannot attend your party; the *reason is that* (not "the reason is because") I have to meet my parents at the airport.

**89. reason why**   The *why* after *reason* is redundant.

*The reason* (not "the reason why") I phoned was to ask you about our homework assignment.

**90. refer back/return back**   The word *back* is redundant in both these phrases.

Please *refer* (not "refer back") to the introduction in your textbooks.

I must *return* (not "return back") the shovel I borrowed from my neighbour.

**91. sit/set**   Set is a transitive verb meaning to place or position; sit is an intransitive verb meaning to be seated.

Please *set* the dial on the oven.

You may *set* the glass on the table.

Because we arrived late, we had nowhere to *sit*.

**92. so**   An overworked word incorrectly used to mean *because* or *therefore*.

*Because* Frank pitched faultlessly, he was given the game ball.

                            not

Frank pitched faultlessly, *so* he was given the game ball.

**93. sure and**   *Sure to* is the preferred phrase in formal writing.

Be *sure to* (not "sure and") call me the minute you arrive.

**94. tasty/tasteful**   Tasty means flavourful; tasteful means showing good taste or judgement.

Yor beef stew was very *tasty*.

Her living room was *tastefully* decorated.

**95. that there/this here**   Both are colloquial phrases for *that* and *this*.

Will you open *that* (not "that there") can of peaches with *this* (not "this here") can opener?

**96. use to**   Colloquial for *used to*.

We are all *used to* (not "use to") physical labour.

**97. wait on**   A colloquial substitute for *wait for*.

I suppose we should *wait for* (not "wait on") Sally.

**98. ways**   Colloquial for *way* or *distance*.

Toronto is a long *way* (not "ways") from Ottawa.

**99. where at**   The *at* is unnecessary in phrases beginning with *where*.

I do not know *where* the telephone directory *is* (not "is at").

**100. with respect to**   A wordy substitution for *about*.

We have some reservations *about* (not "with respect to") our present salary scale.

## Exercise 8.7 — Revising for Effective Diction
Rewrite the following paragraphs by correcting the usage and diction errors.

At times we tend to forget that we have the potential to be excellent communicators due to the fact that each and every one of us has the innate capacity to express our thoughts with clarity and precision. But we seem to be put off by the basic fundamentals of grammar and lose our focus on the more rewarding skills of sentence and paragraph construction.

Utilizing our native language properly is all together a matter of common sense, being as how many of the rules are obvious and logical. For instance, if we realize that we have got to use a verb each and every time we formulate an idea, our attitude toward sentence construction might change; for after all, a sentence is, in the final analysis, a small idea, generated by a verb and completed by other parts of speech. Also alot of the rules of punctuation reflect our habits of speech—the tone we employ, the emphasis we place, and the natural hesitations we use.

Therefore, on condition that we begin perceiving the construction rules of grammar and syntax not in terms of artificial and mechanistic adjuncts to communication, but as necessary guidelines that allow us to think clearly and precisely, we will in the near future gain a new respect for our native tongue.

# CHAPTER NINE

# Preparing an Outline

## A. WHAT IS AN OUTLINE?

An outline is an instrument for organizing ideas and information. It is almost a step-by-step schematic of the way we think when we write. And since all good writing stems from clear thinking, the outlining process can be an invaluable tool for attaining the mental discipline needed for effective prose organization.

However, the outlining process is not an end in itself; that is, it is not a skill that can be set apart from any other skill related to written expression. It is simply one of the mental steps we must take in order to write clearly and efficiently.

## B. THE BENEFITS

Whether you are writing a few short paragraphs, a major essay, or a formal report, the benefits derived from the skill of outlining will be immediate.

**1.** Outlining will help you focus on your main ideas and work out the pattern of their development. It will enable you to anticipate organizational problems before they occur, thus permitting you to keep your ideas in perspective.

**2.** Outlining will help you seek out the logical connection between your principal and subordinate topics. Your ideas will be expressed in parallel form because you will be more sensitive to the skill of coordination; your transitions between paragraphs will be smoother and more efficient because you will be more aware of the pattern of sequential development (subordination) that leads logically to a summary conclusion. Thus your writing will become more proportionate and selective, enabling you to separate the major from the minor, the relevant from the irrelevant, the abstract from the concrete, the direct from the indirect, and the emphatic from the bland.

**3.** Your topic statements and your supporting evidence will be clear, direct, and comprehensive because you will be better able to spot weaknesses in your arguments. Your strict attention to the principles of development will ensure that your data will be complete, containing no gaps in logic or sequence. And as you become more adept at penetrating the organization of written expression, your reading will become more thoughtful and critical.

4. Finally, your sentences will grow forceful and expressive, and your paragraphs controlled and coherent, for you will have a better visual image of your essay's structure and a more precise idea of how to frame your thoughts. In short, you will be working from a structured plan that has its roots in deductive and inductive logic, enabling you to think more intelligently about length, transition, emphasis, tone, precision, and coherence.

In summary, then, we may say that the skill of outlining is directly related to the logic of prose organization. It teaches us how to control our language and order our thoughts so that we can give clear and effective expression to the flow of our ideas.

## C. TYPES OF OUTLINES

There are three common types of outlines representing different levels of thought organization: the scratch outline, the topic outline, and the sentence outline.

1. **Scratch Outline**   The scratch outline is composed of a tentative and random list of topics and ideas. In this outline you write down, almost in a stream-of-consciousness process, everything that you can think about a given topic. This exercise provides you with an important, though rudimentary framework for testing your ideas before attempting to organize them. Thus a scratch outline of an essay on environmental pollution might look like this:

    Industrial waste
    Automobile exhaust
    Lakes are dying
    Soil becomes non-productive
    Factory smoke
    Smog in Montreal
    Bad for lungs: cancer and emphysema
    Acid rain
    Fish die
    Cities are too noisy
    People have nervous disorders
    Noise levels in factories
    Air pollution is dangerous to the elderly
    Mercury found in fish
    Drinking water full of bacteria
    Municipal garbage
    Poisonous chemicals in rivers and streams
    Something must be done

**2. Topic Outline**   The topic outline is the most common type. This outline arranges the random ideas of the scratch outline into headings and subheadings, according to their levels of significance. It is here where you must pay strict attention to the principles of coordination and subordination, as well as to the logic of parallel construction: words with words; phrases with phrases; clauses with clauses. It is here, too, where the topic is focussed into a thesis statement.

**(a) Thesis Statement**   The key word here is "focus," for that is precisely what a thesis statement does. It narrows or limits the topic so that it can be discussed in clearly definable steps. It may also convey your point of view, aligning you closely with one specific section of the topic.* A good thesis statement, then, can show you the direction you should be heading and indicate how far you will have to travel to get there. Here are a few examples of how thesis statements refine and develop topics:

> TOPIC:   Television Advertising
> THESIS STATEMENT:   The television advertising that deals with feminine hygiene products is both tasteless and insulting.

Here the writer has focussed on a specific type of advertising and will demonstrate his or her position under two major headings.

> TOPIC:   Keeping Pets
> THESIS STATEMENT:   Housebreaking dogs need not be difficult if three major points are kept in mind.

Here the writer has limited the topic to a specific kind of pet—dogs—and has chosen three major headings to instruct the reader how to housebreak them.

> TOPIC:   Living in Large Cities
> THESIS STATEMENT:   There are certain cultural advantages to living in a large city.

Here the writer has chosen to talk about city living from only one point of view. The main headings will consist of a number of cultural advantages which may be discussed in detail or simply listed and exemplified.

As you can see from the above examples, the thesis statement implicitly reveals the length and organization of the essay by embodying the central idea that governs sequential development.

*See pages 178 to 187 for a detailed discussion of point of view in relation to the topic sentence.

**(b) Sequence of Symbols**   In the topic outline a set of conventional outline symbols are used. Starting from the largest headings and working downward to the smallest, you use alternate numbers and letters to indicate major and minor topics and sub-topics. The largest sections are indicated by upper case Roman numerals (I., II., III.); then sub-headings take, in descending order of importance, capital letters (A, B, C), Arabic numbers (1, 2, 3), small letters (a, b, c) and then, if needed, lower case Roman numerals (i, ii, iii). Major headings are placed at the margin, and then sub-headings are uniformly indented so that they fall neatly under each other in columns. Thus the skeleton of a topic outline might look like this:

I. _____

   A. _____

      1. _____

      2. _____

         a. _____

         b. _____

      3. _____

   B. _____

      1. _____

      2. _____

      3. _____

II. _____

   A. _____

      1. _____

      2. _____

      3. _____

         a. _____

         b. _____

           (i) _____

           (ii) _____

**B.** _____

    **1.** _____

       **a.** _____

       **b.** _____

       **c.** _____

    **2.** _____

    **3.** _____

**III.** _____

    **A.** _____

    **B.** _____

    **C.** _____

       **1.** _____

       **2.** _____

       **3.** _____

          **a.** _____

          **b.** _____

Most topic outlines you write, however, will rarely go past the third level of indentation. The length of the topic outline is usually determined by the range of the thesis statement. Here is the way a topic outline on environmental pollution might appear after being converted from the scratch outline (on p. 156). Observe how some of the ideas in the scratch outline are rephrased and refined, and how some are placed logically into headings and sub-headings.

            TOPIC:   Our Endangered Environment
THESIS STATEMENT:   *We are making our environment unfit for human habitation.*

### I. Air Pollution
    A. Automobile exhaust
       1. Contributes to lung cancer and emphysema
       2. Causes smog in cities
          a. Montreal
          b. Eastern Seaboard of U.S.

B. Factory Smoke
 1. Kills vegetation near factory towns
 2. Kills lakes and poisons soils
  a. Acid rain kills marine life in lakes
  b. Heavy concentrations of lead make fertile soil barren

**II. Water Pollution**
 A. Industrial Wastes
  1. Pollutes estuaries along sea coasts
   a. Oyster beds become contaminated
   b. Wildfowl lose feeding grounds
  2. Pollutes rivers and streams, and poisons fish
   a. Toxic chemicals in streams and rivers eliminate recreational swimming and boating
   b. Mercury compounds make fish uneatable
 B. Municipal Wastes
  1. Uses up oxygen in fresh water lakes
  2. Causes high bacteria count in drinking water

**III. Noise Pollution**
 A. Airplane noise
 B. Factory noise
 C. Traffic noise in congested cities
  1. Causes nervous disorders in animals
  2. Causes high blood pressure and hypertension in people

Notice that the thesis statement is written as a complete sentence, and that it effectively narrows down and focusses the essay topic. Notice also that every division and sub-division is equally balanced—for every A a B, every 1 a 2, etc.—and that each heading is logically and grammatically parallel. Finally, notice that the first word in each heading is capitalized and that there is no end punctuation after phrases or dependent clauses.

**3. Sentence Outline** In the sentence outline you write headings and sub-headings as complete sentences. This outline is especially useful when you are composing a long essay or a formal report, for it forces you to think through your major sections more thoroughly and to locate the logical relationships of their parts. As a matter of fact, a comprehensive sentence outline could be your final organizational step before the first draft of your essay. The sentence outline of the environmental pollution essay might look like this:

     TOPIC: Our Endangered Environment
 THESIS STATEMENT: *We are making our environment unfit for human habitation.*

 **I.** Air pollution adversely *affects* our health and *destroys* the beauty of our countryside.

A. Automobile exhaust is indirectly related to lung cancer and emphysema and directly related to smog in our cities.
B. Factory smoke *destroys* vegetation, *kills* lakes and *pollutes* soil.
1. Sulphur compounds *denude* vegetation near factories.
2. Acid rain *kills* marine life in lakes.
3. Heavy lead concentrations *destroy* the fertility of top soil.

II. Water pollution *places* toxic chemicals in our rivers and streams, *poisons* our fish, and *infects* our drinking water.
A. Industrial wastes *are responsible* for removing rivers and streams from recreational use and for the high concentrations of mercury found in our freshwater fish.
B. Municipal wastes *are responsible* for the high bacteria count in our drinking water, and for the oxygen starvation of our freshwater lakes.

III. Noise pollution *causes* nervous disorders in animals, and high blood pressure and hypertension in humans.

Notice that each sentence effectively sums up a key idea implicit in the thesis statement, and that each is expressed in proper parallel form.

# D. ORDERING THE OUTLINE

Outlines are usually arranged in one of three ways: analytically, chronologically, or spatially. Depending upon the nature and scope of your topic, you will most likely use one of these three methods of arrangement to organize your essay.

**1. Grouping by Ideas or Analysis**   The analytical outline is one in which the topic and thesis statement are divided into manageable parts according to the logic of your argument. Ideas are grouped into related sections so that each section has a pattern of development. This pattern may take many forms: it may be a simple classification by rank, purpose or degree; or it may be structured according to cause and effect, or statement and example. But no matter which pattern is chosen, it must be used consistently throughout the outline. In the following examples you can see how attention to these principles —manageability of topic divisions, logical development, and consistency of structure—leads to clear, useful outlines.

### Simple Classification

THESIS STATEMENT:   *Our Canadian educational system is both comprehensive and flexible.*

**I. Elementary Schools**
A. Public
B. Private

### II. Senior Elementary Schools

### III. Secondary Schools
A. Public
1. Composite schools
2. Vocational schools
3. Academic collegiates
B. Private
1. Non-denominational
2. Denominational
a. Catholic
b. Protestant
c. Jewish

### IV. Post-Secondary Education
A. Universities
B. Community colleges
C. Technical institutes

## Statement and Example

THESIS STATEMENT:  *Movies are better than ever.*

### I. Better Actors and Actresses
A. Robert De Niro
Dustin Hoffman
B. Katharine Hepburn
Faye Dunaway
Anne Bancroft

### II. Better Directors
A. Francis Ford Coppola
B. Sidney Lumet
C. Martin Ritt
D. Stanley Kubrick

### III. Better Scripts
A. *The Godfather*, Parts I and II
B. *Bonnie and Clyde*
C. *The Sting*

### IV. Better Cinematography
A. *2001: A Space Odyssey*
B. *Butch Cassidy and the Sundance Kid*
C. *The Sound of Music*

## Cause and Effect

THESIS STATEMENT:    *Our dependence on foreign energy is leading us into a major recession.*

### I. Balance of Payments Deficits
A. Increase in interest rates
B. Devaluation of the dollar

### II. High Utility Costs
A. Increase in cost-of-living index
B. Decrease in consumer spending
   1. Less business investment
   2. More unemployment

**2. Arranging Chronologically**    A chronological outline is one in which events are arranged according to a logical time sequence. This type of arrangement is used to write narration, to describe a process, and to write evaluation reports. Time order is the key to this outline.

TITLE:    *How to Plan a Child's Birthday Party*

**I.** Send invitations

**II.** Arrange transportation if needed

**III.** Decorate party room

**IV.** Buy food and beverages

**V.** Prepare party games

**VI.** Purchase plenty of aspirin

TITLE:    *Technical Report Evaluation Procedure*

### I. Purpose of the report
A. Who requested it and why?
B. Is it for external or internal circulation?

### II. Form of the report
A. Is the format appropriate to its function and readership?
B. Are all required formal components included?
C. Are format and substance complementary?

### III. Substance of the report
A. Is the factual information accurate and complete?
B. Are relevant and authoritative sources cited?
C. Does the sequence of the facts justify the conclusion?

D. Are the recommendations reasonable?

E. Are there logical transitions between ideas?

F. Is the style clear and grammatical, and is it appropriate to the occasion and purposes of the report?

G. Is the tone sufficiently technical?

H. Is the visual material completely integrated with the textual information?

I. Does the appendix contain supplementary material unessential to the body of the report?

**3. Arranging by Location and Situation**   In this type of outline the writer organizes things as they appear in space, or as they relate to a specific location. This arrangement usually follows a line of movement in one direction, whether from left to right, top to bottom, north to south, or east to west. This type of arrangement provides a very simple and straightforward way of organizing material, as may be seen in the examples below.

TITLE:   *Post-Secondary Education in Canada*

**I.** Universities in British Columbia

**II.** Agricultural and Technical Colleges in the Prairie provinces

**III.** Community Colleges in Ontario

**IV.** CEGEP's in Quebec

**V.** Colleges of Art in the Atlantic provinces

TITLE:   *Decorating a Study Room*

**I.** Gold rug on floor

**II.** Rust coloured wallpaper on three walls

**III.** Off-white paint on south wall

**IV.** Recessed lighting in ceiling

# E. THE ELEMENTS OF A CONSTRUCTIVE OUTLINE

To determine whether your outline will effectively organize your essay, ask yourself the following questions listed under the headings of balance, unity, and completeness.

## 1. Balance
(a) Are my headings and sub-headings properly coordinated and subordinated?

(b) Are my headings logically and grammatically parallel?

(c) Are there at least two sub-headings under each heading, and are they properly indented?

(d) Is the first word in each heading capitalized?

**2. Unity**
  (a) Have I established a consistent pattern of arrangement?
  (b) Do my ideas fall into a logical sequence?
  (c) Is my language clear and concise?

**3. Completeness**
  (a) Does my thesis statement properly focus my topic?
  (b) Do my headings and sub-headings fully develop my thesis statement?
  (c) Have I used any irrelevant or unrelated material?

## Exercise 9.1 — Preparing an Outline

**#1** In the blanks to the right, or on a separate sheet, arrange the following terms in a logical outline sequence.

**(a)** Sports apparel                    _____

Ski jackets                    _____

Hockey pants                    _____

Summer                    _____

Ski boots                    _____

Golf shoes                    _____

Tennis skirt                    _____

Winter                    _____

Hockey helmet                    _____

Curling shoes                    _____

Bathing suit                    _____

Sailing cap                    _____

Golf glove                    _____

Ice skates                    _____

Toque                    _____


**(b)** Home entertainment                    _____

Radio                    _____

Games                    _____

Tapes                    _____

Euchre                    _____

Stereo set                    _____

Records      _____

Board games      _____

Television      _____

Card games      _____

Monopoly      _____

Bridge      _____

Chess      _____

Poker      _____

Trivial Pursuit      _____

**(c)** Meat      _____

Sirloin      _____

Roasts      _____

Beef      _____

Rump      _____

Steaks      _____

T-Bone      _____

Meat loaf      _____

Eye of the round      _____

Hamburgers      _____

Porterhouse      _____

Ground beef      _____

Cross-rib      _____

Cube      _____

**(d)** Foods of the world      _____

Mexico      _____

Sauerkraut      _____

Spaghetti      _____

France      _____

Chicken Cordon Bleu      _____

Canada      _____

China      _____

North America      _____

Hot dogs      _____

Pea soup     _____

Crepes suzettes     _____

United States     _____

Chow mein     _____

Weiner schnitzel     _____

Tortilla     _____

Italy     _____

Hamburger     _____

Tortiere     _____

Chop suey     _____

Europe     _____

Tacos     _____

Lasagna     _____

Asia     _____

Germany     _____

**#2** Place the proper outline symbols next to the following lists of terms or write this outline on a separate sheet and insert the proper symbols. Begin with Roman numerals.

**(a)** THESIS STATEMENT:    _My father's home and garden tools are taking up more room each year._

Home tools     _____

Hand     _____

Hammers     _____

Pliers     _____

Screwdrivers     _____

Wrenches     _____

Socket     _____

Crescent     _____

Pipe     _____

Power     _____

Drills     _____

Sanders     _____

Saws _____

Band _____

Jig _____

Circular _____

Garden tools _____

Hand _____

Rakes _____

Hoes _____

Shovels _____

Power _____

String trimmer _____

Hedge trimmer _____

Cordless grass shear _____

**(b)** THESIS STATEMENT:    *My literature collection is quite varied.*

Literature _____

Fiction _____

Novels _____

Short stories _____

Poems _____

Lyric _____

Narrative _____

Children's stories _____

Fairy tales _____

Nursery rhymes _____

Non-fiction _____

Biographies _____

Journals _____

Essays _____

Personal _____

Scientific _____

Political _____

**(c)** THESIS STATEMENT: *Professional sports have many specialized terms which are not readily understood by the uninitiated.*

Sports                                    _____

Summer                                    _____

Golf                                      _____

Birdie                                    _____

Par                                       _____

Tennis                                    _____

Love                                      _____

Let                                       _____

Serve                                     _____

Baseball                                  _____

Steal                                     _____

Double play                               _____

Walk                                      _____

Fall                                      _____

Football                                  _____

Blitz                                     _____

Safety                                    _____

Quarterback sneak                         _____

Winter                                    _____

Basketball                                _____

Dribble                                   _____

Dunk                                      _____

Hook shot                                 _____

Hockey                                    _____

Hat trick                                 _____

Slapshot                                  _____

Cross-check                               _____

**(d)** THESIS STATEMENT:    *Our post-secondary educational programs in Canada are second to none in both variety and content.*

Universities         _____

Science         _____

Physics         _____

Chemistry         _____

Computer         _____

Engineering         _____

Civil         _____

Electrical         _____

Chemical         _____

Humanities         _____

Literature         _____

Canadian         _____

British         _____

American         _____

History         _____

World         _____

Canadian         _____

Philosophy         _____

Logic         _____

Epistemology         _____

Community colleges         _____

Applied arts         _____

Child-care worker         _____

Mental retardation counsellor         _____

Business         _____

Accounting         _____

Marketing         _____

Technology         _____

Electronic         _____

Civil         _____

Chemical         _____

**#3** Rewrite the following outlines by correcting the parallel construction errors; make sure the terms within each section are similarly expressed.

(a) THESIS STATEMENT: *Tourists visit vacation resorts for various reasons.*

**I. Social**
   A. Enjoy outings with other families
      1. Picnics
      2. Go on walking tours
   B. Meet people from different cultural backgrounds
      1. Engaging in stimulating conversation
      2. Learn different customs and attitudes
   C. Opposite sexes meet

**II. They want to escape**
   A. Get away from family pressures
   B. Getting away from big-city living
      1. Traffic noise
      2. Overcrowded apartment buildings
      3. The high crime rate is another reason
   C. Break away from daily routines
   D. Pressures of job

**III. Participate in Leisure Activities**
   A. Night club tours
   B. Museum visits are always interesting
   C. Attend concerts and plays
   D. Play sports
      1. Golf
      2. Tennis is good exercise
      3. Badminton
      4. Skiing
         a. Downhill
         b. Skiing cross country.

(b) THESIS STATEMENT: *Causes of juvenile delinquency are rooted in different environmental factors.*

**I. Family**
   A. Single-parent family
      1. No discipline
      2. There may be a lack of moral or ethical direction
   B. Severe tension between mother and father
      1. The spouses may not love each other
      2. Alcoholism in the family

## II. Economic Environment
A. Severe poverty
   1. No jobs available
   2. The family may be on welfare
      a. Low self-esteem
      b. Lacking hope and ambition

## III. Poor Educational Opportunities
A. Classes overcrowded
B. The teachers may be overworked and unmotivated
C. Lacking school counsellors

## IV. Social Environment
A. No social services available
   1. Lack of day-care centers
   2. Recreational facilities
   3. There may be no organized boys' club or sports program
B. Poor choice of companions
   1. Street gangs
   2. High-school dropouts may have a negative influence
   3. Drug dealers are dangerous companions

**#4** Organize the following list of terms into a topic outline; use conventional outline symbols and uniform indentation to indicate coordinate and subordinate relationships.

**(a)** TOPIC:   *Preparing to Vacation in Europe*
Itinerary preparation with a travel agent
List number of tourist attractions to be seen in each country
Language preparation
Arrange guided tours to specific tourist areas in each country
Learn key words and phrases
Bed and breakfast establishments
Car rental
Financial preparation
Learn the tipping customs of each country
Hostels and camping sites
Land transportation
Accommodations
Determine time to be spent in each country
Learn how to read road signs and maps
Purchase travellers' cheques
Tour bus

Hotels and motels
Learn exchange rates for each country visited
Train
Travel and accommodation preparation

**(b)** TOPIC: *Outdoor Occupations*

Bricklayer
Caddy
Construction
Football
Sports
Skiing
Carpenter
Golf
Heavy-equipment operator
Conservation
Referee
Water quality inspector
Greenskeeper
Game warden
Ski instructor
Ironworker
Forest ranger
Coach
Lift-tow operator

**#5** Check the following outlines for errors in coordination, subordination, and parallel structure, and then rewrite them correctly on a separate sheet of paper.

THESIS STATEMENT: *You can travel across Canada in many different ways, depending upon your circumstances and interests.*

### I. By Automobile
  A. Advantages
    1. Costs less than a plane or a train
    2. Riders share transportation and food costs
      a. Accommodations are inexpensive
        i. Sharing motel rooms
        ii. Stay in camping areas
    3. You are able to see the countryside
      a. Can make unscheduled side trips
      b. You can see historic sites
      c. Visiting tourist areas
      d. An opportunity to meet different people en route.

B. Disadvantages must be considered
   1. Must stop often
   2. Cramped quarters; not enough room to move around
   3. Taking a long time to reach destination
      a. There may be hazardous weather and road conditions
      b. Snowstorms
      c. Icy roads are always a possibility
      d. Fog and rain
C. Mechanical failure can happen
D. Higher accident rate

## II. By Train
   1. There are a number of advantages
      a. Room to move around
      b. Seats more comfortable than a car
      c. More social surroundings
      d. One can see the countryside from the windows
      e. Faster than a car
      f. One's sleeping accommodations part of the fare
   2. Disadvantages
      a. Travelling at night
      b. Much slower than a plane
      c. Confined to a rigid schedule and a designated route
         i.   Train routes are not always the most scenic
         ii.  Departure and arrival times may not be convenient
         iii. High noise level
   3. Weather conditions may cause many delays
   4. Food not always well prepared
   5. Costs more than an automobile

## III. Travelling by Plane
   A. Advantages
      1. Planes are faster than both trains and automobiles
      2. Weather not a factor; planes fly above bad weather
      3. Can see a film in flight
   B. Better safety record than train or automobile
      4. Food served at your seat
   C. There are serious disadvantages
      1. Cramped space
      2. No head room
      3. Seats are smaller than seats on the train
      4. Aisles are narrow and restrooms are small
      5. Cannot see the countryside
      6. No opportunity to socialize

    D. High level of boredom

    E. The menus are usually limited

**#6** Convert the following topic outlines into sentence outlines; compose a thesis statement that is effectively developed by each outline.

**(a)** TOPIC:   *Job Interviewing*

THESIS STATEMENT:   _____

  I. Learn all you can about your chosen occupational area
    A. Career choices
    B. Opportunities for advancement
    C. Salary scale

 II. Learn about the company
    A. How old is the company?
    B. How large is the company?
       1. Is it a national or a multi-national company?
       2. How many branches and offices does it have within Canada?
    C. How is it organized and managed?
    D. How many products does it manufacture?
    E. Who are its competitors?

III. Learn the desirable requirements for the job
    A. Educational
       1. University education
       2. Community college training
       3. Specialized skill training
    B. Employment experience
    C. Community involvement

IV. Do a complete personal checklist
    A. What are my major weaknesses and strengths?
    B. Why should the company hire me over someone else with similar qualifications?
    C. Do I work well with people?
    D. What are my salary needs?
    E. What are my long-term goals?
    F. Am I ready to accept responsibility and make decisions?

 V. Prepare a data sheet or resume
    A. Heading
       1. Name and address
       2. Telephone number
       3. Title of job applying for

    B. Educational background
       1. Secondary and post-secondary schooling
       2. Specialized training
    C. Work experience
       1. Part-time and full-time jobs
         a. Last job first
         b. Dates started and finished
    D. Personal information
       1. Height and weight
       2. Age
       3. Marital status
       4. Health
    E. References
       1. Personal
       2. Educational
       3. Employment
VI. Rehearse interview
    A. Before a mirror
    B. With a friend

**(b)** TOPIC:   *Speech Evaluation*

THESIS: ────────────────────────────────────

   I. Content
    A. Topic
    B. Purpose
    C. Details

  II. Organization
    A. Introduction
    B. Body
    C. Conclusion

 III. Language
    A. Vocabulary
    B. Usage and style
    C. Tone

 IV. Diction
    A. Articulation
    B. Pronunciation
    C. Phrasing and emphasis
    D. Tempo and voice control

V. Physical behaviour
   A. Poise
   B. Gestures
   C. Eye contact
   D. Facial expressions

VI. Communication
   A. Projection
   B. Audience response
   C. General impression

**#7** Use three of the following topics to construct an analytical outline, a chronological outline, and a spatial outline. Use no more than three major headings for each outline.

1. How to lose weight
2. How to avoid heart attacks
3. Fast-food restaurants in my city
4. Small business opportunities
5. Travelling through Florida
6. Our city has a number of tourist attractions
7. Setting up a classroom
8. Giving artificial respiration
9. Evaluating a research essay
10. Choosing a ski resort
11. Major automobile manufacturers throughout the world
12. The negative effects of television violence
13. Eliminating the nuclear arms race
14. Decorating a children's playroom
15. Learning how to drive an automobile

# CHAPTER TEN

---

# Constructing Effective Paragraphs

The paragraph is an essential unit of written expression, for it allows the writer to focus on the development of a single idea within the larger context of an essay or a report. Mastering the organization of a paragraph is the first important step towards mastering practically any piece of expository prose.

## A. WHAT IS A PARAGRAPH?

The single paragraph may be defined as a series of related sentences that develops one major idea. Each sentence is logically and structurally joined to the one before it. It is, in effect, a unified whole, with a beginning, a middle, and an end. Each paragraph (in an extended essay) is indented to indicate a shift in thought.

## B. MAKING PARAGRAPHS UNIFIED

The key term in the paragraph definition above is "related sentences," because without a unified sentence structure the paragraph would fall apart like a house of cards. Like the outline pattern, the formal paragraph structure enables you to place ideas into sequential groups that ensure their logical progression. Here is an example of a poorly constructed paragraph.

> My younger brother's room is always a mess. He never learned to be neat.
> Instead of straightening up his room when he returns from school, he'd
> rather go to the schoolyard and play basketball. Even though he is a pretty
> good basketball player, he should try to be a little less sloppy.

There is no sentence continuity in this paragraph, for it is composed of a series of unrelated and disconnected ideas. The sentences wander aimlessly without ever coming to a point, making it impossible for the readers to focus on a unifying idea. Now consider the following paragraph:

My younger brother's room is always a mess. His bed is never made, and there are parts of model airplanes all over his desk and bureau. Dirty clothes are invariably piled in a corner, and chewing gum wrappers are usually scattered beneath his desk. If he doesn't soon clean up his act, my father will discontinue his allowance.

Now the sentences join together to form a unified and coherent paragraph because only one idea is developed—the messy room. Each sentence demonstrates and proves the topic idea, and each leads logically to the concluding statement.

If you think of the paragraph as a delicate structure containing interrelated pieces of information that answer a general question or develop a formal statement, you will realize how irrelevant information disturbs its balance and thereby frustrates your readers.

## Exercise 10.1 Paragraph Unity

Rewrite the following paragraphs by eliminating unnecessary and unrelated ideas and details, and by tightening the sentence structure.

1. I cannot remember when I had a more enjoyable outing. The weather was perfect, and the picnic food delicious. Although I caught a cold after I went swimming in the frigid waters of the lake, I still had a good time. The softball game we played was full of laughs and unexpected excitement, and our marshmallow toast at dusk was the perfect ending of a perfect day. Furthermore, the cold I caught only lasted for a few days. I hope we do it all again next year.

2. Many of us feel that our football team has a good chance to win our division title this year. We are obviously one of the two best teams in the league. All of us are confident we can go all the way this year. Even coaches of other teams admit we are the favourites in our division. Most of our seniors are back this year, and so we have experience on our side. We have the best quarterback and the best linebacking crew. Furthermore, most people agree that our head coach is second to none. If we do not win the title this year, it won't be because we lack the talent.

3. Driving large, gas-guzzling cars is no longer a symbol of prestige, but a sign of irresponsibility. With such a premium placed on energy conservation in Canada, it is almost criminal to drive an inefficient automobile. Some people, of course, have switched to small, fuel-efficient cars, and some have decided to use public transportation to travel to and from work. These people are to be congratulated. Because many people still associate bigness with social importance, they simply ignore the necessity for fuel conservation. Unfortunately, many of them can afford to be wasteful and irresponsible; but the question is, can we afford their irresponsibility? I think not. Perhaps the people who have switched to fuel-efficient cars should be publicly acclaimed and held up as examples to those who are less responsible. We must force our North American car-makers to scale

down the size of their cars and to manufacture more fuel-efficient engines. If responsible behaviour cannot be freely demonstrated by our citizens, then our government will have to legislate it.

4. My favourite reading matter is science fiction because I enjoy using my imagination. When I involve myself in fantastic situations in the distant future, my mind seems to open up, and I feel more alive; my imagination is full of space ships, time warps, anti-matter, and black holes. Maybe that is why I am doing so poorly at school. I simply hate to read dry, technical prose—you know, the kind you find in most textbooks. My teachers think that I am lazy, and some think my speculations are idle daydreams. However, I know that scientific and technological progress is made by people who dream and imagine and speculate—who live at least a part of their lives in the future. That is why I recommend science fiction to anyone interested in developing his or her creative abilities.

5. Your good intentions can sometimes get you into trouble; I learned this valuable lesson when I was only thirteen. My brother, who was three years older than I, was on our high-school basketball team, and I was on my way to see him play. The day was cool, so I was wearing a sweater and a light jacket that my mother had just purchased for me at a department store fire sale. As I approached a busy intersection—I lived in a large city at the time—I noticed an old lady who seemed afraid to cross the street because of the heavy traffic. She had on a heavy black coat that came down almost to her ankles, a blue toque, and extremely thick glasses; she seemed to be squinting at the traffic. Feeling sorry for her, I decided to lend her a hand across the street. Boy, was that a mistake! As soon as I touched her arm, she hit me over the head with her "five-ton" purse and kicked me in the shins. Then she screamed for help. When the traffic cop came running over to where we were standing—he was wearing a leather jacket and high leather boots—she accused me of trying to molest her and demanded my arrest. After a long and involved explanation that included my telling him about my interest in helping other people less fortunate than I was, I finally convinced the police officer that I had made an honest mistake; but he cautioned me to be more careful in the future. He didn't seem to be curious about the woman. You see, the old woman wasn't so helpless after all; in fact, she was working for the city monitoring traffic—she had a traffic counter in her right hand. The lesson I learned was never to offer assistance to anyone unless I was absolutely certain it was needed and would be gratefully accepted.

## C. THE TOPIC SENTENCE: POINT OF VIEW

One of the most important parts of the expository paragraph is the topic sentence, for it contains the controlling idea. And because the controlling idea is the one discussed by the rest of the sentences in the paragraph, the topic sentence must not only state the idea clearly and succinctly but also determine its pattern of development.

A good topic sentence, then, places certain expectations in the mind of the readers by focussing their attention toward a specific attitude or position that you have assumed. It thus informs the readers how you feel, as well as what you think, about the topic idea.

**1. An Effective Topic Sentence**   An effective topic sentence must fulfill two essential requirements: it must be specific enough to convert the topic statement into an idea, and general enough to be broken down, explained, and defended by the rest of the sentences in the paragraph.

(a) If the topic sentence is too general, your paragraph will be loose and unwieldy, and the readers will have trouble distinguishing it from the thesis topic of your essay. Consider the following statements:

Democracy is the political philosophy governing North America.

The highest mountain in the United States is Mount McKinley.

Oil exploration off Canada's east coast is taking place.

These sentences lack direction because they contain no specific idea or point of view. They are merely statements of fact, revealing no sense of purpose and placing no questions in the minds of the readers. They may therefore be dismissed as inert statements, too general and insubstantial to be contained in a single paragraph. Observe how much more solid and interesting they become when given a specific focus:

Democracy in North America is being eroded by special interest groups.

Climbing Mount McKinley can be extremely hazardous.

Oil exploration off Canada's east coast is absolutely essential for the economic health of the Atlantic provinces.

Now each of these topic statements has been given a clear direction. You now know the precise idea you will stress throughout the rest of the paragraph: the first topic sentence focussed on the harmful influence of special interest groups; the second, on the hazards of climbing; and the third, on the promotion of east coast oil exploration. This conversion of the general topic statement into a specific topic idea is illustrated below.

| | | | |
|---|---|---|---|
| TOPIC: | Democracy | TOPIC IDEA: | Hurt by special interest groups |
| TOPIC: | Mount McKinley | TOPIC IDEA: | Hazardous to climb |
| TOPIC: | East coast oil exploration | TOPIC IDEA: | Important to the economic health of the Atlantic provinces |

(b) If the topic sentence is too specific, it will be self-explanatory, and therefore static. It will leave no room for you to expand it into a unified paragraph. Here are a few examples:

My chair is made of wood.

I completed my math test yesterday.

This orange was grown in Florida.

Because these sentences are too narrow and restricted, they literally have no place to go. They cannot be expanded and explored because they lack a general point of view. Now consider these sentences:

Wooden chairs are more decorative than metal chairs.

We are given too many math tests.

Florida oranges are better-tasting than California oranges.

You can now develop these sentences because they contain a general point of view. The initial statement can be justified by giving reasons, examples, and specific details. Adequate arguments can be developed because a clear position has been taken. In short, there is now a solid foundation on which to build a unified and coherent paragraph.

## Exercise 10.2 – Selecting the Topic Sentence

From the lists below, select the number of the sentence that you think would best serve as a topic sentence and write it in the space to the right or on a separate sheet.

Topic
Sentence

EXAMPLE: **1.** My pet cat is named Herman.
**2.** Many people have cats as house pets.
**3.** I swear my cat Herman has a distinct sense of humour.      3

(a) 1. The city of Ottawa attracts many tourists during the summer months.
2. Ottawa offers many attractions for the summer tourist.
3. The Parliament buildings are being renovated.      _____

(b) 1. I enjoy downhill skiing.
2. My ski boots are too tight.
3. Skiing in the spring has many advantages over skiing during the months of December and January.      _____

**(c)** 1. Some women continue their careers after marriage.
    2. My sister is a housewife with two children.
    3. Modern marriage is quite different from the traditional marriage of my grandparents. _____

**(d)** 1. Our city has a new hockey arena.
    2. There is quite a difference between ice hockey and field hockey.
    3. Hockey is the most popular sport in Canada. _____

**(e)** 1. I did not study for today's test.
    2. My teacher assigns too many essays.
    3. Personal essays are more satisfying to write than expository essays. _____

**(f)** 1. My job in the factory is boring.
    2. Ball bearings are used extensively in the auto industry.
    3. Our company manufactures ball bearings. _____

**(g)** 1. Her hairdresser has a good reputation.
    2. Since Sue has changed the style and colour of her hair, she seems to have undergone a personality change.
    3. Sue's hair is now red. _____

**(h)** 1. I love Broadway musicals.
    2. I saw a new musical comedy last night.
    3. My favourite actress did not appear in the starring role. _____

**(i)** 1. Hang gliding is a popular sport in some areas of the country.
    2. My brother broke his leg in a hang-gliding accident.
    3. Hang gliding is a dangerous sport. _____

**(j)** 1. Why do people smoke cigarettes?
    2. One of the causes of lung cancer is cigarette smoking.
    3. My doctor says cigarette smoking takes years off one's life. _____

**(k)** 1. John lied to Mary.
    2. Mary left the party without John.
    3. John cannot decide what he wants out of life. _____

**(l)** 1. I collect rare books.
    2. Collecting rare books is more satisfying and more expensive than collecting match covers.
    3. This book is rare. _____

**(m)** 1. I will never eat in this restaurant again.
    2. Our food was cold when it arrived at our table.
    3. Our waiter was rude and slow. _____

**(n)** 1. My son hates to read.
  2. His English teacher frowns all the time.
  3. There are a number of reasons for the decline of literacy
    in our society.                                              _____

**(o)** 1. Canada's official languages are English and French.
  2. I think Canada should do more to protect its natural
    resources.
  3. Montreal has a number of good French restaurants.          _____

**2. Position of Topic Sentences**   Although the topic sentence is most often placed at the beginning of the paragraph, it can also appear at the beginning and the middle, the beginning and the end, or at the end only. Writers position topic sentences in these different ways according to the way they wish to organize their ideas, the emphasis they wish to place on them, and the tone they wish to convey. However, the developmental details must be clearly arranged so that the reader can follow the logic of the sequence of thoughts, either before or after the topic sentences.

**(a) Topic Sentence at the Beginning**   This type of paragraph structure, which is the most common, introduces the topic idea in the first sentence, so that the reader will know immediately how the rest of the paragraph will be developed.

> *The central symbol for Canada—and this is based on numerous instances of its occurrence in both English and French-Canadian literature—is un-doubtedly Survival*, la Survivance. *Like the Frontier and The Island, it is a multi-faceted and adaptable idea.* For early explorers and settlers, it meant bare survival in the face of 'hostile' elements and/or natives: carving out a place and a way of keeping alive. But the word can also suggest survival of a crisis or disaster, like a hurricane or a wreck, and many Canadian poems have this kind of survival as a theme; what you might call 'grim' survival as opposed to 'bare' survival. For French Canada after the English took over it became cultural survival, hanging on as a people, retaining a religion and a language under an alien government. And in English Canada now while the Americans are taking over it is acquiring a similar meaning. There is another use of the word as well: a survival can be a vestige of a vanished order which has managed to persist after its time is past, like a primitive reptile. This version crops up in Canadian thinking too, usually among those who believe that Canada is obsolete.[1]

In this paragraph the writer uses examples in the body to define precisely what she means by the term "Survival" and its relevance as a Canadian symbol.

**(b) Topic Sentence at the Beginning and End**   In this type of paragraph organization the topic idea is restated in the last sentence so that the reader will clearly understand the writer's position before going on to the next paragraph. You will find this paragraph structure used most often in textbooks or educational journals, where the flow of ideas may be sophisticated and difficult to grasp.

*A child who is made to read, "Nan had a pad. Nan had a tan pad. Dad ran. Dad ran to the pad," and worse nonsense can have no idea that books are worth the effort of learning to read.* His frustration is increased by the fact that such a repetitive exercise is passed off as a story to be enjoyed. The worst effect of such drivel is the impression it makes on a child that sounding out words on a page—decoding—is what reading is all about. If, on the contrary, a child were taught new skills as they became necessary to understand a worthwhile text, the empty achievement "Now I can decode some words" would give way to the much more satisfying recognition "Now I am reading something that adds to my life." *From the start, reading lessons should nourish the child's spontaneous desire to read books by himself.* [2]

By describing the failure of reading lessons in the opening sentence of this paragraph, the writers implicitly tell us what they think the most important goal of such lessons is. Then, they explicitly state this goal in the concluding sentence.

**(c) Topic Sentence at the Beginning and Middle**   This type of paragraph structure is used when the topic idea can be discussed in two parts. First one idea is introduced and developed, and then its opposite or complementary idea is introduced and developed. Paragraphs organized in this manner are usually quite lengthy.

*The future of literacy is ultimately in the hands of the teachers of English.* If they are well enough trained, determined enough, and dedicated enough to the cultivation of literacy, no one can actually stop them from making their students literate. Not every student can be educated to the same degree of literacy, though my own long experience taught me what a great deal can be achieved with what might seem to be unpromising material. But the teacher must have a clear notion of what he is trying to do, and of how to do it, and be constantly imaginative and inventive in his methods. *English is by no means an obsolete industry.* It is an industry which has been suffering from a great deal of confusion about what products it is trying to make and about what its workers are supposed to be doing. Its genuine and proper products should be as valuable and as necessary as ever. [3]

Under the general heading of the future of literacy, the writer first discusses the function and qualities of English teachers; then he goes on to discuss the relevance of English as a subject taught in schools.

**(d) Topic Sentence at the End**   This type of paragraph may be organized in one of two ways: it may contain a series of details or minor statements that are brought together by the final sentence, which serves as the conclusion of the paragraph. Or it may be composed of a number of rhetorical questions that are answered by the final sentence of the paragraph.

The assumption that budget cuts should be made in our social service programs needs careful consideration. In 1978 there were three half-way houses for the needy in our city; in 1982 there were two, and today we have only one. Furthermore, in 1981 we had four day-care centers; today we have only two and both are overcrowded. And finally, the hours our chest x-ray clinic is available to the public have been severely curtailed, and our home for battered wives must now rely on private donations to keep operating. These facts seem to indicate that instead of reducing our social welfare budget, we should significantly increase it.

In this paragraph the author provides the reader with figures and statements of fact that lead logically and inevitably to his topic position in the last sentence.

How long must we endure an increasing debt burden that fuels inflation year after year? How much longer can we go on paying off our mortgages when mortgage rates go up every six months? How much longer do you think our elderly will survive on fixed incomes in a climate of runaway inflation? And how long before our unemployed revolt over the lack of jobs in our sick economy? If action isn't taken soon to halt our high inflation and unemployment, we should call for another election and then vote in leaders who will take decisive political action.

The suggestive questions in this paragraph lead logically to the last sentence which, as a drawn conclusion, functions as the topic idea. There are also paragraphs that do not contain unifying sentences with specific topic ideas. Instead, they gather together enough detailed information to suggest the topic idea without actually stating it. These paragraphs, however, are difficult to write and should be avoided, especially in a closely reasoned essay or report.

In existing capitalisms at any definite time, profit may not be guaranteed for all capitalists but only for a certain number. But this number may be sufficient to keep production up to a level where most workers are employed while those who are temporarily unemployed receive social benefits. Marx was indisputably right in anticipating periodic economic dislocations where the market still operates in an unplanned economy. [4]

This paragraph contains no topic sentence because it is not organized around a single central idea. Rather, it is composed of a series of statements which, when read together, add up to a single thought—that full employment is not a pre-requisite for a capitalist economy.

The point to remember about topic sentences is that no matter where they occur, they must serve as the focus of the paragraph; that is, they must contain the ideas around which the other sentences in the paragraph are organized.

## Exercise 10.3 − Position of the Topic Sentence

In the space to the right or on a separate sheet, place the number of each sentence that contains the topic idea. There may be more than one topic sentence in each paragraph.

**1.** The carburetor malfunctions;   **2.** The break linings are worn;   **3.** One of my headlights is broken;   **4.** I need new shock absorbers, and my front fenders are rusting out.   **5.** I think it is time that I bought a new car.

_____

**1.** Daily jogging is one of the best exercises you can do for your body.   **2.** It develops muscle tone and is excellent for your cardiovascular system, ensuring that your heart and lungs are in prime condition.   **3.** It also burns off a great many calories, preventing you from gaining unneeded weight.   **4.** Yes, nothing beats jogging for keeping you in excellent physical condition, no matter what your age.

_____

**1.** My political opponent has not kept any of his promises to the voters.   **2.** He said that he would not raise taxes, and he did;   **3.** He said he would not oppose our municipal bond issue, and he did.   **4.** Furthermore, he said he would not increase the salary of his personal staff, and he has.   **5.** On the other hand, there were two things he did not do that desperately needed doing.   **6.** He did not repair the potholes in our city streets, and he did not build an extension onto our local retirement home.   **7.** He obviously cannot be trusted.

_____

**1.** Last month our heat went off in the middle of the night.   **2.** Last Wednesday our plumbing failed.   **3.** And now we discover that our roof is leaking.   **4.** I think it is about time that we confront our landlord and force him to meet his obligations to his tenants.

_____

**1.** My uncle is very well respected in our community.   **2.** He is on the Board of Governors of our community college.   **3.** He is the chairman of our United Way committee.   **4.** He is also an active member of the local theatre guild and a coach of our midget hockey team.   **5.** Moreover, last month he was elected Alderman and now sits on our city council.

_____

## D. THREE PARAGRAPH TYPES

Besides the expository or developmental paragraph found in the body of essays, there are other types of paragraphs that, although not independent units of thought, are important for the smooth development of any extended paper. These are the introductory, transitional, and concluding paragraphs.

1. **The Introductory Paragraph**   This paragraph prepares the readers for the body of the essay. It arouses their interest and whets their curiosity. It may also project your attitude toward your subject and thus set the tone for the rest of the essay. In short, it places the readers in a proper frame of mind to accept what you have to say. Here are a few examples of introductory paragraphs:

> If we are going to develop a sensible approach to the encouragement of talent, we shall have to dispose of a good many myths surrounding the talented individual. [5]

> The arguments in favour of a great deal of freedom in education are derived not from men's natural goodness, but from the effects of authority, both on those who suffer it and on those who exercise it. Those who are subject to authority become either submissive or rebellious, and each attitude has its drawbacks. [6]

> There are still no satisfactory answers to many of the general questions which anyone interested in the early eighteenth-century novelists and their works is likely to ask. Is the novel a new literary form? And if we assume, as is commonly done, that it is, and that it was begun by Defoe, Richardson, and Fielding, how does it differ from the prose fiction of the past, from that of Greece, for example, or that of the Middle Ages, or of seventeenth-century France? And is there any reason why these differences appeared when and where they did? [7]

In the above paragraphs the authors clearly define what they intend to write about in the body of their essays. They introduce the statements to be examined and the questions to be answered, so that their readers are able to anticipate how the rest of the essay will be developed.

2. **The Transitional Paragraph**   This type of paragraph allows the readers to move from one section of material to another in an easy and smooth progression. It functions as a signpost that reminds the readers where they have been and where they will go next. These paragraphs are usually brief—sometimes no more than a sentence or two—and are often highlighted by transitional words and phrases that reflect different thought relationships. Here are some examples of transitional paragraphs:

> Having identified four components of a teacher's intellectual and emotional equipment, I would now like to consider a question pertaining to them that has been much debated: Is there a science of education? [8]

So far I have spoken from my own experiences as a teacher in high school, college, and university. But you need not take my uncorroborated word for the deplorable failure of American education. There are many other witnesses who can be called to the stand. [9]

So far so good. But now we must return to the distinction between reading for information and reading for understanding. In the previous chapter, I suggested how much more active the latter sort of reading must be, and how it feels to do it. Now we must consider the difference in what you get out of these two kinds of reading. [10]

These paragraphs remind the readers what was previously covered and what is still to be covered, leading them from one idea to another without an abrupt break in thought. They may be thought of as mental hand-holds that assist readers to maintain their balance through the stacked paragraphs of an essay or a report.

The use of transitional expressions in these paragraphs is very helpful in alerting the readers to the change in the direction of thought. A partial list of such expressions appears on p. 190.

**3. The Concluding Paragraph**   This paragraph sums up the point of the essay by restating the thesis topic. By summarizing some of the development and re-emphasizing topic ideas, you provide your readers with a concise statement of your position.

Concluding paragraphs should maintain the same tone as the rest of the essay, and should refrain from introducing any ideas that were not already discussed in the body. Following are some examples of concluding paragraphs.

Let us sum up again. The majority of young people are faced with the following alternative: Either society is a benevolently frivolous racket in which they'll manage to boondoggle, though less profitably than the more privileged; or society is serious, but they are useless and hopelessly out. Such thoughts do not encourage productive life. [11]

The language of individuality overpromises, and we see the wreckage of its illusions all around us. Only when this happens is individualism's seductive message doubted. It is an insufficient guide to the pursuit of happiness. I suspect we will eventually make our peace with the reality, while, in familiar American fashion, stubbornly continuing to extol the illusion. [12]

The bonuses of "less is more" are vast. The choice facing the American people is not between growth and stagnation, but between short-term and long-term disaster. We can continue to pursue the growth policies of the past and let urban decay, exorbitant prices, and risks to our national security dictate stringent remedial policies a few years from now. Or we can exercise restraint and learn to live comfortably, within our means. [13]

Each of these paragraphs brings the essay of which it is a part to a close. By reviewing some of the ideas that were discussed in the body, and by restating and sometimes redefining the thesis topic, the writer allows the reader to follow the logic of the conclusions drawn from the body of the essay.

---

**Transitional Thought Relationships**

**1. Addition**
again
also
and, and then
besides
further
furthermore
in addition
moreover
too

nonetheless
on the contrary
on the other hand
otherwise
still
unlike
while
yet

**2. Emphasis**
above all
as a matter of fact
certainly
chiefly
doubtless
indeed
in fact
in point of fact
to be sure
unquestionably
without doubt

**5. Example**
for example
for instance
in particular
in this case
namely
to illustrate

**6. Reason**
as
because
for
for that reason
since

**3. Similarity**
in like manner
in the same way
similarly

**7. Result**
accordingly
as a result
consequently
hence
so, so far
then
therefore
thus, thus far

**4. Contrast**
although
but
conversely
however
in contrast
nevertheless

**8. Time**
afterwards
at last
before
immediately
in due time
in the meantime
meanwhile
once
presently
shortly
shortly after
soon
until
while

**9. Chronology**
finally
first, second,
  third, etc.
next
then

**10. Conclusion**
in brief
in conclusion
in other words
in short
to conclude
to sum up

# Exercise 10.4 − Paragraph Types

**A.** Write a brief introductory statement for each of the following development paragraphs. Make sure that your statement is large enough to introduce the ideas discussed in the body of each paragraph:

EXAMPLE: We not only exercise to lose weight but also to improve our muscle tone and strengthen our heart and lungs. Exercise makes us feel physically vital and mentally alert; it is, literally, a life saver.

INTRODUCTORY STATEMENT: The advantages of daily exercise are many and varied, and they cannot be over-estimated.

1. We sell summer sporting equipment for the boater, the golfer, and the tennis player. For the winter sports enthusiast we carry a large line of skiis, ski clothes, and hockey equipment. Of course we also have a large inventory of hunting equipment and fishing gear. Yes, our store services the entire sports-minded community.

INTRODUCTORY STATEMENT: ────────────────────

2. For instance, he knows exactly—almost to the minute—when I must arise and go to work, for every morning at the same time he meows at my bedroom door. He also has good taste in music, for he "sings" along with my recordings of Mozart symphonies. Furthermore, he broods when I pay too much attention to our dog, Kino, and refuses to recognize my presence for a certain period of time. Obviously the word "dumb" cannot be used to describe the complicated behaviour of my cat.

INTRODUCTORY STATEMENT: ────────────────────

3. Our Italian restaurants specialize in veal dishes and pasta. Our French restaurants have achieved recognition for their delicious casseroles and sauces. Our Chinese restaurants serve both Cantonese and Szechwan food, and our German restaurants are noted for their different varieties of schnitzel and wursts. Yes, our city is certainly served well by the international flavour of its eating establishments.

INTRODUCTORY STATEMENT: ────────────────────

4. My English teacher uses a great many overheads to explain different rules of grammar and punctuation. She also uses instructional films and slides to help us learn the principles of paragraph organization and essay writing. On the other hand, my math teacher uses the blackboard extensively to explain different mathematical concepts, and he relies heavily on our textbook for examples of algebraic formulas.

INTRODUCTORY STATEMENT: ────────────────────

5. The characters are dull and flat. The dialogue is artificial and the story line confusing. Furthermore, the motives for action are not sufficiently developed or explained, and the descriptive passages do not provide the reader with a vivid image of important dramatic scenes. I would not recommend this novel to anyone—especially to a high-school English class.

INTRODUCTORY STATEMENT: _____

**B.** Connect the following paragraph fragments with brief, transitional statements. Make each statement serve as a logical bridge between each pair of fragments.

EXAMPLE: Therefore, I think that the shocking obsolescence of our military hardware can be directly traced to the lack of military planning by our government leaders.

TRANSITIONAL STATEMENT: (But the obsolescence of our equipment is not the only problem, nor is it the most serious. There is also the human factor.)

The quality of our military personnel is lower than it has ever been. The men and women are inadequately trained, poorly motivated, and physically unfit.

1. Therefore, my history course was a worthwhile educational experience.

TRANSITIONAL STATEMENT: _____

The physics classroom is overcrowded, and the laboratory is poorly equipped. Our textbooks are out of date and difficult to read, and our teacher is disorganized and lacks enthusiasm.

2. To sum up, our foreign aid budget this year will be comprehensive; it will once again include food relief to several African countries.

TRANSITIONAL STATEMENT: _____

Our military purchases will not include new tanks or fighter planes. And there will be no money for additions to our fleet of light cruisers. Furthermore, our space research projects have been reduced by twenty per cent.

3. When the hockey game finally ended in a 4-4 tie, each coach was extremely unhappy and frustrated.

TRANSITIONAL STATEMENT: _____

Ten fans were arrested for fist-fighting, and four more were charged with destruction of private property.

**4.** Computer technology is here to stay, even though it may have a profound effect on our present workforce.

TRANSITIONAL STATEMENT:  _____

The curricula of our secondary and post-secondary schools must change to accommodate the needed skill levels. More emphasis must be placed on problem-solving and communication skills. Moreover, all of our teachers must become computer literate.

**5.** In Russia, then, Communism is practised in a dictatorial and threatening atmosphere, where material advantages are given to a chosen few.

TRANSITIONAL STATEMENT:  _____

In monastic life, wealth and goods are shared in a spirit of charity and self-sacrifice. Furthermore, rules are made to benefit each member of the community equally.

**C.** Write a concluding statement that logically sums up and completes the ideas and information in each of the following paragraphs.

EXAMPLE: Our city is one of the most beautiful and progressive cities in Canada. It has an abundance of lakes and parks, ample recreational facilities, efficient public transportation, a new arts center, a highly educated and well-motivated workforce, and light industry that does not pollute the environment.

CONCLUDING STATEMENT: Because of all these recreational, cultural, and commercial advantages, I would not choose to live anywhere else—unless, of course, another Canadian city could duplicate these attractions.

**1.** Our school dance was certainly a success. The band we hired played music that everyone enjoyed dancing to. The punch we made received numerous compliments, and we sold every one of our Fifty-Fifty tickets, the proceeds of which will help pay for our class field trip next month.

CONCLUDING STATEMENT:  _____

**2.** None of my electrical appliances seems to work anymore. Yesterday my iron shorted out and blew a fuse. This morning I plugged in my toaster and it started smoking. Then about an hour ago I burnt my dinner because the thermostat in my oven ceased operating.

CONCLUDING STATEMENT: ————————————————————

**3.** Our local ski area needs better management. Our ski tows have broken down four times already this year. Last week the parking lot was not plowed in time to accommodate our weekend skiers. Yesterday the cafeteria ran out of hot chocolate and hamburger patties. Now we are informed that two of our ski instructors are leaving to work at another ski school.

CONCLUDING STATEMENT: ————————————————————

**4.** How much longer must we tolerate a local government that does not care for the aged in our community? How long will we have to put up with inferior schools and sloppy—almost criminal—construction practices? And when will we realize that our city fathers are lining their pockets through influence peddling?

CONCLUDING STATEMENT: ————————————————————

**5.** In 1980 there were 120 students at our college who were studying technology, and we spent $15,000 on laboratory equipment. By 1983 the number of students increased by 10%, but our capital budget decreased 20% to $12,000. Today we have 260 students studying technology in crowded, ill-equipped laboratories, and our budget has just been slashed another 10%.

CONCLUDING STATEMENT: ————————————————————

# E. CREATING PATTERNS OF DEVELOPMENT: THE EXPOSITORY PARAGRAPH

Since the expository or development paragraph controls the direction and the smooth flow of the essay, we must pay particular heed to how expository paragraphs are developed.

Although there are numerous ways to develop a paragraph, some are more common and, for our purposes, more relevant than others. Here are eight of the most useful patterns of development:

**1.** Classification  
**2.** Comparison and Contrast  
**3.** Narration and Description  
**4.** Example  
**5.** Enumeration by Details  
**6.** Cause and Effect  
**7.** Process Description  
**8.** Definition

These are the patterns that you, as a student, will most often have to write. They each serve specific functions, and each has a definite organizational scheme. Your use of one or more of these developmental patterns in your writing will depend upon a number of considerations: 1. What precisely you want to say about a given topic. 2. How you want to arrange your ideas. 3. What effect you want to create in the mind of your reader. 4. How much emphasis you wish to place on certain ideas. 5. How forceful you wish your topic idea to be.

Ninety per cent of the time your opening sentences will contain the topic idea that determines how the rest of the paragraph will be developed. This is illustrated below.

| Topic Sentence | Pattern of Development |
|---|---|
| The term ''behaviour'' can be misleading. | Definition |
| There were many factors that contributed to the outbreak of World War II. | Cause and Effect |
| A cruise ship has many unexpected amenities. | Enumeration by Details |
| I remember my first date. | Narration and Description |
| Our history course was broken into four historical periods that were almost mini-courses in themselves. | Classification |
| Nineteenth-century capitalism, although theoretically the same, functioned quite differently from today's capitalistic system. | Comparison and Contrast |
| Some baseball teams have better facilities and more fan support than other teams. | Examples |
| There is only one way to operate a forklift truck. | Process Description |

Of course, some lengthy paragraphs, or a series of paragraphs, will use a combination of these patterns to develop a topic idea adequately; nevertheless, in most of your expository writing you will have to focus on one pattern at a time in order to write a unified and coherent essay.

**1. Classification** This type of paragraph may not only place its subject term into a class or group to which it belongs, but also divide it into its constituent parts. This pattern of development gives the readers a more precise and comprehensive understanding of the thing or idea being examined, as you can see in the examples below.

     *In the earlier epochs of history, we find almost*
Topic *everywhere a complicated arrangement of society into*
Sentence *various orders, a manifold gradation of social rank.* In
     ancient Rome we have patricians, knights, plebians, slaves;
Classification in the Middle Ages, feudal lords, vassals, guild-masters,
by Social Rank journeymen, apprentices, serfs; in almost all of these
     classes, again, subordinate gradations. [14]

*Topic*
*Sentence*

*A useful rhetorical classification divides sentences into those which make a major point near or at the beginning of the sentence and then add to that point—the loose sentence—and those which delay, by interruption and qualification, the major point 'til the end of the sentence—the periodic sentences.* The basis for this division is essentially grammatical. The loose sentence will usually begin with a complete simple sentence and

*Classification*
*by Function*

add phrases, clauses or more sentences. On the other hand, the periodic sentence will usually not complete the central grammatical structure until the end of the sentence. [15]

**2. Comparison and Contrast**   In this type of paragraph the idea in the topic statement is related both to terms that are similar and to those that are distinct. The comparison terms, which are usually more obvious and concrete, place the topic statement in a familiar context; and the contrasting terms emphasize the uniqueness of the topic statement.

These developmental terms are usually examined point by point: either all the comparison details are presented and then all the contrasting details —AAA—BBB (as seen in the first example below)—or the contrasting and comparing details are presented alternatively—ABABAB (as seen in the second example below). But whatever organizational scheme is used, a closely-reasoned relationship must exist between the subject term and its supporting details.

*Topic*
*Sentence*

*Historically, the engagement of craftsman and professional was analogous.* A craftsman was accepted into the guild of his peers by making a masterpiece and, just as

*Comparison*
*Details*

with the professional, this achievement signalized a long growth, by apprenticeship, into a career that had become second nature. Usually he would have a prior disposition to the craft, by family, or locality, or personal talent. Thus,

*Contrasting*
*Details*

induction into a job was a process of personal engagement, not unlike the doctor's ring and kiss. It must be said, however, that unlike the humane professions, attachment to a craft or mechanic trade could easily produce a craft-idiot or drudge. Up to a point, "alienation" from this situation was liberating both from narrow ideas and long hours. [16]

*Topic*
*Sentence*

*Consider our lives. All other activities we share with the other inhabitants of the planet.* Animals, birds, reptiles, fish and insects also struggle for power, as we do. They

*Comparison*
*Details*

organize themselves into social groups. Many build. Some control their own environment by ingenious inventions. Some of them, like some of us, collect wealth. They fight. They make love. They play games. Some have powers we

*Contrasting Details*  shall never possess and can scarcely comprehend. Cunning and skillful, that they are. Yet collectively they learn little that is new, and individually almost nothing. Their skills are intricate, but limited. Their art, though charming, is purely decorative. Their languages consist of a few dozen signs and sounds. Their memory is vivid but restricted. Their curiosity is shallow and temporary, merely the rudiment of that wonder which fills the mind of a human scientist or poet, or historian or philosopher. They cannot conceive of learning and knowledge as a limitless activity administered by the power of will. Only human beings really learn, and know, and remember, and think creatively as individuals far beyond the limitations of any single group or the dominance of any single need. Knowledge acquired and extended for its own

*Comparison Details*  sake is the specific quality that makes us human. Our species has the hair and the lungs of animals, reptilian bones, and fish-like blood. We are close indeed to the beasts; often

*Contrasting Details and Conclusion*  we are more cruel. But we are fundamentally different from them in that we learn almost infinitely, and know and recollect. We are *Homo Sapiens:* Man the Thinker. [17]

**3. Narration and Description**  These two developmental patterns almost always go together. A narration, of course, tells a story or relates an event, and a description provides a sensual impression of that story or event.

In this type of paragraph the reader is made to stand at the elbow of the writer, so that the reader can see and feel what the writer sees and feels. That is why the sensual quality of the language is so important here—it conveys to the reader not only what happened but what it looked, sounded, and felt like.

To enhance the sensual dimension of the narrative, you will often need to employ similes and metaphors that exemplify what you are describing. A *simile* is a direct comparison of two essentially different things or ideas, usually joined by the words ''like'' or ''as'':

Hearing him relate his boring and repetitious war-time experiences is like listening to the eternal dripping of a leaky faucet.

This knife is as sharp as a gust of winter wind.

A *metaphor*, on the other hand, is a figure of speech that makes its comparison by transfering the qualities of one thing directly onto another thing:

Jack is a tiger when he is angry.

Her mind was a vast treasury of historical knowledge.

In narrative or descriptive writing your task is to convey experiences precisely and, in the process, to make them vivid, meaningful, and dramatic. The following two paragraphs exemplify these qualities.

*Opening*      *I set about gaining Piquette's trust.* She was not
*Narrative*   allowed to go swimming, with her bad leg, but I managed to
*Statement*   lure her down to the beach—or rather, she came because
              there was nothing else to do. The water was always icy,
*Descriptive*  for the lake was fed by springs, but I swam like a dog,
*Details*     thrashing my arms and legs around at such speed and with
              such an output of energy that I never grew cold. Finally,
              when I had enough, I came out and sat beside Piquette on
*Narrative*   the sand. When she saw me approaching, her hand squashed
*Details*     flat the sand castle she had been building, and she looked
              at me sullenly, without speaking. [18]

*Opening*      *That beach is a vast and preternaturally clean and
*Descriptive*  simple landscape.* It is like a piece of the moon. The surf had
*Statement*   pounded the floor solid, so it was easy walking, and
              everything left on the sand had been twice changed by the
*Descriptive*  waves. There was the spine of a shell, part of a broomstick,
*Details*     and part of a brick, both of them milled and broken until
              they were nearly unrecognizable, and I suppose Lawrence's
*Narrative*   sad frame of mind—for he kept his head down—went
*Details*     from one broken thing to another. The company of his
              pessimism began to infuriate me, and I caught up with him
              and put a hand on his shoulder. "It's only a summer day,
              Tifty," I said. "It's only a summer day. What's the matter?
              Don't you like it here?" [19]

**4. Example**  Paragraphs that use examples as their pattern of development
usually expand and support an explanation in the topic sentence. These
paragraphs narrow down general and abstract statements into concrete sections
that enable the reader to focus clearly on the writer's argument, as in the
following example.

*Topic*        *And yet poverty, even the poverty of an entire society,*
*Statements*  *is not an insurmountable barrier to education if people are*
              *determined to learn and prepared to sacrifice. An entire*
              *society can raise its standards within fifty years by a*
              *concerted effort, or maintain them for centuries against*
*First*       *persistent discouragement.* Finland is one of the poorest
*Example*     nations in Europe, but it has splendid schools, and its
              citizens are far more cultivated than many a richer nation.
*Second*      Scotland was never wealthy; yet she has supported four
*Example*     universities ever since the Renaissance, and the annals of
              each of them are filled with tales of peasant boys reared in
              grinding poverty and scarcely able to buy a suit of clothes,
              still winning their way to college, living there on a sack of
              oatmeal and a few salt herring brought from their cottage
              homes, and rising to distinction as scholars and inventors.

*Third*   Most astonishing of all, perhaps, is the tenacity with which
*Example*  the Jews, living for many generations in the poor ghettoes of
Eastern Europe, kept up their own school system, transmitted their books faithfully through the centuries, and added to
them a mass of explanation, symbolism, and decoration
which is a monument to the power of the human mind as well
as an act of homage to God. [20]

*Topic*     *Technological modesty, fittingness, is not negative. It*
*Statement* *is the ecological wisdom of cooperating with nature rather*
*than trying to master her.* A well-known example is the
*First*  long-run superiority of partial pest control in farming by
*Example* using biological deterrents rather than chemical ones. The
living defenders work harder, at the right moment, and with
more pin-pointed targets. But let me give another example
*Second* because it is so lovely—though I have forgotten the name of
*Example* my informant: A tribe in Yucatan educates its children to
identify and pull up all weeds in the region; then what is left
is a garden of useful plants that have chosen to be there and
now thrive. [21]

**5. Enumeration by Details**  In this type of paragraph the topic sentence is
always placed at the beginning, and is large enough to be supported by a
substantial number of details, which may be statements of fact, statistics,
examples or minor definitions. The topic sentence states an idea or affirms an
opinion, and the following sentences develop and support it. When using this
pattern of development, you must be certain that your supporting information
adequately develops your topic idea.

*Topic*     *A husband should try to remember where things are*
*Statement* *around the house so that he does not have to wait for his wife*
*to get home from the hairdresser's before he can put his*
*hands on what he wants.* Among the things a husband is
*A series*  usually unable to locate are the iodine, the aspirin, the nail
*of amusing* file, the French vermouth, his cuff links, studs, black silk
*development* socks and evening shirts, the snapshots taken at Nantucket
*details*  last summer, his favorite recording of "Kentucky Babe," the
borrowed copy of *My Cousin Rachel*, the garage key, his own
towel, the last bill from Brooks Bros., his pipe cleaners, the
poker chips, crackers, cheese, the whetstone, his new
raincoat and the screens for the upstairs windows. [22]

*Topic*     *The principle of decentralism is that people are*
*Statement* *engaged in a function and the organization is how they*
*First Detail* *cooperate.* Authority is delegated away from the top as much
as possible and there are many accommodating centers of
*Second Detail* policy making and decision. Information is conveyed and
discussed in face-to-face contacts between field and head-

*Third Detail*     quarters. Each person becomes increasingly aware of the
whole operation and works at it in his own way according to
*Fourth Detail*    his capacities. Groups arrange their own schedules. Historically, this system of voluntary association has yielded most
*Concluding*     of the values of civilization, but it is thought to be entirely
*Statement*    unworkable under modern conditions and the very sound of
it is strange. [23]

**6. Cause and Effect**    In this type of paragraph the writer demonstrates in a
causal sequence how one event is necessarily the result of another event. The
reader is shown why something has occurred in the past and may occur in the
future. Each step in the sequence depends upon a preceding step, and the
developmental details must logically follow from the topic sentence when it
occurs at the beginning of the paragraph, or lead up to it when it falls at the
end of the paragraph.

     This cause-and-effect pattern of development may be organized around
a statement of fact or an opinion, and its causal sequence may vary: one cause
may have one or more effects, or several causes may have a single effect, or in
a long paragraph there may be an involved sequence of causes and effects.

     At the end of the paragraph, however, the reader must be convinced that
every term in the cause-and-effect sequence has satisfactorily demonstrated
the topic idea.

*Topic*     *The perfection of gene splicing, as one offshoot of biological*
*Sentence*   *engineering, could cause dangerous social changes in the*
*twenty-first century.* For instance, it may lead to a biological
*Sequence of*   class system in which, say, blond hair and blue eyes would
*Causes and*   indicate a certain socio-economic group, and heavy upper-
*Effects*   body musculature another socio-economic group. I.Q. levels
may be intentionally reduced so that certain people could be
matched with repetitious, low-level occupations. And the
ability to *grow* new organs would dramatically increase life
expectancy which, in turn, would spur population growth
and place intolerable burdens on food production and energy
consumption.

*Topic Sentence*     *On balance, one is compelled to say that the advances*
*in technology already made and to be made promise that*
*mankind's future, with effective population control, can be*
*much brighter than its past.* If technology makes highly
*First Effect*   destructive world wars possible for the first time in this
century, it is also true that for the first time in this century
the technological conditions are such that world government
has become a practicable project. If technology results in
*Second Effect*   uncontrollable industrial expansion and sometimes wasteful
affluence, it is also true that our power to produce con-
sumable wealth has reached the point that for the first time

in this century, the elimination of poverty is even con-
ceivable; more than that, this is the first century in which
any steps have been taken to reduce its extent. [24]

**7. Process Description**   This paragraph pattern describes a series of successive events that leads to specific result. Each step in the series must necessarily lead to the next, and the final results must be the logical outcome of the series. Also, the specialized terms used in describing the process must be adequately defined.

    This type of development is most often used in a report that explains how a given task is accomplished by following a number of procedural steps in chronological order.

> **How to Saw a Board**   There is only one correct way to saw a board. First, measure carefully with a ruler or a tape and then use a pencil and a square to draw your line across the top edge of the board. Second, place the board on two sawhorses, keeping the pencil line on the outside, but allowing a few inches of clearance for the saw. Third, start the cut near the handle of the saw at the far end of the board, and when you have a groove, saw toward yourself at a 45° angle. Remember to saw outside the line, because if you saw on the line the kerf (the width of the cut) will cause the board to be too short.

> **Cleaning a Paint Brush**   Cleaning a paint brush can be easy if you follow the correct procedure. After you finish using the brush remove excess paint with a scraper. Then soak the brush in a can of paint thinner, working it back and forth against the bottom of the container so that the thinner soaks through. Next, squeeze the bristles between your thumb and forefinger to loosen the paint in the center of the brush. Rinse it again in the thinner to make sure that all the paint has been removed. After rinsing thoroughly, press out the water with a stick, and then comb the bristles carefully with a wire comb. Allow the brush to dry by suspending it from the handle or by laying it flat on a clean, flat surface. Finally, wrap the dry bush in heavy paper to keep the bristles straight and store suspended by its handle. If you follow this simple procedure, your brush will be clean and ready to use when you need it again.

**8. Definition**   This type of paragraph is the most flexible, for it may use more than one pattern of development. Because the developmental details supporting the topic sentence must be simpler and more concrete than the term defined, the writer will often use examples, comparisons, analogies, or synonyms to convert general and abstract ideas into specific and concrete information.

    The definition of the subject term should be comprehensive, containing all the necessary details that not only place it into a specific category, but also distinguish it from any other term in its class. It should tell the reader what something is and how it differs from anything else with which it might be confused. An orange, for example, may be defined as a citrus fruit, but its difference from other citrus fruits, such as a grapefruit, can be described according to its colour, size, and taste.

Ideally, then, at the end of the paragraph the reader should know precisely the important and unique characteristics of the defined term and be familiar with the context in which it was defined.

| | |
|---|---|
| *Topic Sentence* | *I think that what we mean in practice by reason can be defined by three characteristics.* In the first place, |
| *First Definition Detail* | it relies upon persuasion rather than force; in the second place, it seeks to persuade by means of arguments which |
| *Second Definition Detail* | the man who uses them believes to be completely valid; and in the third place, in forming opinions, it uses |
| *Third Definition Detail* | observation and induction as much as possible and intuition as little as possible. [25] |

| | |
|---|---|
| *Topic Sentence* | *The term 'class' in Marx is used in various senses, not at all strictly derivative from each other.* Sometimes its defining feature is the role a group plays in production, |
| *Sequence of Definition Details* | sometimes it is their common mode of life, including culture and traditions, sometimes the source of their income or the level of their income, sometimes their vocation or, in the case of the unemployed, their lack of any. [26] |

## Exercise 10.5 – Topic Sentence and Patterns of Development

From the list below select the pattern of development that you think most logically develops each topic sentence; then write it in the space to the right or on a separate sheet. Choose only one pattern for each topic sentence.

Classification
Comparison and/or Contrast
Cause and Effect
Narration and Description

Example
Enumeration by Details
Definition
Process Description

EXAMPLE:   There is only one logical method of
organizing an essay.          _Process Description_

**Topic Sentence**                    **Pattern of Development**

**1.** There are many reasons for high mortgage
rates and runaway inflation in our country.          *C + E*

**2.** Tina had an interesting experience when she
visited Greece last summer.          *N + D*

**3.** My father sells furniture for every room in
the house.          *C*

**4.** Bravery during wartime has several common
characteristics.          *D*

5. My dentist's new office is not as spacious as his old office, but it is certainly better equipped.

    *C & C*

6. Excessive nationalism in some countries is often confused with traditional patriotism.

    *D*

7. Computer programming offers many interesting job opportunities.

    *E*

8. Performing a winter checkup on your car can be done easily if you follow the proper procedure.

    *P D*

9. Canadian and American football, although similar in many ways, have some important differences.

    *C & C*

10. The meaning of "pedagogy" may differ, depending upon the level of education one is talking about.

    *D*

11. The enemy was getting closer, and we were almost out of ammunition.

    *N + D*

12. Our marina sells many different kinds of pleasure craft, the purchase of which will depend upon your nautical experience and your financial circumstances.

    *C*

13. Our new car has a number of luxury options which added 10% to the base purchase price.

    *E by D*

14. My sociology textbook is much better than Peter's.

    *C & C*

15. Pasta can compliment many different kinds of meals.

    *N + D*

16. I'll never forget the Christmas we spent in Banff, Alberta.

    *E*

17. My brother's athletic accomplishments have earned him the reputation as the best all-round athlete in our school.

18. There is only one correct way to learn how to play golf.

    *P D*

19. Our city has many interesting tourist attractions.

    *E by D*

20. The technology course I am taking is quite different from the technician's course that is offered in the same semester.

    *C & C*

## Exercise 10.6 – Selecting Topic Sentences and Constructing Patterns of Development

Select four topic sentences from the list below, or use four similar topic sentences of your own, and write four paragraphs that use the following patterns of development: Classification, Comparison and/or Contrast, Cause and Effect, and Narration and Description.

1. My older brother and younger sister share many of the same personality traits.

2. Many women perform three different functions: that of a homemaker, a mother, and a business executive.

3. I shall never forget the day I bought my first car.

4. I'll never try to hitchhike to Toronto again.

5. Canada's three largest cities—Toronto, Vancouver and Montreal—each offer different attractions for the visitor.

6. I don't know which is more detrimental to your health—nicotine or alcohol.

7. The tremendous influx of oil revenues has resulted in many social and economic changes for the exporting countries.

8. Jogging through neighbourhoods inhabited by dog owners can be dangerous to your health.

9. The major power blackout on the Eastern Seaboard of the United States had both humorous and tragic results.

10. Canadian and American football each has strengths and weaknesses as a spectator sport.

11. Individualized instruction and classroom discussion, as alternative learning methods, are used in our school to meet the needs of different students.

12. The industrial pollution of our rivers and lakes has resulted in many economic hardships and health hazards for the people who depend upon these water sources for their livelihood.

## Exercise 10.7 – Selecting Topic Sentences and Constructing Patterns of Development

Select four topic sentences from the list below, or use four similar topic sentences of your own, and write four paragraphs that use the following patterns of development: Examples, Enumeration by Details, Process Description, and Definition.

1. Tom was the stingiest man I ever knew.

2. Censorship often implies a loss of personal freedom.

3. Knowing how to shop for the right car can save you time, money, and frustration.

4. The management of our plant does not care about the health and safety of the workers.

5. Our company's profits have been declining for the past five years, even though our sales have increased 10%.

6. The terms "education" and "training" reflect different kinds of learning experiences.

7. There are a number of time-saving steps that will help you study for final examinations.

8. We had our summer cottage built in one of the most desirable locations in Eastern Ontario.

9. Since the Vietnam war, the term "Conscientious Objector" has acquired a measure of legitimacy it never had before.

10. I shall now tell you how one goes about organizing a car pool.

11. Our firm makes many different products for the handyman.

12. The educational background of the teachers in our school is quite impressive.

## ENDNOTES

1. Margaret Atwood, *Survival: A Thematic Guide to Canadian Literature* (Toronto: House of Anansi Press, 1972), p. 32. Reprinted by permission of House of Anansi Press Limited.

2. Bruno Bettelheim and Karen Zelan, "Why Children Don't Like to Read," *The Atlantic* (November, 1981), p. 26. Excerpt from *On Learning to Read* published by Alfred A. Knopf, Inc. Reprinted with permission.

3. F.E.L. Priestly, "English: An Obsolete Industry?" *In the Name of Language*, ed. Joseph Gold (Toronto: Macmillan of Canada, 1975), p. 145. Copyright © The Macmillan Company of Canada Limited, 1975. Reprinted by permission of Macmillan Company of Canada, a Division of Gage Publishing Limited.

4. Sidney Hook, *Marx and the Marxists* (New York: Van Nostrand Co., 1955), p. 42. Reprinted by permission of the Wadsworth Publishing Company.

5. John Gardner, *Excellence: Can We Be Equal and Excellent Too?* (New York: Harper and Row, 1962), p. 58.

6. Bertrand Russell, "Education and Discipline." *In Praise of Idleness* (London: Unwin Books, 1960), p. 127. Reprinted by permission of George Allen & Unwin Ltd.

7. Ian Watt, *The Rise of the Novel* (Pelican Book, Chattos and Windus, 1974), p. 9. Reprinted by permission of Chattos & Windus Ltd.

8. James B. Conant, *The Education of American Teachers* (New York: McGraw Hill, 1963), p. 117. Reprinted by permission of McGraw-Hill Book Company. Copyright © The McGraw Hill Book Company, 1963.

9. Mortimer J. Adler, *How to Read a Book* (New York: Simon and Schuster, 1967), p. 54. Copyright © 1940, 1967 by Mortimer J. Adler; Copyright © 1972 by Mortimer J. Adler and Charles Van Doren. Reprinted by permission of Simon & Schuster, a Division of Gulf & Western Corporation.

10. *How to Read a Book*, p. 35. Reprinted with permission (see above).

11. Paul Goodman, *Growing Up Absurd* (New York: A Vintage Book, Random House, 1960), pp. 33-4. Reprinted with permission.

12. Thomas Griffith, "Party of One," *The Atlantic Monthly* (1979), p. 32. Copyright © 1979 by The Atlantic Monthly Company, Boston, Mass. Reprinted with permission.

13. Stewart Udall, "The Last Traffic Jam," *The Atlantic Monthly* (1972), p. 65. Copyright © 1972 by The Atlantic Monthly Company, Boston, Mass. Reprinted with permission.

14. Sidney Hook, *Marx and the Marxists*, p. 134. Reprinted with permission (see above).

15. Tom E. Kakonis and James C. Wilcox, *Forms of Rhetoric: Ordering Experience* (New York: McGraw-Hill, 1969), p. 222.

16. Paul Goodman, *People or Personnel* (New York: A Vintage Book, Random House, 1968), p. 132. Reprinted with permission.

17. Gilbert Highet, *Man's Unconquerable Mind* (New York: Columbia University Press, 1954), pp. 7-8. Reprinted by permission of Columbia University Press.

18. Margaret Laurence, "The Loons," *Double Vision: An Anthology of Twentieth-Century Stories in English*, selected by Rudy Wiebe (Macmillan of Canada, 1976), p. 21. Reprinted by permission of The Canadian Publishers, McClelland and Stewart Limited, Toronto.

19. John Cheever, "Goodbye, My Brother," *The Stories of John Cheever* (New York: Alfred A. Knopf, 1978), p. 18.

20. Gilbert Highet, *Man's Unconquerable Mind*, pp. 72-3. Reprinted with permission (see above).

21. Paul Goodman, "Can Technology Be Humane?" *Technology and Man's Future*, Albert H. Teich, ed. (New York: St. Martin's Press, 1972), p. 186. Reprinted with permission.

22. James Thurber, *Thurber Country* (New York: Simon and Schuster, 1965), p. 47. Copyright © 1953, James Thurber. From *Thurber Country*, published by Simon and Schuster, New York.

23. Paul Goodman, *People or Personnel*, p. 4. Reprinted with permission (see above).

24. Mortimer J. Adler, *The Time of Our Lives* (New York: Holt, Rinehart and Winston, 1970), p. 215. Copyright © 1970 by Mortimer J. Adler. Reprinted by permission of Holt, Rinehart and Winston, Publishers.

25. Bertrand Russell, "The Ancestry of Fascism," *In Praise of Idleness*, pp. 55-56. Reprinted with permission (see above).

26. Sidney Hook, *Marx and Marxists*, p. 39. Reprinted with permission (see above).

CHAPTER ELEVEN

# Composing an Expository Essay

The skills involved in organizing and writing the expository essay are precisely those needed to organize and pattern sentences, construct topic outlines, and compose unified and coherent paragraphs. The pattern of organization may be broader and more complex, and the ideas more involved and segmented, but the thinking process is essentially the same. The primary difference is that, in organizing the essay, you must use a number of different skills to achieve a singular result.

## A. WHAT IS AN EXPOSITORY ESSAY?

Because the word "exposition" means to point out or explain something, the essay should answer a specific question or questions about its subject. Therefore, as soon as you construct a thesis statement, you must justify that statement by responding to questions like these: What is it? How does it work? What is its significance? What values does it convey? Why is it important? Why should someone find it interesting? If you fulfill this purpose, readers should leave the essay quietly, with their curiosity satisfied and their imagination inspired.

## B. PREPARING TO WRITE

Because a number of important planning decisions must be made before you begin writing your essay, you can divide your preparation time into a series of specific planning steps. These steps will involve outlining, subject focus, thesis statement, tone, method of development, and summary conclusion.

**Step One:   Make a Scratch Outline**
Whether your topic is self-chosen or assigned by an instructor, your starting point will be the same. Write down everything you know or think you know about your topic; do not be concerned about relevance or logical sequence. The fact that you are jotting down words and phrases that bear some relationship—however distant—to your topic means that you have already begun the necessary process

of organizing your essay. At this initial planning stage your most important concern is getting started, and the scratch outline format can serve as a useful crutch.

**Step Two:   Focus Your Subject**

Assuming that you have already chosen or been assigned an essay topic, and that you have written down everything you know about it, you must now start thinking about the length of your paper. Remember, your subject must be narrow enough to be handled in a given space and within a given time; do not overextend yourself.

You may begin the process of narrowing the subject by eliminating ideas that are too broad or too vague from your scratch outline. This process of elimination will help you think about point of view and allow you to pose questions that give your subject more substance: "What can I draw from my own reading and experience that will help me develop this topic? What portion of it should I stress? How do I want my reader to respond? How much outside reading must I do to adequately cover my topic?" These questions and others like them will enable you to develop your outline as the functional skeleton of your essay. And as you eliminate some ideas and include others, you will gradually bring the subject of your essay clearly into focus.

**Step Three:   Write a Thesis Statement**

After choosing — even tentatively choosing — the aspect of the topic you wish to stress, you must attempt to state the central idea or theme of your essay in one or two sentences. Nothing you write during these preparatory stages will be more important than your thesis statement; for, like the topic sentence in a paragraph, it will serve as the framework on which everything else in your essay will hang. It is essential not only because it defines more clearly your essay's limits but also because it keeps your mind fixed on its central theme. Therefore, once your statement is formulated, the rest of the essay will begin taking shape in your mind. And gradually the weak skeleton of random thought fragments that you started with will give way to a more substantial structure of logically sequenced ideas.

**Step Four:   Plan the Body and Prepare a Topic Outline**

The functional question you will ask yourself in planning the body of your essay will be this: "How can I break down, define, and exemplify my thesis statement?" In posing this question, you will use your outline to list your major points, because at this stage you will be thinking of your essay as a series of topics and sub-topics. The following list of questions should occur to you as you begin the process of expanding your thesis statement: "How many major sections will my essay require, and what will be the approximate length of each section? How many examples or illustrative details will I need to fully develop my central idea? What method of development should I use to successfully exploit the implications in my thesis statement, and what tone should I properly employ?" As your essay begins taking shape in your outline, you will be thinking more clearly about the organization of your ideas: how they will lead into one another, and how they will begin and end. You will also be thinking about the structure of your paragraphs — their length, unity and coherence. At this point you will be well into the final planning stages of your essay and in firm control of its direction.

### Step Five:   Plan Your Conclusion

Ideally, your concluding statements should flow easily and naturally from the ideas in the body. In reality, however, this process often works in just the reverse manner. Your progress in developing the ideas in the body of your essay may well depend upon how carefully you have planned your concluding statements. Thus, even when still in the process of organizing your essay, you should have some idea of how you wish to end it. Here are a few questions that may help you formulate your final remark: "How can I summarize the main sections of my essay so that the logic of my conclusions will be explicit? How can I restate my central idea so that it has a conclusive impact on my reader? And in what frame of mind do I want my reader to leave the essay?" Even though you have only a vague idea of how you want your essay to end, jot down some ideas or a few phrases you may wish to use. This exercise will keep you working toward a goal, so that by the time you are ready to write your conclusion, you will be better able to summarize your major ideas and rephrase your thesis statement.

### Step Six:   Write and Revise

After you have composed the first draft of your essay from your topic outline, read aloud what you have written. Try placing yourself in the mind of your reader by asking yourself the following questions: "Have I a well-articulated thesis statement? Do my ideas hold together? Is my tone consistent and my word selection adequate? Does my introduction clearly prepare the reader for the discussion in the body of the essay, and is my conclusion a logical extension of my development? Can I express any of my ideas more clearly and emphatically?" And finally, "If I were the reader, would I be interested in the content of the essay?" Once you have answered these questions to your satisfaction and made the proper structural revisions, reread your essay for grammar, spelling, and mechanics. Remember, one of the keys to good essay writing is an orderly process of revision; if you do a thorough job, your first and last drafts should be quite different.

## C. THE PARTS OF THE ESSAY

One of the most common prescriptions for a well-constructed essay is that it must have a beginning, a middle, and an end. At first glance this statement may seem obvious and simplistic, but upon further reflection we realize that its importance cannot be overemphasized; for each of these divisions serves a specific function, and without all of them our essays would almost certainly be unreadable. Here is a brief description of what each section of the essay should accomplish.

1. **The Introduction**   The introduction has one primary function: it persuades your reader to read the rest of your essay. It does this by arousing interest in its purpose and significance and by informing the readers, in clear, precise prose, of the central idea that will organize it. Unless they have specific knowledge of what you intend to say and how you intend to say it, they may not be inclined to read further. The introduction, then, in sales vernacular, is "the grabber."

2. **The Body**   The body of the essay develops the central idea in your thesis statement. It is written in sections, with each section dealing with one aspect of your central idea. If you are discussing, say, the future of nuclear energy as a power source, you might devote one paragraph to operating costs, one to safety procedures, and one to waste disposal. In this way the main idea in the introduction is broken down and discussed in separate, but related development paragraphs.

3. **The Conclusion**   The conclusion should simply restate the central idea (or ideas) in the introduction and briefly summarize the major points in the body. But it should not, under any circumstances, contain anything new. Nothing is more frustrating to the readers than finding ideas in the conclusion that were not suggested in the introduction and discussed in the body. It may also contain several general remarks designed to ease the readers out of the essay. These remarks may suggest other areas and other circumstances where your discussion may be relevant, or they may simply restate a general point made in the introduction.

## D. THE WELL-CONSTRUCTED STUDENT ESSAY

The following writing sample illustrates the organizational characteristics of the brief expository essay. Its three sections are obvious and well-defined. It has a clear introduction with a central thesis idea, a body that breaks down and exemplifies different aspects of the idea, and a conclusion that sums up and restates the idea.

### The Various Skills and Responsibilities of Executive Secretaries

1.   After observing the daily activities of three different executive secretaries, I have come to realize that these secretaries must possess a wide variety of skills to do their jobs effectively. Among their most essential skills are the ability to communicate, an acute sense of organization, and an intimate knowledge of different types of office equipment.

2.   Communication skills include both oral and written communication, for executive secretaries must represent their supervisors in many different business situations. Orally, for instance, they are required to speak effectively on the telephone, which means using proper diction and an effective

tone. They must also be able to greet and converse intelligently with each of their supervisor's clients and transmit his or her instructions accurately and concisely. Their written skills comprise a detailed knowledge of the rules of grammar and a familiarization with syntax. Duties in this area would include taking minutes of meetings and translating rough notes into accurate and readable prose. Correcting improper English in any outgoing correspondence and writing letters from bare outlines may also be part of their communication responsibilities. It is obvious, then, that executive secretaries must master a broad range of oral and written communication skills before they can represent their supervisors properly.

**3.**        Another important skill that executive secretaries must have is a keen sense of organization. The day-to-day responsibilities that test this skill would be arranging transportation and accommodations for their supervisor's out of town visitors, keeping his or her appointment calendar up to date, *Transitional* and arranging staff meetings and conferences, both inside and *Statement* outside the building. But perhaps their most important skill, which comes under the general heading of organization, is the ability to set priorities. Since they are given a number of various duties, some requiring immediate action, they must make judgements that provide for their supervisors' time restrictions. In this way they ensure that their supervisors do not waste time dealing with unessential information.

**4.**        Finally, because modern business offices use the latest audio-visual and electronic equipment, executive secretaries must have ''hands on'' knowledge of this equipment. Making overheads, setting up projectors, and using electronic calculators are some obvious examples, but they must also be familiar with video display equipment and word processors. Their skills in accessing and transmitting information effectively will depend on their keeping abreast of the latest electronic information technology which, in turn, will increase productivity and lower costs.

**5.**        Therefore it is obvious that executive secretaries do much more than simply type and take dictation. Rather, they should be thought of as executive assistants who keep the office running smoothly by controlling the working environment. And this control is directly related to their ability to communicate, to organize, and to use modern office equipment.

## Analysis of Paragraph Development

**1.** In the introductory paragraph the student sets up her thesis, which explicitly informs the reader that the essay will be divided into three parts — communication, organization, and office equipment.

**2.** Under communication she makes a further breakdown into oral and written, and provides specific examples of each skill. Notice also that in this paragraph two topic sentences are used — one at the beginning and one at the end.

**3.** Under organization she not only discusses the daily external duties of secretaries, but also their internal judgement in setting priorities. Here the student uses a transitional sentence to link the two ideas.

**4.** The third section talks about executive secretaries having to use modern office equipment to save time and money.

**5.** Her conclusion restates her thesis idea and sums up the three-part analysis in her body.

## E. EXAMPLES OF EFFECTIVE ESSAYS

The following examples of the expository essay are written for different audiences and therefore have slightly different organizations. One deals with an abstract human quality, one with concrete observation, and one with personal speculation. But although each has a different level of formality, all have an identifiable organization that permits the reader to follow the writer's thoughts.

### Men versus Insects

The first exemplary essay, which is by Bertrand Russell, is personal and speculative.[1] In it, he wanders easily through history, giving us facts of survival and extinction. He discusses insects as a possible threat to mankind to get us thinking about man's vulnerability. We are given the impression that he is thinking aloud, wondering how much longer the human race will survive with its rage and lust for power. He ends by suggesting that man, through his irrationality and penchant for war, may forfeit the earth to the insects and micro-organisms.

**1.** Amid war and rumours of wars, while 'disarmament' proposals and non-aggression pacts threaten the human race with unprecedented disaster, another conflict, perhaps even more important, is receiving much less notice than it deserves — I mean the conflict between men and insects.

**2.** We are accustomed to being the Lords of Creation; we no longer have occasion, like the cave men, to fear lions and tigers, mammoths and wild boars. Except against each other, we feel ourselves safe. But while big animals no longer threaten our existence, it is otherwise with small ones. For many ages dinosaurs ranged unconcerned through swamp and forest, fearing nothing but each other, not doubting the absoluteness of their empire. But they disappeared, to give place to tiny mammals — mice, small hedgehogs, miniature horses no bigger than rats, and suchlike. Why the dinosaurs died out is not known, but it is supposed to be that they had minute brains and devoted themselves to the growth of weapons of offence in the shape of numerous horns. However that may be, it was not through their line that life developed.

The mammals, having become supreme, proceeded to grow big. But the biggest on land, the mammoth, is extinct, and the other large animals have grown rare, except man and those that he has domesticated.

**3.** Man, by his intelligence, has succeeded in finding nourishment for a large population, in spite of his size. He is safe, except from the little creatures — the insects and the micro-organisms.

Insects have an initial advantage in their numbers. A small wood may easily contain as many ants as there are human beings in the whole world. They have another advantage in the fact that they eat our food before it is ripe for us. Many noxious insects which used to live only in

**4.** some one comparatively small region have been unintentionally transported by man to new environments where they have done immense damage. Travel and trade are useful to insects as well as to micro-organisms. Yellow fever formerly existed only in West Africa, but was carried to the Western hemisphere by the slave trade. Now owing to the opening up of Africa, it is gradually travelling eastward across the continent. When it reaches the east coast it will become almost impossible to keep it out of India and China, where it may be expected to halve the population. Sleeping sickness is an even more deadly African disease which is gradually spreading.

Fortunately science has discovered ways by which insect pests can be kept under control. Most of them are liable to parasites which kill so many that the survivors cease to be a serious problem, and

**5.** entomologists are engaged in studying and breeding such parasites. Official reports of their activities are fascinating; they are full of such sentences as: 'He proceeded to Brazil, at the request of the planters of Trinidad, to search for the natural enemies of the sugar-cane froghopper.' One would say that the sugar-cane froghopper would have little chance in this contest. Unfortunately, so long as war continues, all scientific knowledge is double-edged. For example, Professor Fritz Haber, who just died, invented a process for the fixation of nitrogen. He intended it to increase the fertility of the soil, but the German government used it for the manufacture of high explosives, and has recently exiled him for preferring manure to bombs. In the next great war, the scientists on either side will let loose pests on the crops of the other side, and it may prove scarcely possible to destroy the pests when peace comes. The more we know, the more harm we can do each other. If human beings in their rage against each other, invoke the aid of insects and micro-organisms, as they certainly will do if there is another big war, it is by no means unlikely that the insects will remain the sole ultimate victors. Perhaps, from a cosmic point of view, this is not to be regretted; but as a human being I cannot help heaving a sigh over my own species.

## Analysis of Paragraph Development

**1.** Introduction suggesting potential conflict between man and insects.

**2.**⎱ Discussion of how large mammals have disappeared and how man has
**3.**⎰ managed to survive.

**4.** List of the many advantages insects have over men.

**5.** Lengthy conclusion observes that modern science will continue to control insects and micro-organisms unless man, through war, unleashes them and wipes out the human species.

### Motivation

John Gardner's essay deals with the fairly abstract idea of human motivation, how it is encouraged and frustrated. [2] As an example he uses the American post-secondary educational system; he discusses its positive and negative effects and how it meets or fails to meet the requirements of individual motivation. His examples are meant to persuade us that a problem exists and that a solution should be found. (Please note that italics have been used to emphasize particular sentences; these do not belong in the original text.)

**1.** Dan, who was twelve years old and the best ballplayer in his school, was undergoing a psychological interview. The psychologist said, "What is the thing you feel you need to change to be the kind of person you'd like to be?" Dan replied, "Learn to spell. Learn to throw a knuckler that hops."*

**2.** If all young people were as capable as Dan of putting first things first, some of the perplexing problems facing American education would resolve themselves.

**3.** *Everyone agrees that motivation is a powerful ingredient in performance.* Talent without motivation is inert and of little use to the world. Lewis Terman and Catherine Cox found that historical geniuses were characterized not only by very high intelligence but by the desire to excel, by perseverence in the face of obstacles, by zeal in the exercise of their gifts.†

**4.** Some people may have greatness thrust upon them. Very few have excellence thrust upon them. They achieve it. They do not achieve it unwittingly, by "doing what comes naturally"; and they don't stumble into it in the course of amusing themselves. *All excellence involves discipline and tenacity of purpose.*

*The problem of motivation raises some questions of social strategy which are extremely perplexing* — so perplexing that Americans have never been willing to face them squarely. Consider, for example, the presence in our colleges of large numbers of boys and girls who really "couldn't care less" about higher education but are there

*P.S. Sears, "Problems in the Investigations of Achievement and Self Motivation," *The Nebraska Symposium on Motivation,* University of Nebraska Press, 1957. (NP)

†Catherine M. Cox et al. *The Early Mental Traits of Three Hundred Geniuses* (Genetic Studies of Genius, Vol. II), Stanford University Press, 1926. (NP)

because it's the thing to do. Their presence creates prob-

**5.** lems which, if honestly faced, would be the grounds for genuine concern. We avoid that unpleasantness by the simple expedient of not facing the problems honestly. This is to be

*Transitional* commended on grounds of comfort, but it is not the path that
*statement* leads on to wisdom. *Let us explore some of the issues.*

*Over the past thirty years, we have made it easier and easier for young people to enter our colleges and universities.* We have scattered colleges so liberally that no student need go far for an education. We have lowered the financial barriers in the hope of easing the way for the qualified boy or girl who

**6.** could not possibly pay for higher education. Many of our institutions have held academic requirements as low as possi- ble in order to salvage talented young people from poorer secondary schools, and in the hope that able youngsters who loafed through high school would "wake up" in college.

Now that we are entering a period of overcrowding in our colleges, the trend toward lowered barriers to higher

**7.** education appears to have reversed itself — at least temporarily. But over the past three or four decades — for the country as a whole — the trend has been clear.

Important social benefits have flowed from these policies. They have brought into the colleges a considerable number of bright and ambitious youngsters who might not

**8.** otherwise have continued their education. *But with every step*
*Transitional* *we took along this path we also increased the flow into the*
*statement* *system of youngsters with little or no real concern to educate themselves. . . .*

Anyone who has ever taught could comment on the vivid differences between *eager* and *apathetic* students. A Chinese proverb says "To be fond of learning is to be at the

**9.** gate of knowledge." It is almost impossible to prevent the interested student from learning. He meets the teacher more than half-way — all the way if necessary. He seeks out the situations in which he can learn. He gets an education in the most active sense of that term.

The apathetic student, if he is at all affected by schooling, receives an education. To say that teachers must

**10.** meet him more than half-way understates the case: they must block all exits and trap him into learning. They must be wonderfully inventive in catching his attention and holding it. They must be endlessly solicitous in counselling him, encour- aging him, awakening him and disciplining him. Every professor has observed what Lounsbury once described as "the infinite capacity of the undergraduate to resist the intrusion of knowledge. . . ."

*The flow of languid and indifferent youngsters into the colleges is not wholly indefensible.* In many instances, lack of interest in education is traceable to handicaps of home background that the school and college must try to remedy.

**11.** Bright youngsters with low motivation do represent a potential national resource, and it is important to discover whether that resource is recoverable. It is our obligation to salvage those who can be salvaged. Furthermore, there are social reasons why a society might wish to provide higher education even for those youngsters who care little about it. *But we* *should be aware of the consequences of what we are doing.* *Education of the aimless and half-hearted is very arduous,* *very expensive and — most important — totally different* *process from education of the highly motivated.*

*Transitional* *statement*

As the number of apathetic students in a college increases, there is a fundamental change in the tone of the **12.** educational process. There occurs a gradual but inevitable shift in the entire educational approach — in teaching methods, and in the nature of assignments, in the curriculum and in the methods of handling students. As the institution re-orients itself toward educational practices suitable for youngsters of low motivation, it all too often forgets the art of dealing with youngsters of high motivation.

It applies to eager and alert youngsters the practices which it uses on less spirited individuals — assignments which do not stretch the mind, and procedures which assume a considerable degree of individual apathy. The attitude which comes to dominate a school is reflected in the forthright assertion of one progressive educator: "The school should *meet* the demands of the nature of childhood, not *make* demands."* In short, the classroom comes to reinforce the attitude which is cultivated by the rest of our prosperous society; namely, that the individual should never be faced with a severe challenge, that he should never be called upon for even minor sacrifices, that asking him to undertake arduous duties is a form of injustice.

One might say that this makes very little difference because eager and ambitious individuals will drive them- **14.** selves to achieve, and the apathetic ones will not drive themselves in any case. In short, one might argue that our bland treatment of all young people does no harm and is at the very least humane. But the difficulty is that the degree of motivation which the individual possesses at any given time is very much affected by what is expected (or demanded) of him. Every emergency, every crisis reveals unsuspected resources of personal strength in some people and evokes heightened motivation in almost all. In speaking of the hero born of such a crisis, people say, "I didn't know he had it in

*Marietta Johnson, *Youth in a World of Men*, The John Day Co., 1929, p. 261.

him.'' But most of us, in fact, have a better, stouter-hearted, more vigorous self within — a self that's deliberately a little hard of hearing but by no means stone deaf.

15.     We all know that some organizations, some families, some athletic teams, some political groups inspire their members to great heights of personal performances. In other words, high individual performance will depend to some extent on the capacity of the society or institution to evoke it. And woe to the society that loses the gift for such evocation! When an institution, organization or nation loses its capacity to evoke high individual performance, its great days are over.

## Analysis of Paragraph Development

1.
2. An anecdote used as an introduction to exemplify the theme of the essay.

3. Thesis of essay expressed alternatively in the first and last sentences in the
4. next two paragraphs.

5. Motivation problems introduced and exemplified.
6. Reasons why young people find it easier to attend college.
7. Transitional paragraph introducing effects of social trends.
8. Good and bad effects of social trends.

9.
10. Qualities of eager and apathetic students.

11. Social benefits of present educational system and transitional statement indicating changes in educational process if system continues.

12. Discussion of important process changes in education resulting from lower
13. standards of present system.

14. Further clarification of motivation difficulty in relation to expectation of others.

15. Concluding reaffirmation that society must evoke the individual's desire to excel if it is to remain healthy and viable.

### The Changed and Unchanging

Barbara Tuchman's essay, unlike Gardner's, is a narrative and deals with observable events and norms of behaviour.[3] As an observer, she tells us what she has seen and what she thinks it means. In doing so she uses a great deal of vivid description to let us see and feel what she has seen and felt. Through her sometimes sensuous observations she enhances our understanding of China and its people.

1.     The two most striking physical features of China today are the new tree-planting and the old transportation by animal and man-drawn cart.

2.     Willows, sycamores, and countless varieties of poplars and cypress in multiple and flourishing rows, often under-planted with shrubs and hedges, supply shade and greenness in the city streets and

extend for miles along the roads outside. Trees have been richly planted in parks, on campuses, factory grounds, new housing lots, airports, military barracks, dam sites, river banks. In the new part of Chengchow the avenues lined with double rows of sycamores already thirty feet high are spectacular. Nanking and Scuchow have no street without shade. Nurseries of thin saplings can be seen everywhere. The "greening" campaign, as it is called, is said to have lowered the implacable summer heat in the baked cities of the north and the muggy cities of the Yangtse Valley by two degrees. In the hills it has begun to get a grip on the soil that had been allowed to erode and slide away in the rivers unchecked for centuries.

**3.** Afforestation is one of those civic works that was simply not undertaken in China before what is officially called "Liberation," that is, the Communist takeover in 1949. In Manchu times, local officials lived by the cut they could take out of tax collecting and were disinclined to spend any of it on projects for the public welfare. After the Revolution of 1911, the "People's Welfare" was one of the Three Principles of the Kuomintang Party founded by Sun Yat-sen and inherited by Chiang Kai-shek, but it got lost in the difficulties of consolidating political power and of invasion by the Japanese. Until now the Yangtse was never bridged—not at Nanking although it was the national capital during 1929-49; nor upstream at the triple city of Wuhan where railroad cars on the main north-south line had to be carried over by ferry; nor farther up at Chungking, Chiang Kai-shek's wartime capital for eight years. Now bridges carry traffic across the river at all three places.

**4.** In Honan, province of the ghastly famine of 1942-43, a canal that took ten years to build has been cut through rock and mountain to carry water and electric power to stony Linhsien Country whose people used to walk six miles to fetch water by bucket. Less spectacular but in the same spirit, a 400-man factory in Loyang has developed from twelve original workers and one sewing machine to make rubber-soled shoes for soldiers and peasants who once walked on straw.

**5.** How far China remains from its goal of modernization, however, lies under one's eyes every day in the endless procession of two-wheeled carts moving in and out of the provincial cities. This, not the trucks that serve Canton, Shanghai, and Peking, is the wider reality of China. Drawn by mixed teams of tandems of donkey, mule, and horse or by the straining muscles of a man between the shafts, with added pulling rope around a shoulder pad, the carts carry gravel, manure, bricks, building stone, sand, iron, pipes, bottled drinks, earthenware jars, mountainous piles of scallions, red onions, melons, and other produce, roped loads of tires, boxes, chairs, waste paper and rags, bags of grain, bags of fertilizer, blocks of ice, baskets of coal, heavy tree trunks twenty feet long, and everything else the country sends to the city and vice versa.

Some, pulled by children, carry grandma sitting under an umbrella; some, pulled by grandma, carry children. Every animal-drawn cart carries, in addition to the driver, a second figure sprawled

asleep on top of the load. Whole lives must be thus spent plodding along the roads, at such creeping pace when the load is heavy that once
**6.**    we drove past two haulers of scrap iron in the morning and on returning three hours later saw the same men only a few blocks farther on. Though some of the plodders are brawny young men, most are thin, muscular, workworn, soiled, and sweating toilers who may no longer have a landlord to oppress them but whose labour has not been much alleviated since the old days. A scrawny old woman bent against the weight of a load of wire rods bears little relation to the sturdy rosy ever-smiling maiden idyllically picking grapes who represents ideal proletarian womanhood on China's magazine covers. Often the heaviest loads are pulled by the oldest men as if (whisper it not in Mao's land of "struggle") the Marxist young, like any other, may have little inclination for the hardest work.

In the canal area, transportation is by barge, much of this too propelled by manpower. While some barges in the long trains are
**7.**    pulled by tugs on the Grand Canal, others are dragged by rope by plodders along the bank. On the smaller canals, single scows are moved by a man poling at snail's pace or bending his back to an oar pushed back and forth on a fulcrum at the stern.

How will all this human labour be used when and if China's transportation gradually becomes mechanized? The goal is so far from realization that it is hardly a worry, yet there are already signs that urban labour is underemployed. China's boasted record of full employment, which they like to tell you is the result of a planned economy as against the evils of our competitive private enterprise, is only achieved by assigning large numbers to more or less nominal jobs with no real function. Retinues of junior assistants follow every "leading cadre"
**8.**    like a claque, and a superabundance of personnel stands around in hotel corridors vaguely waiting for something to do. No fewer than six staff members of a "Friendship" store for foreigners clustered around the foreign exchange desk to supervise the cashing of one American Express check. At the Nanking Observatory nine staff members at one time were engaged in moving a bag of sand—which one could have handled—to mend a terrace. The cost of keeping people employed must be as great if not greater than our system of supporting the unemployed on welfare. The burden looms heavily over the future.

## Analysis of Paragraph Development
**1.** Introduction giving examples of the changed and the unchanging in modern China.
**2.** Numerous examples of how tree planting has changed the face of China.
**3.**⎫Reason why progress was slow in coming and what is being accomplished
**4.**⎭today.
**5.**⎫
**6.**⎬Discussion of the unchanging mode of transportation in China, with vivid
**7.**⎭descriptions and examples.

**8.** Conclusion wondering how China's large, underemployed labour force will be supported after China becomes modernized.


## F. A NOTE ABOUT FOOTNOTES AND BIBLIOGRAPHY

For longer essays requiring library research, you will need to cite your sources in footnotes and collect them in a bibliography. Therefore you should be aware of the rules and conventions that govern proper footnote and bibliographical entries.

**1. Footnotes**   Footnotes are numbered references that explain your statements or identify the sources of your information. They must be either placed at the bottom of the page, where their reference numbers appear, or collected on a separate sheet entitled "Notes" at the end of the essay. The separate-page listing method is more convenient for the writer but may inconvenience the reader. Therefore placing footnotes on the same page as their reference numbers is usually preferred.

Footnotes generally contain the following information: the author's name in normal order (i.e., given name first and surname second), title of publication, publishing data in parentheses (i.e., the place of publication, the name of the publishing company, and the year in which the particular edition was published) and page number(s). Information on the proper format for both footnoting and bibliography is taken from the *MLA Handbook for Writers of Research Papers, Theses, and Dissertations* (see List of Useful Reference Books, p. 246). This source is commonly used in the humanities; other academic disciplines may use slightly different formats. Check with your instructor for specific format directions.

### (a) General Guidelines for Writing Footnotes
   (i) Footnote numbers appear *after* the quoted material and about a half space above the line—like this. [4]
   (ii) Footnotes are numbered consecutively throughout the essay and are placed outside all punctuation.
   (iii) Footnote entries are single-spaced but separated from a preceding footnote by a double space.
   (iv) Footnotes at the bottom of the page are located four spaces below the last line of the text, and the first line is indented five spaces.

### (b) Some Sample Footnotes
**BOOKS:**

Brain Moore, *The Doctor's Wife* (Toronto: McClelland and Stewart Limited, 1976), p. 67.

Note: No comma before parenthesis enclosing publishing information, and colon separates place of publication and name of publisher.

**ARTICLES IN PERIODICALS:**
> Louis Peters, "Modern Perceptions of Tragic Drama," *The Quarterly Review,* 12 (Fall 1965), 102.

Note: Volume in arabic numbers and no abbreviated form of "page(s)" (p, pp.) used with periodical page number.

**ARTICLES IN ENCYCLOPEDIA:** no author
> "Laser," *The Encyclopaedia Britannica,* 1977.

Note: Since all encyclopedia articles are alphabetized, no volume or page numbers are given unless referring to a specific section in a multi-page article.

**ARTICLES IN A COLLECTION OR ANTHOLOGY WITH AN EDITOR:**
> John Diebold, "The Magnitude of Automation," *This Cybernetic Age,* ed. Don Toppin (New York: Human Development Corporations, 1976), 73-79.

Note: Title of article in quotation marks and collection title underlined (to indicate italics) and followed by a comma.

**GOVERNMENT PUBLICATIONS:**
> Department of Indian Affairs, *Mercury Pollution in Northern Ontario* (Ottawa: Queen's Printer, 1967), p. 123.

Note: Government department substitutes for author's name.

For further footnote conventions, see the *MLA Handbook.*

2. **Bibliography**    A bibliography is an alphabetized list of all the sources that were used to write an essay or a report. This material may include books, journals, magazines, government documents, newspaper articles, films, and other published or unpublished material that you consulted in researching your essay. Each reference item should include the following information: the author (surname first), title of work, name and location of publisher, and the publishing date.

(a) **General Guidelines for Writing a Bibliography**
   (i) The list of entries is alphabetized but not numbered.
   (ii) Titles of works without authors are placed in the alphabetical sequence, using the first letter of the title word.
   (iii) Entries are single-spaced and separated from preceding entries with double spacing.
   (iv) The second and following lines of each entry are indented five spaces.
   (v) The second reference to an author's name (and all succeeding references) is represented by a series of hyphens, indicating ditto marks.
   (vi) Only the first author's name is inverted when a work has two or more authors.

See the *MLA Handbook* for further bibliographical conventions.

**(b) Sample Bibliography**

Atwood, Margaret. *Survival: A Thematic Guide to Canadian Literature*. Toronto: Anansi Press Ltd., 1972.

*Double Vision: An Anthology of Twentieth-Century Stories in English*. Selected by Rudy Wiebe. Toronto: Macmillan of Canada, 1976.

Frye, Northrop. *Anatomy of Criticism*. New York: Atheneum, 1968.

Gold, Joseph, ed. *In the Name of Language*. Toronto: Macmillan of Canada, 1975.

Kakonis, Tom E. and James C. Wilcox. *Forms of Rhetoric: Ordering Experience*. New York: McGraw-Hill, 1964.

McFee, Oonah. *Sandbars*. Toronto: Macmillan of Canada, 1977.

Nowattny, Winifred M.T. "Justice and Love in Othello," *Univ. of Toronto Quarterly*, 21 (1950-51), 330-44.

O'Connor, Flannery. "The Displaced Person." In *Flannery O'Connor: The Complete Stories*. New York: Farrar, Straus, and Giroux, 1979, 194-235.

Rowse, A.L. *The Elizabethan Renaissance: The Cultural Achievement*. London and Basingstoke: Macmillan London Ltd., 1972.

Shakespeare, William. *Shakespeare: The Complete Works*. Ed. Peter Alexander. London and Glasgow: Collins, 1951.

_____. *The Poems*. Arden Shakespeare. Ed. F.T. Prince. London: Methuen, 1960.

Staines, David, ed. *The Canadian Imagination: Dimensions of a Literary Culture*. Cambridge, Mass: Harvard Univ. Press, 1977.

Trilling, Lionel. "Manners, Morals, and the Novel." In *Approaches to the Novel*. Collected and edited by Robert Scholes. San Francisco: Chandler Publishing Company, 1961.

# ENDNOTES

1. Bertrand Russell, "Men versus Insects," *In Praise of Idleness* (London: Unwin Books, 1960), pp. 124-5. Reprinted by permission of George Allen & Unwin Ltd.

2. John Gardner, "Motivation," *Excellence: Can We Be Equal and Excellent Too?* (New York: Harper & Row, 1962), pp. 92-6. Reprinted by permission of The Sterling Lord Agency, Inc. Copyright © by John Gardner.

3. Barbara Tuchman, "The Changed and the Unchanging," *Notes from China* (New York: Collier Books, 1972), pp. 23-27. Reprinted by permission of The Associated Press.

# CHAPTER TWELVE

# Writing a Report

The fundamental difference between the expository essay and the technical or business report is that the report is organized into discrete units of specific and highly visible information. This format enables the reader to peruse any section of the report without having to read the body in detail.

Most reports are designed to convey and record information which will be of practical use to the reader; therefore you must persuade with clear and explicit explanation. You do this by captioning all your headings and sub-headings and by placing complex technical information into visual formats—figures, charts, graphs, and so on. Also, keep your organization logical and your language exact. Thus, when compiling technical information, consider the following points:

1. Use simple and precise language. Your presentation must be objective and informative, not argumentative and theoretical; therefore avoid simplistic generalizations, confusing nomenclature, and imprecise superlatives. Remember, it is an accurate account of the subject matter, not the personality of the author, that should be paramount in any report.

2. Construct sentences that are unambiguous and concise, and that obey the rules of parallel structure. Make your paragraphs short and to the point, and place your topic sentence at the beginning so that the reader can locate your main ideas quickly.

3. Use clear, descriptive headings and sub-headings, and place exceptionally detailed information in point form. Also, use enough transitional words and phrases to enable your reader to move from one thought to another smoothly and efficiently.

# A. INFORMAL REPORTS

Depending upon their length and complexity, technical and business reports can be divided into formal and informal reports. Informal reports are short, and deal with a specific problem or piece of information, and they are normally written to a single individual or department. They may be divided into the letter report and the memorandum.

**1. The Letter Report**   The letter report is usually written to someone outside the company and may vary in degrees of formality, depending upon its subject matter and the position of the person to whom it is being sent. Because these letters deal with specific, sometimes technical information, they do not waste time with prefatory remarks or background details. Thus the introduction may only be a sentence or two—just enough to state the purpose; the body may contain only the necessary details—sometimes in point form—to clarify the problem; and the conclusion may simply propose a solution or make recommendations. See the two examples of the letter report; notice how they vary in degrees of technicality while essentially following the same format.

**2. The Memorandum**   The memorandum, unlike the letter report, is normally used for communications within the organization, and its format is unique. The tone is more conversational, and it is more obviously divided into specific sections: the Heading, the Introduction, the Findings (or Body), and the Conclusions (or Recommendations).

(a) The Heading contains the date, the name of the person to whom the report is being sent, the writer of the report, and the subject of the report.

(b) The Introduction states the reason why the memorandum is being sent and the problem or point of information that it will deal with.

(c) The Findings (or Body) contains the specific data necessary to understand, and act on, the problem. The data, for purposes of clarity, may be placed in point form and is often presented visually in charts, groups, tables and so forth.

(d) The Conclusion simply sums up the results of the findings and contains recommendations that warrant immediate action.

The memorandum has no formal closing; in fact, the writer will often use his initials in place of his signature. Although the memorandum and the letter report differ somewhat in format and style, they have one thing in common: they both deal with a specific problem or point of information that should be acted on promptly. Thus their express purpose is to transmit instructions or request information as efficiently and succinctly as possible.

# Sample 12.1—Letter Report

October 19, 19xx


Mr. J.T. Turner
Vice-Principal
Sherwood College
2675 King Street
Ottawa, Ontario
K6V 9Y5

Dear Mr. Turner:

### Guide to Interlibrary Loan and Photocopy Service

The Canada Institute for Scientific and Technical Information has a
non-circulating policy for journals. However, with some exceptions,
monographs may be borrowed for two weeks.

#### How to Obtain Material:

If the reference you want is from a CAN/DLE computer or an offline printout,
simply cut it out and attach it to a piece of 5 x 8 paper with your name and
address at the top. Then photocopy it twice and submit the three (3) copies
to our Interlibrary Loan and Photocopy Service.

All other items should be submitted on a standard library request form. These
forms are available from the address below for three cents each. Telephone
calls or Telex messages are equally acceptable. (Please be sure that your
Telex operator has a copy of the Library Telecommunications Code.)

>        Interlibrary Loan and Photocopy Service
>        Canada Institute for Scientific and Technical Information
>        Bldg. M-55, National Research Council
>        Ottawa, Ontario  K1A 0S2

#### Costs:

The charges for photocopy are two dollars and twenty cents ($2.20) minimum, up
to ten (10) pages, and twenty-two cents (22¢) for each additional page. A
duplicate microfiche is two dollars and twenty cents ($2.20) per document or
twenty-two cents (22¢) a page for a blowup. Prepayments are not allowed, but
a deposit account may be established; otherwise separate invoices will be
sent. Remittances should be made payable to the Receiver General of Canada,
credit National Research Council.

May I remind you that full information, including source of reference, is
essential to ensure the best possible service.

Sincerely, *Martha Howatt*

Martha Howatt
Librarian

# Sample 12.2—Letter Report

*Provincial Power Commission Research Division*

File:  STR/13/025
November 26, 19xx

Mr. John C. Dunn
Director of Research

Subject:
  A Taped Termination For Paper-Insulated Cable

  A method of terminating single-conductor PILC (or PIAC)
  cable, using taping techniques to replace porcelain
  potheads, has been developed.  This report describes an
  extension of the terminating method suitable for application to metallic-sheathed paper-insulated cable.

Background:

Over the past several years, work has been in progress on the development and
evaluation of taped splicing and terminating techniques applicable to
polymeric-insulated cable.  This work has been recorded in a series of
progress reports culminating in the publication of <u>Distribution Standards
Bulletin</u> Number 68 of August 19xx, and IEEE Transactions Paper No. 64-32, "A
Universal Method for Splicing and Terminating Polymeric-Insulated Cables" by
Kelly and Ross, published in the August issue of <u>Power Apparatus and Systems.</u>

Procedure

In July 19xx, taped terminations were applied to the ends of two twelve-foot
lengths of 1/C 4/0 PILC Type H 23-kv cable.  The methods described in the
publications referred to above were used, but with varnished-cambric tape
stress-cones, and with four different oil barrier tapes over the paper to
protect the polyethylene tape from contact with the oil or compound.  The
layer of barrier tape was covered in each case with self-amalgamating
polyethylene tape (SAPT).  An outer layer of self-bonding silicone rubber tape
was applied to complete the termination.

The cables were thermally cycled 6 cycles a day for one month by circulating
current sufficient to raise the sheath temperature to 75°C.  This was followed
by cycling for one month to a maximum sheath temperature of 90°C.  No
deterioration or oil leakage was noted at any termination, nor could any
permanent deformation of the sheaths be found.

Storage and Exposure:

The specimens were stored for one year under standard laboratory conditions,
then exposed for one month to 100 per cent humidity conditions.  The effects
of the latter exposure were assessed by the measurement of dissipation factor
to 25 kv with the Schering Bridge.  No change in the DF/voltage curve
occurred.

- 2 -

The terminations were finally dissected and examined carefully for indications of oil leakage and for the effectiveness of the adhesion to the cable insulation and sheath. Best performance was obtained with a self-amalgamating neoprene barrier tape.

The flashover and impulse strength of the terminations are a function of the general geometry and dimensions. Suitable values have been determined in the previous work, and these are incorporated in the proposed termination method to be included in the next report.

Conclusions:

1.  A method of applying a taped termination to paper-insulated, metal-sheathed cable has been developed and subjected to laboratory evaluation.

2.  This method of termination may be used for compound or oil-filled cable to 25-kv line-to-line voltage rating, using the specified dimensions.

3.  Until further field experience is obtained, the use of a taped termination is not recommended for an oil-filled cable where pressure heads, due to differences of evaluation greater than 20 feet, may be encountered. Nor is it suitable for compound-filled cable where heads of 40 feet or more may be present.

4.  A detailed termination method will be transmitted to all managers in the next report.

Approved:                                                Respectfully Submitted:

*J.V. Stanhope*                                          *Martin Keller*

J.V. Stanhope                                            Martin Keller
Engineer in Charge                                       Dialectrics Engineer
Electrical Research Dept.                                 Power Division

MK/1s

# Sample 12.3 — The Memorandum

MEMORANDUM

From:  Allan Jones                    Date:  March 28, 19xx

To:  Ann McFadden, Dean              Subject:  IBM 3101 Terminal Replacement


As you know, we are presently using 15 IBM PC stand-alone computers for our computer literacy program. At the same time, however, we are requiring our first-year business students to use 3101 terminals connected to our mainframe.

I believe we could vastly improve our teaching environment and make more effective use of our learning resources if we replace these 3101 terminals with IBM PC's. The portion of our capital budget this year that has been set aside for computer purchases has not yet been used; therefore we have the necessary funds to purchase at least 12 more stand-alone computers.

This purchase would enable us to offer our business students a series of introductory programming and package learning procedures without requiring them to learn another operating system. And through the retention of our 3270 terminal equipment link to the mainframe, we would still be able to allow our technical programmer students to get the necessary computer time.

In considering this request, please be advised that a purchasing decision must be made within the next thirty days if we are to have these computers in place by next semester.

Thanks.

*allan*

# Sample 12.4 – The Memorandum

MEMORANDUM

TO:        All Faculty

From:      Doris Anderson, Development Officer

Date:      February 19, 19xx

Subject:   Development Fund

As you are aware, the college sets aside funds for special projects in its
"Development Funds."  The intent is to provide funding for projects that have
implications for the college as a whole, rather than for a specific campus.
Therefore, to be approved, a project must be relevant to all of our campuses.

Examples of Previous Applications:

  a) A project to develop a core curriculum for programs and/or courses that
     are common to all campuses.

  b) Develop a college-wide orientation program suitable for cross-campus
     use.

  c) Computer personnel to provide college-wide development on our systems.

Some issues and/or operating problems reach across departments or campuses and
therefore require resolution at a level beyond the local operating
environment.  These development funds are intended not only to provide
resources for problem solving but also to open up new opportunities for
professional development.

If you have ideas for projects that meet these broad requirements, please
submit a preliminary proposal for discussion by the end of the present
semester.

Thank you.

*Doris*

DA/le

# B. THE FORMAL REPORT

The formal report is used for complex technical subjects that require background knowledge and extensive research. It may be written by one person or by a team of people, and may be circulated within a single organization or throughout many different organizations. It contains both technical and non-technical sections, and its information is presented in well-defined segments so that a reader can understand its purpose and results without having to read the entire report.

Depending upon the length, complexity, and formality of the report, organization will vary, some reports having more sections than others. A long and complex report may contain all of the following sections: Cover, Title Page, Cover Letter, Letter of Transmittal, Abstract or Summary, Table of Contents, Introduction, Discussion or Body, Conclusion, Recommendations, References, and Appendix.

1. **Cover Letter**   The cover letter merely identifies the report and discusses briefly why the report is being submitted. It may also explain why and under what circumstances the report was written and acknowledge any assistance received in its preparation. It is never bound within the report, but is attached to the outside cover or submitted in a separate envelope.

2. **Cover**   The cover has two purposes: to protect the contents of the report and to inform the reader of its subject. The cover material may be heavy cardboard printed in different colours or a three-ring binder with a gummed label. The front of the cover should contain only the title of the report and perhaps the name of the organization that originated it.

3. **Title Page**   This page usually has four pieces of information: the report title, the name of the person, department, or organization for whom the report is intended, the name of the author (or authors), and the completion date. It may also have several lined spaces for approval signatures.

4. **Letter of Transmittal**   This letter may function as a foreword or brief summary of the report and is often written by someone other than the writer of the report. It may also include suggestions and follow-up recommendations by management. It is always bound inside the cover, usually after the title page.

5. **Abstract or Summary**   This is one of the most important sections, for it is here that the heart of the report is summarized: The major arguments are discussed, the conclusions reviewed, and quite often the recommendations presented. And because this is the section of the report that the reader will survey before he reads the body, its language and organization must be clear, precise, and to the point. Its information must be expressed in non-technical terms, and it should be written in a narrative style.

6. **Table of Contents**   This page lists the subject matter of the report and reveals its organization. Major sections or chapters are listed in order of appearance, along with their respective page numbers, and it may also include

an appendix and a list of illustrations at the bottom. The organization of both headings and sub-headings may use the formal conventions of the outline. (See pp. 158.)

7. **Introduction**  This section prepares the reader for the body of the report. It includes a brief statement of purpose, some background information the reader may need to understand the subsequent discussion, and the scope and objectives of the report. In effect, it prepares the reader to receive the technical information that follows.

8. **Discussion or Body**  This section, the longest, is largely self-explanatory. In it the writer informs the reader or readers what was done, how it was done, and what was found out. He or she presents the detailed information—facts, arguments, lab procedures, test results, and mathematical equations—that the reader needs to understand the subject under discussion. The writer must not, however, include background data not necessary for the discussion at hand; this subsidiary information must be placed in the appendix.

9. **Conclusion**  The conclusion briefly summarizes the findings in the discussion and states their major implications. The concluding statements must be based entirely on the evidence in the foregoing discussion and must never advance arguments unrelated to the stated purpose of the report. The conclusion may also propose further action if the report does not contain a separate section for recommendations.

10. **Recommendations**  This section is included when the report's findings suggest that additional work must be done in order to arrive at a satisfactory conclusion or to accomplish a given task. These recommendations may include an outline of methodology, or a list of procedural steps, required to meet the objectives proposed in the conclusion. This section of the report always points the reader in a certain direction and to a specific action.

11. **List of References**  This is the most acceptable way for listing sources in technical reports. The sources are either listed alphabetically or, if they are numerically referenced in the body of the report, numbered sequentially. The list contains the books, journals, articles, and other sources that were used to prepare the report.

12. **Appendix**  This is the section that contains the data not necessary for understanding the arguments or ideas proposed in the discussion. It usually includes ancillary visual material such as charts, graphs, equations, drawings, or tables that support, but do not explain, the findings in the Conclusion. If the amount of supporting information the report requires is great, this section may be broken into a number of subsections (Appendix A, B, C, etc.) and designated by the plural heading *Appendices*.

Your report may not require all of these sections, but it is essential that you know what kind of information they include, and how they enhance the clarity of the final product.

# Sample 12.5 — The Formal Report

## Covering Letter

---

*Ontario Water Resources Commission* _____

April 18, 19xx

Mr. M.D. Trudel, P. Eng.
Supervisor
Department of Sanitary Engineering

Dear Mr. Trudel:

Enclosed is my team report No. 80-201 on Simulated Thermal Effluent into Lake
Ontario.  This report was prepared in response to your department's urgent
request in October for an effluent simulation study of Lake Ontario.  Our
budget was approved in November and our team was assembled under project
#207B.

Our study predicts the dispersion pattern of Duffin Creek water into Lake
Ontario; the experimental model we used was applied to an existing thermal
generating station.  We were able to predict maximum temperature to within 25%
of measured values, which satisfies the parameter requirements of our
measurement guidelines.

If you wish a further thermal simulation study done for a proposed industrial
plant relocation, please notify our unit by June 1 so that a team can be
assembled and a budget prepared before the end of August.

In the meantime, if you would like a further discussion of the report's
contents and, more specifically, the need for further field studies, please do
not hesitate to call my office.

Sincerely,

John Silburn, P. Eng.
Water Quality Surveys Branch

JS:de
enc.

---

## Title Page

SIMULATED THERMAL EFFLUENT

INTO LAKE ONTARIO

APRIL, 19xx

J.B. Silburn
Water Quality Surveys Branch

## Abstract

SIMULATED THERMAL EFFLUENT

INTO LAKE ONTARIO


ABSTRACT


    The dispersion pattern of Duffin Creek into Lake Ontario was determined
under two different wind conditions in the spring, when the flow was 180 cfs
and 5°f warmer than the lake water.  Continuous dye injection was used to
trace the plume.  Based upon experimental results, a model was developed which
predicts maximum concentrations within 25 per cent for distances up to 4000
feet from source.  Maximum dye concentrations were proportional to
(distance)-0.8.  The model applied to an existing thermal generating station
at Lakeview was capable of predicting maximum temperatures within 25 per cent
of measured values.

i

## Table of Contents

TABLE OF CONTENTS

Appendices

A - List of Symbols
B - Table 1:  Wind Conditions, Duffin Creek
C - Figure 1:  Field Set-Up*

*Figures 2 through 9 have been omitted for space considerations.

# Introduction

<u>INTRODUCTION</u>

There is relatively little information available that allows one to
predict what effect an effluent released at the shore will have on adjacent
areas. Obviously, this type of information is mandatory for the proper
locating of municipal service intakes and outlets as well as the effect of
industry on adjacent areas. The information must be formulated in such a way
that it can be used for different loading and longshore currents, and distance
from the source. In addition, the formulas incorporate a temperature
difference between the effluent and the receiving body, which is likely to be
the case for most discharge conditions. Equations were developed from
controlled experiments in the field, then checked by applying them to a
completely different area. They were also compared to results from similar
studies on Lake Huron as a test of their general application. While the
equations developed are obviously not universal or capable of handling all
physical situations, they do provide a valuable prediction vehicle for small
discharges at the shore. As more field studies are conducted, it will be
possible to expand the equations to incorporate more physical factors and
produce more accurate predictions. An interim approach to the problem would
be to check the application of the prediction equations with limited field
surveys, then decide whether it is necessary to conduct full studies or accept
the existing equations. In each case, the results should be such that they
can be extended through the use of long-term meteorological data.

1

# Discussion or Body

OUTLINE OF PROBLEM

At present, a thermal generating plant is under construction at Perkinton. The plant, on completion in 19xx, will discharge warm cooling water (10-25°F above lake temperature) at a rate of 1200 cfs. A study was conducted at the mouth of Duffin Creek to estimate the dispersion pattern. This stream, which is a tributary to Lake Ontario, was selected because of its geographical proximity to the plant, the lack of a well formed delta, and the large marsh just upstream of the mouth that ponds and routes the flow. To simulate a thermal effluent, the study was conducted in the spring when the flow was 180 cfs and 5°F warmer than the lake water.

EXPERIMENT

Rhodamine B dye was injected (see Fig.1) at a rate of approximately 200 ppb (a flow gauge existed two miles upstream of outlet). The distribution of the dye was not uniform at the outlet due to the non-uniform mean velocity (see Fig.4). The surface layer and the eastern side of the creek were actually flowing upstream due to the wind conditions. Consequently, the mass flow was determined by integrating the concentration and velocity profiles at the outlet. The longshore currents were measured by tracking drogues at a two-foot depth. They were placed 500 feet directly south of the outlet while wind velocities were measured with an anemometer (Table 1). Once the direction of the current was determined, marker buoys were established at the various range lines (constant distances from creek outlet) using an optical range finder. Dye was continuously injected at a steady rate. Once the plume had reached approximately 6000 feet from the source, sampling was started on the nearest range line. The boat traversed the dye plume sampling at a depth of two feet to determine the location of the maximum concentration in the "Z" direction. At this point, samples were taken at one foot intervals (y-direction) to determine the depth to the maximum concentration. Positions were determined from the shore, using a transit-mounted optical range finder with a one meter base. All concentrations were measured with a fluorometer.

Dye was normally injected for about three hours, with the result that the wind conditions varied little (see Table 1). Two runs were made under different wind conditions, resulting in a western and eastern dispersion pattern; but in each case, the temperature of the creek water was 44°F and the lake temperature 500 feet offshore was 39°F.

2

RESULTS

In both studies, the maximum concentration of dye remained very near to the shoreline at each range line.  Sampling was restricted to depths of approximately 1.5 feet, due to the draft of the small boat.  It was observed that the dye plumes were more widely dispersed at 500 feet than at 1000 feet. This is probably due to the inertia of the creek flow, which is directly south and has a mean velocity of 0.5 fps.  The inertia of the creek water must be dissipated, then redirected to conform with the wind-driven lake currents along the shore.  Beyond this initial spreading at the mouth, the concentrations on the average varied as x-0.7 in the westerly direction and as x-0.78 in the easterly direction.  G.T. Csanady[1] found that the concentration varied between approximately x-1.0 and x-0.7.  The confinement of the thermal regime produced higher concentrations in a narrower zone along the shore.

The dye concentration profiles at the various distances from the mouth are presented in Figs.2, 3, 4, 5 and 6, and the variances ($\bar{\sigma}^2$) for each profile appear in Fig.7.  The distribution of dye with depth is fairly uniform and appears to have a constant variance of approximately one foot (see Fig.6). This is probably due to the bottom having a uniform away-from-shore gradient.

PREDICTION MODEL

To apply the prediction model, it was necessary to develop a relationship between the variance and distance from the outlet.  J.E. Foxworthy[2] fitted a straight line to a plot of log $\sigma$ vs. log x.  However, this method produces erroneous results when applied to Duffin Creek, due to the initially large plume at 500 feet from the creek mouth.  A two segment line was fitted to the measured variances by joining the variance at the creek outlet and the variance at 1000 feet; then a second line was fitted for distances greater than 1000 feet.  This method produced a good prediction model for maximum concentration for Duffin Creek, but failed to define the initial large spreading of the plume at the creek outlet, which would probably be dependent on the creek flow and cross section.  This study also failed to define the relationships between variances and different thermal lakewise temperature gradients which are likely a factor, since Csanady's concentrations vary approximately at x-1 to x-0.7 in the summer[3] while the Duffin Creek study varies approximately as x-0.8.  Further, the study failed to define the relationship between variances and longshore currents.

3

MODEL COMPUTATIONS - WESTERN PLUME

The model maximum concentrations were computed by substituting the following values into equations 5 and 6:

| X<br>feet | Q<br>lbs/sec | $\bar{U}$<br>fps | $\bar{\sigma}_y$<br>ft | $\bar{\sigma}_z$<br>ft |
|---|---|---|---|---|
| 0 | $11.1 \times 10^{-4}$ | 0.58 | 3.16 | 5.36 |
| 500 | $11.1 \times 10^{-4}$ | 0.43 | 0.94 | 36 |
| 1000 | $11.1 \times 10^{-4}$ | 0.33 | 0.97 | 42 |
| 2000 | $11.1 \times 10^{-4}$ | 0.33 | 0.97 | 42 |
| 4000 | $11.1 \times 10^{-4}$ | 0.33 | 0.97 | 108 |

The variation in velocity downstream was accounted for by employing dimensionless velocity ratios to equation 5. The results are as follows:

| Distance<br>ft | $C_{max}$<br>Measured<br>ppb | $C_{max}$<br>Model<br>ppb | Per cent<br>Difference<br>% |
|---|---|---|---|
| WESTERN PLUME | | | |
| 500 | 130 | 150 | 18 |
| 1000 | 205 | 170 | 17 |
| 2000 | 130 | 112 | 14 |
| 4000 | 72 | 70 | 3 |
| EASTERN PLUME | | | |
| 500 | 140 | 175 | 25 |
| 1000 | 100 | 94 | 6 |
| 1500 | 60 | 70 | 13 |

4

A temperature and drogue study, conducted in May at an existing thermal generating station (Lakeview) with a cooling water flow of 1160 cfs at a temperature of 62.6°F, showed that the warmer water stays near the surface and the shore (see Fig.9). The sub-surface cooling water had acquired lake temperature by 4000 feet, while the surface cooling water was still 4°F warmer than the lake water at 4000 feet. The Duffin Creek dye plumes were similar in configuration to the measured Lakeview thermal plumes.

The Duffin Creek model was applied to the Lakeview thermal plant site to predict maximum downstream temperatures. This application was based on temperature and flow data at the outlet (assuming constant along-shore currents and heat as a complete conservative, with no atmospheric heat transfer.) The following results were obtained:

| Distance from the Outlet | Predicted Maximum Temperature | Measured Maximum Temperature | Difference |
|---|---|---|---|
| feet | °F | °F | % |
| 500 | 60.5 | 62.6 | 7 |
| 1000 | 57.0 | 62.6 | 18 |
| 2000 | 53.4 | 60.8 | 25 |
| 4000 | 50.7 | 53.4 | 12 |

It must be appreciated that the transposed model is an estimate which can only be applied to along-shore plumes. A more comprehensive model would take into consideration current regimes, thermal stratification, atmospheric transfer, and probably wave considerations.

5

## Conclusion and References

CONCLUSIONS

A mass flow model based on measured concentration profiles for continuous constant dye injection was developed for a creek with a flow of 180 cfs into Lake Ontario. The model was done in the presence of a thermal difference of 5°F between the creek and the lake. The model predicts dye concentrations within 25 per cent of measured values in the effluent plume for a mile from the outlet, which will vary as the (distance) -0.8. The developed model was then used to predict the maximum temperatures in the effluent plume of an existing thermal generating station and was capable of predicting maximum temperatures to within 25 per cent of the measured values.

REFERENCES

[1] G.T. Csanady, Hydrodynamic Studies on Lake Huron at Baie du Dore, Summer, 1964. Water Resources Institute, University of Waterloo and Great Lakes Institute, p.19.

[2] J.E. Foxworthy, Dispersion of a Surface Waste Field on the Sea. Water Pollution Control Federation. Vol.38, No. 7, December, 1967, p.117.

[3] Csanady, p.19. (See also Douglas Point Saturation Run. University of Waterloo, Great Lakes Institute, 1967, p.213.)

6

# Appendices

<u>APPENDIX A</u>

<u>LIST OF SYMBOLS</u>

x     —   distance measured in the direction of the dye plume movement — feet

y     —   depth measured from the surface — feet

z     —   distance measured parallel to the water surface and perpendicular to x — feet

$\bar{U}$    —   mean velocity in x direction fps

$\bar{\sigma}^2$    —   variances in y and z direction $ft^2$

Q     —   mass flow rate of dye lbs/sec

fi    —   frequency

c     —   concentration ppm

APPENDIX B

TABLE 1

WIND CONDITIONS

DUFFIN CREEK - APRIL 10/xx

| Time | Force (Knots) | Direction | Activity |
|------|---------------|-----------|----------|
| WESTERN | | | |
| 0900 | 4 | 245° | |
| 1000 | 7 | 280° | dye injection |
| 1115 | 10 | 285° | |
| 1330 | 10 | 280° | sampling |
| 1500 | 11 | 280° | |
| 1540 | 7 | 280° | |
| | | | |
| EASTERN | | | |
| 0700 | 5 | 110° | |
| 0815 | 5 | 110° | |
| 0930 | 4 | 95° | |
| 1110 | 3 | 95° | |
| 1150 | 8 | 113° | |
| 1330 | 15 | 60° | |
| 1430 | 11 | 50° | dye injection |
| 1700 | 1 | 50° | |
| 1815 | 0 | 0° | sampling |

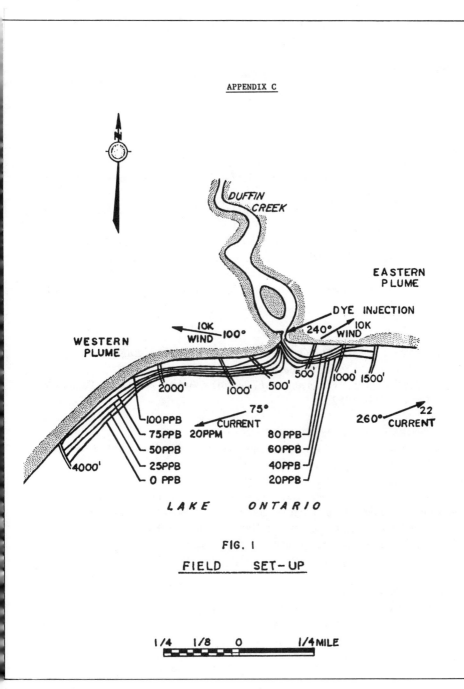

APPENDIX C

FIG. I

FIELD   SET-UP

# Some Useful Reference Tools

**DICTIONARIES**

*Dictionary of Canadian English: The Senior Dictionary.* Toronto: W. J. Gage Limited, 1973.

*Funk & Wagnall's New Standard Dictionary.* New York: Funk & Wagnall's Publishing Co., 1963.

*The Oxford English Dictionary.* Oxford: Oxford University Press, 1971.

*Webster's New Collegiate Dictionary.* Springfield, Mass.: G & G Merriam Co., 1976. (desk size)

*Webster's New International Dictionary.* Springfield, Mass.: G & G Merriam Co., 1961.

**THESAURI**

Dutch, Robert A., ed. *The Original Roget's Thesaurus of English Words and Phrases.* New York: St. Martin's Press, 1965.

Roget, Peter M. *Roget's International Thesaurus,* 3rd ed. New York: Thomas Y. Crowell Co., 1952.

**HANDBOOKS AND REFERENCE MANUALS**

Brusaw, Charles T., Gerald J. Alfred and Walter E. Oliu. *Handbook of Technical Writing.* New York: St. Martin's Press, 1976.

Dallas, Richard J., and James M. Thomson. *Clerical and Secretarial Systems for the Office.* Englewood Cliffs, New Jersey: Prentice-Hall, Inc., 1975.

Messenger, William E. and Jan de Bruyn. *The Canadian Writer's Handbook.* Scarborough, Ontario: Prentice-Hall of Canada, 1980.

Sabin, William A. *Reference Manual for Secretaries and Typists.* Toronto: McGraw-Hill Ryerson, 1978.

**STYLE BOOKS**

*A Manual of Style.* Chicago: University of Chicago Press, 1969.

*MLA Handbook for Writers of Research Papers, Theses & Dissertations.* New York: Modern Language Association, 1977.

*Turabian's Manual for the Writers of Term Papers, Theses, and Dissertations.* 4th ed. Chicago: University of Chicago Press, 1973.

# Exercise Answers

## Exercise 1.1 — Distinguishing Parts of Speech

1. The footbridge hangs *between* large cliffs which are studded with *caves*.                                                          5     1

2. *Follow* that car *down* the yellow brick road.                                                                                       7     4

3. The Christmas tree was decorated by two *young* boys who lived across the street from *us*.                                            3     2

4. Ted *and* Carol both *won* prizes for their paintings at the art show.                                                                6     7

5. *We* will visit Vermont in the fall *when* the leaves change colour.                                                                  2     4

6. *Try* to be *on* time tomorrow.                                                                                                       7     5

7. *When* shall *we* meet?                                                                                                               4     2

8. Toronto is the *largest* city in *Ontario*.                                                                                           3     1

9. Michael *plays* hockey, *but* Brenden prefers soccer.                                                                                 7     6

10. *My* father's sailboat *capsized* yesterday.                                                                                         2     7

11. Please remain *in* the classroom until the *bell* rings.                                                                             5     1

12. *Which* subject do *you* prefer? English or French?                                                                                  3     2

13. I know *where* the *best* restaurants are located in our city.                                                                       4     3

14. *Dr. Thomson* was only thirty years old when he was appointed a *full* professor at our university.                                  1     3

15. All of the rooms were booked, *so* we had to move to another *hotel*.                                                                6     1

16. The toy *was broken* when we opened the *damaged* parcel.                                                                            7     3

17. I don't know *when* we will visit *our* friend, Helen.                                                                               4     2

18. Our hockey team won *its* first game; *however* our basketball team was beaten very soundly.                                         2     4

19. Please *read* the next chapter in the text *for* tomorrow.                                                                           7     5

20. My brother sold his stereo set *after* he lost *all* of his money gambling.                                                          4     3

## Exercise 2.1 – Locating the Subject and Verb

| | Subject | Verb |
|---|---|---|
| 1. Into the classroom walked the students. | students | walked |
| 2. One of my mother's pies is missing. | one | is |
| 3. Call the team together for a meeting. | (you) | call |
| 4. Where is Winnipeg in relation to Calgary? | Winnipeg | is |
| 5. The fertilizer was spread on the garden yesterday. | fertilizer | was spread |
| 6. Telling lies is a disgusting habit. | Telling lies | is |
| 7. Some of our tomatoes were picked too early. | Some | were picked |
| 8. There are not enough textbooks in the bookstore. | textbooks | are |
| 9. My sister's birthday falls on Tuesday this year. | birthday | falls |
| 10. Who was here yesterday? | Who | was |
| 11. Near the schoolyard were several tennis courts. | tennis courts | were |
| 12. Skiing and ice skating are my favourite winter activities. | skiing, ice skating | are |
| 13. Several of our teachers are at a remedial reading conference in Toronto. | Several | are |
| 14. Here is the winning number. | winning number | is |
| 15. Diane, fighting to stay in contention, sank a thirty foot putt on the eighteenth green. | Diane | sank |
| 16. Some of the trees we planted are now infested with budworm. | Some | are |
| 17. On the roof of our house there is a robin's nest. | robin's nest | is |
| 18. Failing to answer the test questions in the allotted time, James flunked his final math quiz. | James | flunked |
| 19. Please follow the dotted line. | (you) | follow |
| 20. When did this happen? | this | did happen |
| 21. How many chairs are there in the room? | chairs | are |
| 22. Who fired the first shot? | Who | fired |
| 23. More than two volunteers are needed for next week's project. | volunteers | are needed |
| 24. There are not enough tables in the cafeteria. | tables | are |
| 25. The cause of the accident is still under investigation. | cause | is |
| 26. Inside the barn, the fire spread rapidly. | fire | spread |
| 27. Many of our former students have won scholarships. | Many | have won |
| 28. Jogging keeps me in good physical shape all year round. | Jogging | keeps |
| 29. Struggling to free himself from the clinging vines, Roger hacked desperately with his | | |

machete as the pursuing cannibals gained
on him.

|  |  |
|---|---|
| Roger | hacked |

**30.** Outside the cabin, the snowstorm intensified.

|  |  |
|---|---|
| snowstorm | intensified |

## Exercise 2.2 — Recognizing Phrases

**1.** Bob wants *to tour Europe next year.* — Inf.

**2.** I enjoy ice skating *on the frozen canal in Ottawa.* — Prep.

**3.** *Before the math quiz,* we reviewed our notes in the library. — Prep.

**4.** The woman *wearing the blue skirt* is my sister. — Part.

**5.** *Running five miles every day* is quite an achievement. — Ger.

**6.** *To eliminate acid rain* will cost hundreds of millions of dollars. — Inf.

**7.** Betty's greatest thrill was *piloting a jet plane.* — Ger.

**8.** The dinner rolls, *purchased yesterday,* are already stale. — Part.

**9.** *Writing well* is always a difficult task. — Ger.

**10.** My classmates eat their lunch *before noon every day.* — Prep.

**11.** *Surprised by the expensive gift,* Sheila was at a loss for words. — Part.

**12.** *Taking music lessons* was not what Carl had in mind. — Ger.

**13.** The warehouse *near the railroad tracks* burned down last night. — Prep.

**14.** *Worn by a world famous model,* the designer jeans were an instant
success. — Part.

**15.** We enjoyed *skiing with Pat and Frank.* — Ger.

**16.** The man *sitting by the exit sign* is my stepfather. — Part.

**17.** Our cat ran *after a field mouse yesterday.* — Prep.

**18.** Pete certainly enjoys *swimming in his backyard pool.* — Ger.

**19.** The workers decided *to join the local craft union.* — Inf.

**20.** *After staying awake all night with a raging toothache,* Claudia was
completely exhausted. — Prep.

**21.** *To win at chess* one must concentrate intensely. — Inf.

**22.** *Sought by the police in two provinces,* the criminal left the country. — Part.

**23.** *Baking award-winning pies* was Martha's claim to fame. — Ger.

**24.** Susan studied all summer *to compete for the French language
scholarship.* — Inf.

**25.** *Frustrated by his slow start,* Don quit the race after only three laps. — Part.

**26.** The large house *near the lake* was sold yesterday. — Prep.

**27.** *Learning computer programming* was Sylvia's year-long project. — Ger.

**28.** *To start his own business* remains my brother's burning ambition. — Inf.

**29.** The hockey puck rolled *into the net.* — Prep.

**30.** The city of Quebec decided *to host the winter games.* — Inf.

## Exercise 2.3 — Identifying Clauses

**1.** *After I finished the test,* I went to the student lounge. — Adv.

**2.** The mechanic *who repaired my car* was a former student. — Adj.

3. We think *that nuclear war is suicide*.                            N.

4. *What we accomplished* is beyond belief.                           N.

5. *Before you start your car*, be sure to fasten your seatbelt.      Adv.

6. The carpenter *who repaired our coffee table* is a first-rate tennis
   player.                                                            Adj.

7. Mr. Zuccarelli bought the truck *that we traded in last year*.     Adj.

8. *When our basketball team scored in the last two seconds of the
   game*, the fans went wild.                                         Adv.

9. Tony Woo, *who is our computer programmer*, has won another
   science award.                                                     Adj.

10. *If our company cannot meet the deadline*, we will surely lose
    the contract.                                                     Adv.

11. I believe *that it is your serve*.                                N.

12. We will repair your television set *as soon as the parts arrive*. Adv.

13. *That our City Council will meet its civic responsibilities* is beyond
    question.                                                         N.

14. We are not interested in *what her religious beliefs are at the moment*. N.

15. Our school ordered ten dozen arborite tables *that were made
    in Poland*.                                                       Adj.

16. *When Michael entered the room*, everyone stood at attention.     Adv.

17. *If you do not participate in class discussions*, you will be given
    a written examination.                                            Adv.

18. I am certain *that we are scheduled for our field trip tomorrow*. N.

19. Lift the crystal punch bowl off the table *as gently as you can*. Adv.

20. The red and white convertible *that was in the major accident* is still
    being driven.                                                     Adj.

21. We are certain *that Helen can still win the academic prize*.     N.

22. I arrived at the committee meeting *as soon as I could*.          Adv.

23. Jack White, *who owns the corner grocery store*, was robbed
    last night.                                                       Adj.

24. Who knows *what his position will be on this issue?*              N.

25. Victoria, B.C. is one city *that I want to revisit*.              Adj.

26. The fire started *after we left the room*.                        Adv.

27. *That he will win the mathematics scholarship* is almost guaranteed. N.

28. Fred Vandergriffe, *who has recently joined our faculty*, is a former
    chess champion.                                                   Adj.

29. *Whoever is responsible for our delay* should be disciplined.     N.

30. We did not attend the company picnic *because our supervisor
    made us work over the weekend*.                                   Adv.

# Exercise 2.5 – Detecting Fragments

1. Writing to express ourselves is an important activity.             C

2. Because it allows us to personalize knowledge.                     F

3. It may also develop our critical faculties.                        C

**4.** By allowing us to explore new ideas and areas of speculation. _____F_____

**5.** Writing to explore, then, can be an important part of self-expression. _____C_____

**6.** It may even be an essential step in our intellectual development. _____C_____

**7.** Writing this way obliges us to put new ideas into our own words. _____C_____

**8.** Which are added to and combined with our existing body of knowledge. _____F_____

**9.** We are then able to discover what we know. _____C_____

**10.** And more importantly, what we don't know. _____F_____

**11.** This knowledge eventually leads to self-realization. _____C_____

**12.** Making us more aware of our relationship to the world around us. _____F_____

**13.** Finally, we develop our potential to become independent learners. _____C_____

**14.** And creative problem solvers. _____F_____

● ● ●

**1.** Teaching report writing can be simple and effective. _____C_____

**2.** If an example-oriented approach is used. _____F_____

**3.** In this approach, students are given laboratory reports with varying degrees of completeness. _____C_____

**4.** The degree of completeness decreases with each successive experiment. _____C_____

**5.** With each report serving as an example for the completion of the next laboratory report. _____F_____

**6.** Thus the student is asked to complete a portion of his next report. _____C_____

**7.** Using the first report as his model. _____F_____

**8.** This process continues until the last few reports are reached. _____C_____

**9.** At which time the student is asked to complete these reports completely on his own. _____F_____

**10.** This approach ensures that the student learns by example. _____C_____

**11.** Rather than being told by an instructor what he has done wrong. _____F_____

**12.** Time is saved not only for the instructor but also for the student. _____C_____

**13.** Furthermore, educational objectives are not sacrificed. _____C_____

# Exercise 2.6—Correcting Run-Together Sentences

**1.** Here comes the store manager, she will tell us where to cash our cheque. _____R_____

**2.** Sam drove the pick-up truck, and Phil followed him in our family car. _____C_____

**3.** Our city applied for a Wintario grant, however its application was denied. _____R_____

**4.** History is an important subject, I find it fascinating. _____R_____

**5.** We searched long and hard for qualified computer programmers, but we couldn't find any. _____C_____

**6.** We have a swimming pool on our property we also have tennis courts.        R

**7.** Please turn off the television set, there is nothing on that is worth watching.        R

**8.** The bank teller made a mistake she gave me too much money.        R

**9.** Our living quarters were extremely cramped; nevertheless we stayed for two nights.        C

**10.** When I saw the storm approaching I ran for shelter; however, I was too slow and was caught in the downpour.        C

**11.** The Prime Minister of Canada is leaving for England next week, he will meet the British Prime Minister.        R

**12.** Please turn in your reports this Friday, I intend to mark them over the weekend.        R

**13.** That gray automobile is not mine, nor is it Susan's, it must be Lorraine's.        R

**14.** George bought an electric guitar, but his mother made him sell it.        C

**15.** Our corn crop is small this year, perhaps we haven't had enough spring rain.        R

**16.** She could never succeed at tennis, however hard she tried.        C

**17.** The team does not need a new locker room it needs a better coach.        R

**18.** While reviewing last year's budget, Harold discovered a serious error that bordered on criminal negligence.        C

**19.** The men brought the food the women brought the eating utensils.        R

**20.** I cannot drive more than three hours at a time, for some reason my left leg develops a cramp.        R

**21.** The library closes at 9:00 p.m., however, it opens again at 8:00 a.m.        R

**22.** Seven students failed the final examinations, they will have to repeat the course.        R

**23.** Nathalie received a traffic ticket because her car's left turn signal was not working.        C

**24.** Chalk and erasers are not needed, we will use an overhead projector and a flip chart.        R

**25.** What do you think of our plan should we alter it in any way?        R

**26.** Alice reported in sick, therefore we shall continue without her.        R

**27.** Wanting to get more studying done, Jim locked himself in his room for three hours.        C

**28.** Joy's Meat Market is now located near the river, the owner moved his store last week.        R

**29.** The city was devastated by an earthquake, but its citizens are determined to rebuild it from the rubble.        C

**30.** You help the children, I'll call the fire department.        R

## Exercise 2.7 — Revising Sentences in the Paragraph

Education is generally regarded as an experience that happens at a specified time in someone's life — and then recedes. It is too often considered an institutional process, providing us with certain definable skills that are directly associated with a specific occupation or a certain social status. Thus, for many of us, education becomes an outside activity with measurable benefits and rewards.

However, education's true nature is quite different; it is, in fact, an internal human function, one that implies intellectual and emotional growth. If we can think of it as an expansive process that allows us to deal thoughtfully with our culture and society, we will appreciate its dynamism. For if education means anything, it means change. It means a continuous interaction—a creative interaction—between man and his global environment. Therefore, in this context, we must not think of ourselves (educated people) as merely adapting to a patterned society, as if our culture were fixed and rigid — as if it were perfect, instead of perfectable.

What, then, are the real qualities and consequences of education? Well, for one, it is uncomfortable, for it never settles down. It calls up a seemingly infinite number of questions that do not have simple, quantifiable answers. It almost never provides but always demands. It suspects certainty, rejects equivocation, and resists conformity. It is, at best, disquieting and, at worst, frustrating and annoying.

In view of these qualities, it follows that educated people are never really satisfied. They are never, finally, at peace within their surroundings because they are constantly changing. Through the absorption of new and diverse ideas and perceptions, they seek meaningful relationships between different branches of knowledge. They are not interested in simply acquiring bits of information, but in testing ideas. Nor are they content with adapting to a specific societal value system, but are interested in developing their own values consistent with the larger reality of the global human family.

From this brief overview of the qualities of education, it can be seen that the phrase "getting an education" can never be transitional or confined to a certain period of time. "Education" is a word for all seasons and for all the ages of humanity.

## Exercise 2.8 — Recognizing Sentence Patterns

1. We found the lost camera, but we could not find its expensive attachments. — Cd

2. Don Hall works as a reporter for our local newspaper. — S

3. We finally relaxed after the election. — S

4. Sheila will have to work long hours if she expects to earn a company bonus. — Cx

5. The football game ended, but the excited fans refused to leave the stadium. — Cd

6. Paula was surprised when she was elected to the student council. — Cx

7. The intense snowstorm delayed our flight, but we managed to
check into a motel that was just one mile from the airport.        Cd-Cx

8. John Trask and Peter Soames cleaned and polished their new
sports cars.                                                        S

9. Turn left at the next traffic light; our office building is located on
the corner.                                                        Cd

10. Before you decide to buy a new car, please read the latest consumer reports; you may save yourself a great deal of time and
trouble.                                                           Cd-Cx

11. After the film we had dinner at an expensive restaurant.        S

12. We do not want special favours; we want only what is fair and
equitable.                                                         Cd

13. Tom is intellectually astute, but emotionally immature.         S

14. Please refrain from smoking in the restaurant.                  S

15. Phil found an urgent message when he returned home last night.  Cx

16. When the janitor saw the smoke pouring from the basement
window, he phoned the fire department; however the firefighters
arrived too late to save the building.                            Cd-Cx

17. I don't care who wrote the letter; it is too long and ungrammatical.  Cd

18. Don't forget to feed our pet canary.                            S

19. Last Saturday Steven mowed the lawn, trimmed the hedge, and
washed the car.                                                    S

20. Our school has a good academic reputation but a mediocre sports
program.                                                           S

21. If we cannot settle our differences without violence, then our
so-called civilized society will not survive.                     Cx

22. Our athletic club is now accepting new members; however, you
have only one week to apply.                                       Cd

23. Tina's new car, which she purchased only last week, has faulty
brakes and a leaky exhaust system.                                Cx

24. My brother has just graduated from university; he earned an "A"
average, which pleased my parents very much.                      Cd-Cx

25. The motorcycle skidded on the gravel, knocked over a lawn
chair, and tore up our flower garden.                             S

26. Stan Wojek, to his credit, never overcharges his customers; that is
why he has such a successful plumbing contracting business.       Cd

27. Chris and Don both swim and jog, but they do not enjoy team
sports.                                                            Cd

28. Calvin, who weighs only 95 pounds, is trying out for our football
team.                                                             Cx

29. Listening to classical music can be restful, if there are no
distractions.                                                     Cx

30. Our farm is losing money; therefore my father is selling it.    Cd

# Exercise 2.9 — Coordination

(Since there is no one correct revision, answers may vary; the following corrections reflect only one revision approach and may serve as a guideline.)

1. Sue might be young, but she is not immature.
2. We are reading short stories, essays, and modern drama.
3. Our school has three separate buildings, and each building has its own cafeteria; however, there is only one library.
4. Tom is either a professional athlete or a health club instructor.
5. Kathy is a writer and an actress, but she does not like being referred to as a movie star.
6. Our workers dug drainage ditches, laid cement pipe, repaired the overpass, and then ate their lunch.
7. Our city is not only clean and attractive but also prosperous.
8. My nephew is both a famous athlete and a radio sportscaster.
9. I was warned not to climb alone; however I did, and fell and broke my leg.
10. Her sister is neither a fashion model nor an actress, but a clothing designer in New York City.
11. The college basketball team will practise either on Thursday evening, or Saturday afternoon.
12. I bought a new notebook, sharpened all my pencils, and even turned my stereo off; nevertheless, I still have trouble writing.
13. We were told that the department store would be closed for inventory and to shop by using the mail-order catalogue; however, the store opened earlier than expected because of customers' complaints.
14. Dick is neither a university professor nor a high-school teacher.
15. I planted flowers, mowed the lawn, and even trimmed the hedges; but my property still needs professional landscaping.
16. Doris is either a good writer or a plagiarist.
17. Our home might be old, but it is not poorly constructed.
18. We were told to turn in our final essays on Friday; however, we ignored the deadline and were placed on academic probation.
19. Peggy cooked breakfast, fed the baby, reviewed her notes, and then wrote her newspaper article.
20. I am neither angry nor upset.

# Exercise 2.10 — Subordination

(Since there is no one correct revision, answers may vary; the following corrections reflect only one revision approach and may serve as a guideline.)

1. The hurricane destroyed more than fifty homes before it finally diminished.
2. Computer technology has advanced dramatically in the last five years.
3. The last major Montreal exposition was in 1967.

**4.** Our modern college gymnasium was used for a professional basketball game last winter.

**5.** The allies finally landed on the Normandy beaches in France on June 6, 1944.

**6.** I saw the bomb explode on Friday afternoon while sitting by my bedroom window.

**7.** Our community built an indoor ice-skating rink with the Wintario grant it received last year.

**8.** Aunt Martha arrived on a skateboard when she visited us last week.

**9.** I observed thousands of people protesting against the nuclear arms race last summer while hitchhiking through British Columbia.

**10.** The young girl nearly drowned because she was swimming in the lake without proper supervision.

**11.** The river, which was swift and relentless, overflowed its banks.

**12.** Our trailer home, which was located in a valley, was swept away by the surging waters.

**13.** We saw the mudslide begin while standing on a hillside that overlooked the town.

**14.** My family moved to Halifax, Nova Scotia, in 1965.

**15.** Our school, which once employed over twenty-five teachers, will be closed down next week.

**16.** Our hockey coach benched our two best players because he wanted to teach us a lesson on teamwork.

**17.** The experimental racing car, while attaining a speed of more than 175 miles per hour, blew a gasket and began smoking.

**18.** Sally saw an old lady being robbed by a gang of youths while she was on a theatre tour in New York City.

**19.** Michael discovered that the painting he bought at an auction was a masterpiece.

**20.** Our school bus was hit in the rear by a tractor-trailer while we were going to Cornwall on a field trip.

## Exercise 3.1 – Making Subject and Verb Agree

**1.** Neither of Paula's brothers (is/are) coming with us this evening. — is

**2.** The student counsellor, as well as the school principal, (was/were) given the award for excellence during our convocation. — was

**3.** Neither the nurses nor the doctor (is/are) responsible for hospital routine. — is

**4.** Each student, teacher, and administrator (favours/favour) the construction of a fully equipped gymnasium. — favours

**5.** There (was/were) discovered in the reading laboratory two comic books and a motorcycle maintenance manual. — were

**6.** In the center of the shopping plaza (is/are) a water fountain and a newspaper stand. — are

**7.** There certainly (is/are) more than one way to skin a cat. — is

**8.** The store's refrigerators, as well as its stoves, (come/comes) in a harvest-gold colour. — come

**9.** (Is/Are) *Julius Caesar* or *Antony and Cleopatra* scheduled for production this year?

is

**10.** In our Canadian Literature course, Alice Munro, as well as Mordecai Richler, (is/are) on our reading list.

is

**11.** None of the students (was/were) sufficiently prepared for the examination.

was

**12.** The number of automobile accidents (has been/have been) increasing the last five years.

has been

**13.** Everyone who attended our school dance (was/were), I am certain, impressed by the rock band.

was

**14.** Sandra and I are among the few who (takes/take) studying seriously.

take

**15.** Anyone who thinks he or she (deserves/deserve) special consideration had better think again.

deserves

**16.** Participating in the essay contest (were/was) one of the members of the basketball team.

was

**17.** Neither my textbook nor my class notes (was/were) permitted in the test room.

were

**18.** *The Thorn Birds* (is/are) on my summer reading list.

is

**19.** Only one athlete in ten (require/requires) more than eight hours sleep.

requires

**20.** Bruno, together with his sister Frieda, (have/has) enrolled in the computer literacy course.

has

**21.** Neither Helen nor I (are/am) responsible for the broken desks in the classroom.

am

**22.** The Disciplinary Committee (are/is) meeting behind closed doors.

is

**23.** The concerns of the parents for traffic safety (reflect/reflects) our City Council's concerns.

reflect

**24.** Phil's patience, as well as his determination, (enable/enables) him to be a first-class chess player.

enables

**25.** Every man, woman, and child (has been/have been) given explicit instructions.

has been

**26.** We were told that either the Ottawa Rough Riders or the Hamilton Tiger Cats (was/were) scheduled to play in our stadium this Sunday.

was

**27.** Susan, together with her friend, Leslie, (have/has) finally completed nursing training at our local community college.

has

**28.** Neither the convicts nor the prison administration (want/wants) additional security measures.

wants

**29.** After a full day of minding little children, peace and quiet (is/are) all that Martha desires.

is

**30.** Anybody who anticipated an easy essay question on the test (were/was) certainly disappointed, to say the least.

was

## Exercise 3.2—Making Pronouns Agree with Nouns

1. The technology class is trying to arrange (its/their) field trip next week.

its

2. Anyone who wants to attend the concert this Saturday should purchase (his/their) own ticket.

his

3. The young camper was told that (you/he) had to get up at 6:00 a.m. and make (his/your) own bed.

he-his

4. Everyone in the lecture hall was asked to turn in (their/his or her) test booklet when leaving the room.

his or her

5. Any actress not presently employed will receive (their/her) audition card tomorrow.

her

6. Mr. Johnson, along with his fellow workers, was asked to contribute some of (their/his) free time to work on the United Fund drive.

his

7. After debating with one another for hours, the team could not decide on (their/its) strategy for the next game.

their

8. Anyone who does not wish to participate in the touch-football game will be asked to arrange (their/his or her) own transportation to our annual picnic.

his or her

9. Everyone but Frank completed (their/his) two-mile run this morning.

his

10. Neither of the lawyers could account for (their/her) client's whereabouts last Tuesday.

her

11. Neither the sales agent nor the buyers could get (their/his) price for the merchandise.

their

12. The rules covering student behaviour can be found in (its/their) entirety in the Student Handbook.

their

13. No member of the teaching staff will be permitted to take (his or her/their) holidays in the fall.

his or her

14. Our school's hockey team lost (their/its) final game.

its

15. Both Jan and Carol received (their/her) scholastic awards at the banquet last night.

their

16. Each member of the audience must watch (their/his or her) TV monitor for the applause sign.

his or her

17. Neither the department manager nor her staff members expected (their/her) budget to be slashed.

their

18. Those who want to use our houseboat next weekend must pay (his/their) share of the rent.

their

19. As I entered the bank, the sign directed (you/me) to follow the painted arrows on the floor.

me

20. If anyone wishes to enjoy (himself/themselves/theirselves), (he/they) should visit Banff National Park.

himself-he

21. Every member of the school band received (his or her/their) due recognition as a qualified musician.

his or her

22. Nobody would refuse if (he or she/they) were offered a chance to attend the winter Olympic Games.

    he or she

23. The *Ottawa Citizen* assigned (its/their) most experienced journalist to the kidnapping story.

    its

24. Either of my classmates will be happy to lend you (their/his) biology notes.

    his

25. When I joined the exercise program, I was told that (you/I) had to have a gym suit and cushioned running shoes.

    I

26. Neither the arbitrator nor the union members could submit (his/their) salary recommendations before the strike deadline.

    their

27. The student body will choose (its/their) next president tomorrow.

    its

28. The jury (have been/has been) deliberating for three days.

    have been

29. Our school principal, together with her academic chairmen, will be submitting (her/their) budget recommendations to the Board of Governors next week.

    her

30. Every team member will memorize (his/their) blocking assignments by tomorrow.

    his

## Exercise 3.3 – Review of Agreement

1. Someone is in the auditorium; it sounds as if (they/he) (is/are) bouncing a basketball.

    he      is

2. The teacher will tutor any member of the class who (wants/want) to improve (their/his or her) math score.

    his or her      wants

3. Our purchasing department (was/were) working ten-hour days since (its/their) budget was slashed twenty per cent.

    its      was

4. One of the weather forecasters in our meteorological section (predict/predicts) that (their/his) function will be taken over by the new weather satellite.

    his      predicts

5. Either Lisa or Marie will sponsor the new legislation when (they/she) (returns/return) home from the West Coast.

    she      returns

6. A book of lottery tickets (were/was) lost in the men's locker room. (They/it) should be taken to the lost and found department.

    it      was

7. Neither Peter nor Vincent (is/are) aware that (he/they) won lottery prizes.

    he      is

8. Any person in our department who (exceed/exceeds) the speed limit will have (their/his or her) driver's licence revoked.

    his or her      exceeds

9. Both Clarence and George thought that (he/they) (were/was) refused membership in the country club because of racial discrimination.

    they      were

10. Common sense, as well as decisiveness, (is/
    are) necessary for someone to do (his/their) job
    properly in our organization.

    his      is

11. If either our teacher or our administrators (fail/
    fails) to take into account (his/their) academic
    responsibilities, then our class will not be pre-
    pared for the competition in the technology fair.

    their      fail

12. Among Kelly's favourite films (are/is) *Star
    Wars* and *Raiders of the Lost Ark*; she has
    seen (them/it) many times.

    them      are

13. A string of firecrackers (was/were) found in the
    classroom, but none of our students was re-
    sponsible for (their/its) presence.

    its      was

14. Dr. Slaughter is one of those people who
    (enjoys/enjoy) both jazz and country music for
    (its/their) unique appeal to different ethnic and
    racial backgrounds.

    their      enjoys

15. (Was/were) there further recommendations by
    anyone at the meeting who wanted (their/his
    or her) views known to the safety committee?

    his or her      were

16. Everyone must write a final examination if
    (they/he or she) (expect/expects) to get credit
    for the course.

    he or she      expects

17. Joan is one employee in ten who (listens/listen)
    carefully to the instructions given to (them/her)
    by the plant supervisor.

    her      listens

18. The college camera club (are/is) meeting next
    week to discuss (its/their) budget.

    its      is

19. No one has experienced frustration until
    (they/he or she) (try/tries) to learn the sport of
    golf.

    he or she      tries

20. Each of my nephews (live/lives) in a different
    Canadian city, but (he/they) will return to
    Ottawa for our family reunion.

    they      lives

21. Our English teacher, along with several of her
    students, (are/is) decorating (her/their) class-
    room for the crafts display next Monday.

    her      is

22. There (wasn't/weren't) anyone in the football
    stadium who did not receive (his or her/their)
    free bumper sticker.

    his or her      wasn't

23. Our neighbour, in addition to several other resi-
    dents, (belong/belongs) to the Neighbourhood
    Watch Committee, and each person is assigned
    (their/his or her) specific area.

    his or her      belongs

24. Neither the firefighter nor the building super-
    visor (was/were) aware that (he/they) did not

|  |  |  |
|---|---|---|
| have the correct key to the garage where the fire was located. | he | was |

**25.** Both Kim and her sister's friend, Beverly, (was/were) certain that (she/they) were going to receive athletic scholarships. — they — were

**26.** Each doctor, nurse, and laboratory assistant (wear/wears) (their/his or her) own radiation suit when working in the nuclear medicine laboratory. — his or her — wears

**27.** Each of our new sales girls (performs/perform) (their/her) duties with enthusiasm and good will. — her — performs

**28.** Neither Bill nor I (are/am) sure that both Denise and Jo Anne will pay for (their/her) own lunch. — their — am

**29.** Every citizen in our community who (fail/fails) to register to vote by next Tuesday will receive a telephone call at (their/his or her) residence by one of our volunteers. — his or her — fails

**30.** The jury (are/is) in closed session and won't announce (their/its) verdict until at least next Monday. — its — is

## Exercise 3.4—Revising the Paragraph for Agreement

Since the invention of the atomic bomb, control of nuclear weapons has become not only desirable but absolutely essential. In the past, any nation at war was able to kill its enemy without physically affecting the rest of the world. After all, since the end of the Second World War there have been quite a few small-scale wars around the globe, and those people not directly affected hardly suffered at all: their lifestyle did not radically change; their social environment remained relatively stable; and they were able to do business as usual. Our response to these wars — from the war in Vietnam to the Falkland Islands — was generally revulsion and disgust at the obscenity of someone slaughtering his fellow man. But at the same time people knew that so long as these wars were restricted to conventional weapons, they were relatively safe — that the bombs, land mines, and artillery shells, along with the new Exocet missile, were capable of devastating only a limited geographical area.

With the proliferation of nuclear weapons, however, the odds against a small war being limited are lowering. Too many nations are storing nuclear weapons. Too many many nations use war as the only means of solving problems, and almost none, it seems, values human rights over militarism. So long as any one of these war-like countries was fighting with swords and spears, other nations were relatively safe. Now, however, fanaticism has risen to the surface and is gaining access to nuclear technology. As a consequence, our planet has never been more at peril.

Today our so-called civilization seems to have embraced war as a logical — even a moral — alternative to the political process. One cannot get through a twenty-four hour day without reading about a new international crisis caused by military action. No nation trusts its neighbour; there is no rational dialogue, no common sense, no moral commitment to peace, and certainly no political leadership. So we are caught in a psychological bind from which there does not seem to be any means of escape. But if we do not soon find a solution to this insane nuclear arms race, our children will be the endangered species.

# Exercise 4.1 — Choosing Verb Forms

1. Please (set/sit) the statue on the pedestal.                                 set

2. The police officer (lay/laid) wounded on the floor while the bank robbers cleaned out the vault.                                 lay

3. Here is the woman who was (suppose/supposed) to carry our flag in the Canada Day parade.                                 supposed

4. George is the man who (swum/swam) across Lake Ontario last year.                                 swam

5. When Deborah and I were university students, we (use/used) to study together.                                 used

6. By the time our friends returned from their fishing excursion, we had already (ate/eaten) our lunch.                                 eaten

7. My brother had never (flew/flown) on a jet airplane before today.                                 flown

8. Susan has already (rang/rung) for room service.                                 rung

9. There are twenty-four paintings to be (hanged/hung) before the art auction can begin.                                 hung

10. Please (sit/set) the dishes in the sink after you finish your breakfast.                                 set

11. Harold's cabin cruiser (sprang/sprung) a leak when he grazed a rock while avoiding a speedboat.                                 sprang

12. Paul and Sarah were severely sunburned because they had (lain/laid) on the beach all afternoon.                                 lain

13. Our baseball game had already (begun/began) when the thunderstorm arrived.                                 begun

14. We were (suppose/supposed) to turn in our laboratory assignments yesterday.                                 supposed

15. The team members left their equipment (laying/lying) all over the locker-room floor.                                 lying

16. After procrastinating for two weeks, I have finally (wrote/written) to my sister in Calgary.                                 written

17. The murderer was finally (hanged/hung) after his appeal was denied by the Supreme Court.                                 hanged

18. Just as the jury members were (rising/raising) from their seats the judge dismissed the witnesses and declared a mistrial.                                 rising

19. Our student government had already (chose/chosen) a president before the school semester began.                                 chosen

**20.** The mayor of our city (don't/doesn't) cast a vote in city council
deliberations, unless there is a tie.                                    doesn't

**21.** I do not think that she has ever (come/came) to one of our
meetings on time.                                                        come

**22.** The athletic director has (spoke/spoken) very highly of Jane's
gymnastic ability.                                                       spoken

**23.** If the second baseman had (threw/thrown) the ball to the catcher,
the runner would have been out at home plate.                           thrown

**24.** We already (seen/saw) the science-fiction film, *Star Wars*.        saw

**25.** The singer, during the course of the evening, (sang/sung) many
protest songs of the sixties.                                           sang

**26.** We could have all (went/gone) to the theatre together if Jack and
Sue had arrived on time.                                                gone

**27.** The majority of the people at the picnic thought they had
(saw/seen) a flying saucer.                                             seen

**28.** The sales agent (rung/rang) the bell a number of times, but nobody
answered the door.                                                     rang

**29.** If we had only (knew/known) the combination to the lock,
we could have saved a great deal of time and trouble.                  known

**30.** The jury members were (swore/sworn) to secrecy before they
were allowed to enter the jury room.                                   sworn

## Exercise 4.2 — Correcting Verb Errors

| | | |
|---|---|---|
| **1** | | |
| Last summer I worked on a construction crew in | C | |
| **2** | | |
| the province of Nova Scotia. We had built | 2 | built |
| **3** | | |
| roads and repaired bridges, and sometimes | C | |
| **4** | | |
| have worked ten hours a day. When I started | 4 | worked |
| **5** | | |
| the job, in early May, I weigh one-hundred and | | |
| eighty-five pounds, but by the end of August I | 5 | weighed |
| **6** | | |
| lost twenty pounds as well as two inches around my | 6 | had lost |
| **7** | | |
| waist. I earned enough money to pay for my | C | |
| **8** | | |
| university tuition, and I even have had enough | | |
| left over to buy a used motorcycle. I would | | |
| recommend construction work to any student who | 8 | had |

**9**

had to earn money during the summer months to
finance his or her education. I would suggest,          9          has

**10**

however, that he or she were in excellent
physical condition; for the work, although          10          be

**11**

financially rewarding, will be extremely strenuous
and exhausting.          11          is

## Exercise 4.3 − Using the Proper Pronoun Case

1. No one asked Tom and (I/me) to try out for the swimming team.          me
2. There is no one as well qualified to lead our group as (her/she).          she
3. Just between you and (me/I), there doesn't seem to be any chalk in the classroom.          me
4. There was a great deal of support for (him/his) being named the valedictorian at our graduation ceremony.          his
5. I believe it was (him/he) who wore the orange sneakers to class.          he
6. (Whoever/Whomever) is ready to eat lunch may get his or her hamburger from the barbecue.          Whoever
7. The scoring title was shared by Stephen and (I/me/myself).          me
8. (Us/We/Our) having to wait for the umpire to arrive was the reason our baseball game was delayed.          Our
9. (Whom/Who) do you think will win the beauty contest this year?          Who
10. We think that the chores should be shared equally between (he and she/him and her).          him and her
11. (We/Us) office workers should form a union before it is too late.          We
12. Everyone but (him/he) contributed to our auction sale.          him
13. Do you think Bikash is a better student than (I/me)?          I
14. It was (her/she) who found the silk purse.          she
15. The best runners in the history of our marathon race were (them/they).          they
16. Please give this enrollment sheet to (whomever/whoever) enters the room.          whomever
17. The teacher (hisself/himself) told us that class was cancelled next Friday.          himself
18. Verna saw (him/his) copying someone else's homework.          him
19. The broken desk was placed between Fred and (I/me/myself).          me
20. The political leaders (theirselves/themselves) are contributing to our high inflation rate.          themselves
21. It was she, I believe, (whom/who) was selected to represent our school at the academic conference in Toronto.          who
22. Phil earned more money than (me/I/myself) over the summer.          I
23. Our team members are not as well coached as (them/they).          they

24. (Them/Their) agreeing to sell lottery tickets came as a big surprise.    <u>Their</u>

25. Everything will be ready for you and (she/her) when the curtain is raised and the footlights go on.    <u>her</u>

26. We shall share our prize money with (whomever/whoever) we wish.    <u>whomever</u>

27. Both Jennifer and (I/me) bought the same hat.    <u>I</u>

28. Ivan as well as (I/me/myself) will serve drinks at our parents' anniversary party.    <u>I</u>

29. I think Claire is much more talented than (her/she).    <u>she</u>

30. (Them/They) and the school janitor are responsible for the security of the building.    <u>They</u>

## Exercise 4.4 — Confusing Adjectives and Adverbs

1. My sister was once a (real/really) fine commercial artist.    <u>really</u>

2. These pickles taste (bitter/bitterly).    <u>bitter</u>

3. The child's birthday party certainly went very (smooth/smoothly).    <u>smoothly</u>

4. The dog appeared (vicious/viciously), so the mailman did not approach the front lawn of the house.    <u>vicious</u>

5. Our soccer team played very (well/good) last Saturday.    <u>well</u>

6. The team's desire to win was (real/really) intense during the second half of the football game.    <u>really</u>

7. The tragedies of Shakespeare (surely/sure) must be in our school library.    <u>surely</u>

8. The teachers acted (different/differently) outside the classroom.    <u>differently</u>

9. The lunch bell sounded (shrill/shrilly) throughout the empty hallways.    <u>shrill</u>

10. She is the (most silliest/silliest) girl I know.    <u>silliest</u>

11. We feel (joyful/joyfully) as the Christmas season approaches.    <u>joyful</u>

12. Marg and Betty felt (bad/badly) when they heard that Sam's mother was seriously ill.    <u>bad</u>

13. If he had given directions more (accurate/accurately) we would have arrived much earlier.    <u>accurately</u>

14. Viola felt (good/well) after she received the results of her blood test.    <u>good</u>

15. She writes (quick/quickly) but speaks slowly.    <u>quickly</u>

16. Patricia's essays are (more neatly/neater) done that Pam's.    <u>more neatly</u>

17. The quiz-show contestant looked (strange/strangely) after he won the first prize.    <u>strange</u>

18. Our hockey coach works more (diligently/diligent) at our practice sessions than your hockey coach.    <u>diligently</u>

19. This (loose/loosely) tied bundle will not survive the trip.    <u>loosely</u>

20. The passenger train went (slow/slowly) as it approached the overpass.    <u>slowly</u>

21. Our teacher made the essay test (easier/more easy) than the multiple-choice quiz.    <u>easier</u>

22. Wally must be one of the (most laziest/laziest) people I ever met.    <u>laziest</u>

| | |
|---|---|
| **23.** This is the (worse/worst) winter we've ever had. | worst |
| **24.** I feel (sick/sickly) whenever anyone mentions raw oysters. | sick |
| **25.** Her banana-cream pie is (more sweet/sweeter) than her coconut-custard pie. | sweeter |
| **26.** The recently polished coffee table felt (smooth/smoothly). | smooth |
| **27.** Our physics laboratory is certainly (more clean/cleaner) than their chemistry laboratory. | cleaner |
| **28.** She behaved (differently/different) from anyone in the room. | differently |
| **29.** We did not realize that you felt so (strongly/strong) about nuclear disarmament. | strongly |
| **30.** Bert played (awful/awfully) in the final game of our annual bridge tournament. | awfully |

## Exercise 4.5 — Revising the Paragraph to Solve Special Problems

When my friend Peter and I tried out for a professional football team, we expected to be treated no differently from anyone else. We thought that if we worked hard and wanted to make the team badly enough, we would be given an impartial trial like everyone else. Boy, were we mistaken. I never knew what the term "rookie" implied until Peter and I reported to our first training camp.

Our receiving a different colour jersey from the rest of the players was the first indication that we would be treated differently. Then we were told not to talk to the veteran players unless they spoke to us first. Next, we were seated in the gloomiest end of the team cafeteria and were always served last.

Also, almost every day Peter and I had to help the trainers lug the tackling dummies and the blocking sleds on and off the practice field. And during calesthenics the veterans would often stand around and jeer at us for being clumsy and inept. Furthermore, sometimes they and the coaches, who were veteran players themselves, would make us do extra laps around the track because we moved too slowly when carrying practice equipment.

Peter and I were made to feel that we were outsiders who were trying to join a close-knit fraternity who had earned their unique status in combat. They had the scars of battle, and all we had was a burning desire to play a game we loved with the best players available.

## Exercise 5.1 — Improving Pronoun Reference

(The revisions that replace or remove pronouns will vary; the following revisions may serve as guidelines.)

**1.** I spend most of my spare time on tennis lessons because tennis is my favourite sport.

**2.** Sue told Jane that Jane's dog was in the yard without a leash.

**3.** The stereo my uncle gave me for my birthday pleased me a great deal.

**4.** I have not played soccer since graduating from high school, but I am still very much interested in the game.

5. Because Christine's older sister is a nurse, nursing is the profession that Christine wants to enter.

6. We inquired about our concert tickets at the information booth, but the clerks couldn't tell us when the tickets would be mailed.

7. After I parked my truck next to the limousine, I noticed that the truck's tire was flat.

8. Whenever I telephone City Hall, the operator puts me on hold.

9. As our football team entered the crowded stadium, the fans rose and gave us a deafening cheer.

10. Correct.

11. My brother tried out for the school basketball team, but he was informed that he was not big enough to play basketball.

12. Nothing we do ever pleases her, which makes us angry.

13. Correct.

14. I never saw a real volcano, but I am certainly fascinated by volcanos.

15. The seacoast had snow because of a low pressure system to the south of us.

16. Because coffee is the national beverage of Brazil, the people of Brazil drink it every day.

17. The flight attendant asked the passengers if the flight had been comfortable.

18. The lawyer said to the client, ''Your case is coming to trial next Friday.''

19. Sheila's volunteering to donate her time to the Muscular Dystrophy campaign was appreciated.

20. The menu has a special on roast beef.

21. Our committee could not reach a decision yesterday on the budget because the deliberation was too difficult.

22. Steven flunked his biology examination; he therefore enrolled in summer school.

23. I phoned the police department and told the police officer about my car being stolen.

24. After living in an apartment for many years, I have come to dislike apartment living.

25. Gloria, in her latest magazine article, writes about communal living.

26. Dan told Mel that Mel's garden needed weeding.

27. After my cousin returned from Saudi Arabia, he could not stop commenting on the religious fervour of its people.

28. Helen's continuous talking during the concert recital disturbed the person sitting next to her.

29. Fran was annoyed when she was told to keep her opinions to herself.

30. I know I am not supposed to eat this chocolate bar, but I can't stop snacking on chocolate bars.

## Exercise 5.2 — Revising the Paragraph for Clear Pronoun Reference

1. The day the circus came to our town was one of the most important events of the season. As a young boy I felt that circus people were somehow magical, endowed with mysterious abilities. As I watched the tents being raised and the performers practising, I thought that this

activity was one of the most exciting things I had ever seen. In the lion tamer's cage, for instance, the lion tamer was holding back three ferocious lions with only a whip and a chair. And the clowns' acrobatics were something to behold; I thought surely the clowns would break their necks jumping off those high ladders. But to me the most thrilling experience of the day occurred when I was allowed to ride an elephant. The handlers made the elephant kneel, and then they lifted me onto a huge saddle strapped on its back and told me to hang on. They then led the elephant around a track close to the main tent while I waved at all of the performers. After this experience, the formal opening of the circus was almost anti-climactic. To this day I can still recall the excitement that only a young boy of thirteen could feel who was allowed, for a time, to experience the magical world of the circus.

2. Mass confusion existed the day our school had a fire drill. The fire wardens led our class into the hall and made us wait there until all of the other classes were assembled. By this time the hall was full of laughing and shouting students. Also the bell continued ringing, which prevented us from hearing the wardens' instructions. Even the teachers were disgusted at the way the drill was organized. When we were finally led outside—at least ten minutes after the bell had begun ringing—we were left standing in the rain while the wardens checked to see if everyone was out of the building. This drill spoiled the entire afternoon, for once we were back inside the classroom, it was too late to see the film that the teacher had started to show us before the fire drill began. I guess the school administrators learned their lesson, though, for a confusing drill like that never happened again for the rest of the semester.

# Exercise 5.3 — Misplaced Modifiers

(Corrections may vary.)

1. With much enthusiasm the opera singer sang the aria.
2. Phil told Martha they would leave for their lakeside cottage on Saturday.
3. In the new restaurant we ate seafood chowder that had too much garlic in it.
4. Frequently, a person who sings is happy.
5. Please indicate on the back of the order form if you wish us to send you our latest product directory.
6. If the weather is pleasant, Henry intends to go golfing on one of the Thousand Islands.
7. Correct.
8. At our community college, we heard the debate on waste disposal sites.
9. By the end of the week I had earned almost a hundred dollars in tips.
10. On Tuesday our insurance agent told us to decide if we wanted to update our insurance policy.
11. We collected nearly three thousand signatures on our petition.
12. Correct.
13. I purchased my bicycle with chrome fenders from Canadian Tire.
14. The visiting hockey player from Winnipeg stayed overnight at our house.

15. Only Sophie and Vic finished their novels by the assigned date.

16. I sing in the shower almost every day.

17. Never purchase a personal computer with a built-in disk drive from a department store.

18. With only a brief smile of goodbye, he left on his expedition to the Antarctic.

19. Often, jogging strengthens the heart and lungs.

20. We intend to enter the beauty contest, whether or not you approve.

21. We listen almost every evening to rock music on the radio.

22. In the school library Sandra read a novel that contained romance and adventure.

23. Mother told us to mow the lawn and trim the hedge on Friday.

24. Who was that woman with purple shorts who gave you the canary?

25. Paul drove his motorbike nearly two hundred miles to Toronto.

26. With great sorrow, our teacher showed us our marks.

27. Often, eating causes obesity.

28. Last summer my girlfriend from Germany stayed at our school dormitory.

29. We finally found our motorcycle with a broken windshield in the school parking lot.

30. Only Tracy and Kim were selected to audition for the new dramatic play.

# Exercise 5.4 — Revising the Paragraph to Correct Misplaced Modifiers

My sister ran almost twenty-four miles in the marathon race on Sunday. Her performance was remarkable when you consider that she practised only two weeks before the race and never ran more than ten miles. She intended to enter the twelve-mile race if there were any more spaces, but that race had a full complement of runners. Nevertheless, she was the only one of five racers over the age of thirty-five to run more than twenty miles.

Everyone in our family is extremely proud of her, and we now know that, with a little determination, we can also aspire to what she accomplished on Sunday. Most people know that by jogging often, one's cardio-vascular system and muscle tone are improved, but not many people realize that frequent running also improves one's self-image. Therefore, starting Monday, I intend to follow my sister's example by jogging at least five miles every day.

# Exercise 5.5 — Dangling Modifiers

(Revisions may vary.)

1. Because Bill was reluctant to put all his weight on the damaged ankle, the coach removed him from the game.

2. While sailing on Lake Winnipeg, we saw many beautiful boats.

3. While I was skiing downhill without goggles, my eyes were stung by sleet and snow.

4. To attain high marks in computer science, one must spend many hours of practice on the computer terminal.

5. After sitting for two hours in the doctor's office, I was finally called into the examining room.

6. While I was jogging slowly through the woods, my eye was caught by a scampering woodchuck.

7. Correct.

8. Once he was out of the city, the air pollution no longer made his eyes water.

9. Correct.

10. While travelling from Halifax, Nova Scotia, to Saint John, New Brunswick, we saw many quaint farmhouses.

11. After hearing her arguments for nuclear disarmament, I have changed my position on nuclear proliferation.

12. As one of the leaders in our community, he must challenge this slander.

13. Because Dorothy was afraid to eat any more pickle relish, she had the waiter remove the relish tray from her table.

14. After he was finally introduced to one of Canada's leading actors, they found nothing to talk about.

15. To win at poker, you must take many risks.

16. Correct.

17. Like many of today's students, Magda believes that financial security is a high priority.

18. After reading five chapters of her latest novel, I think her theme is still unclear.

19. Correct.

20. Great dedication and perseverance are necessary for one to become a first-class gymnast.

21. When I was only two years old, my family moved from a large city to a small farming community.

22. After installing the muffler, you must clamp the tailpipe properly.

23. When the cake was thoroughly risen, Mother removed it from the oven.

24. Correct.

25. After I danced for twenty-four hours in the marathon, the doctor told me to soak my feet and have my head examined.

26. To obtain all your rights as citizens, you must know the laws of our country.

27. Before you swim in the ocean, make sure there are lifeguards on duty.

28. After I examined my shopping receipts, it became obvious that I was overcharged at the clothing store.

29. Correct.

30. Once he was out of the office, the piped-in music no longer gave him a headache.

# Exercise 5.6 — Revising the Paragraph to Remove Dangling Modifiers

The computer applications conference I attended in Toronto was certainly a worthwhile experience. I met some very important and interesting people working in today's computer environment. The knowledge I gained about systems management while attending the seminars, which were conducted by highly trained professionals, will, I feel, be invaluable in the future. Since I am a former computer programmer, this training experience allowed me to realize the enormous potential for computers in a modern office environment. To be successful in today's competitive marketplace, we must all pursue professional development as an intrinsic part of our working lives.

Therefore, I would highly recommend that everyone in our management group attend the next conference because, like many of today's managers, we must realize that knowledge of computer applications is our bread and butter. Also, for your convenience, I have attached to my letter a detailed evaluation of the seminars I attended. If you have any questions or require further information, my office will be happy to respond.

## Exercise 5.7 — Correcting Faulty Parallelism

(Revisions may vary.)

1. I decided to live in this city because I wanted a better job, an active social life, and a clean environment.
2. My sister was a teacher, a school principal, and finally a successful business executive.
3. Carl not only wants to compete but also to win a gold medal.
4. Our next door neighbour, who is a shy and quiet man and who is a member of the local Rotary Club, was once a commando in the Canadian Armed Forces.
5. She is neither young nor inexperienced.
6. My father's car is sporty, fast, expensive, and also quite comfortable.
7. Correct.
8. Our school's computers are more advanced than the computers in your school.
9. Soccer, which is Europe's most popular sport, is becoming more popular every year in North America.
10. I am either going to study electrical engineering at university or electrical technology at our local community college.
11. Correct.
12. My parents always have voted and always will vote in the national election.
13. She contributes to and works for the peace movement in Canada.
14. Fernando practises strenuously every day.
15. Dominic not only works hard but studies hard.
16. Jake helps his wife by dusting and by cooking his own meals.
17. Correct.
18. She plays either a flute or an oboe in the symphony orchestra.
19. Our city's buildings are not as modern as the buildings in your city.
20. Both our teachers and our students wanted the gymnasium repainted.
21. My favourite teacher, who is a native of Australia and who is also our tennis coach, is moving to another city next semester.
22. An industrial plant with well-motivated and qualified workers and with the latest high-technology equipment will succeed in today's competitive marketplace.
23. My sister asked for the family car and for permission to stay out after twelve o'clock.
24. If I had my choice of seeing a rock concert or an opera, I would choose the opera.

**25.** My teacher asked me to state my opinion of the short story and to talk about the main character.

**26.** Correct.

**27.** Sky-diving is extremely hazardous and requires great skill and concentration.

**28.** My mother studied physics and mathematics, and now she is studying world history.

**29.** Maria not only collects old coins but also stamps.

**30.** Hockey in Canada is more popular than hockey in the United States.

## Exercise 5.8 — Revising the Paragraph to Improve Parallelisms

**1.** The introduction should not only motivate readers to read the body of your report, but should contain the purpose of the report, the background and limits of the problem, and the guidelines of the solution. There may be instances, however, when your introduction need only include the purpose of the report; for example, your readers may have already familiarized themselves with the general areas of your research and are conversant with the technical context of your development and proposed solution. You must be careful, though, not to give the impression that you will deal with larger problems than your report actually covers; for nothing is more frustrating to readers than being led to expect more than they are actually given. Readers always have rebelled and always will at being misled by promises in the introduction that are not developed in the body and fulfilled in the conclusion.

**2.** What can we do to improve the image of science and technology as something that can be understood and controlled by ordinary men? Well, we can start by educating the public, both in and outside of school, in the way in which scientific discoveries affect our daily lives. We may pursue this educational process in a number of ways: in our schools we can arrange student field trips to high-technology industries so that students can see for themselves the direct applications of scientific developments; we can invite speakers working in the mainstream of science who can talk about their work in progress; and we can organize more scientific forums where different students can exchange ideas. In the non-academic sector, we can devote more newspaper and magazine space to news stories that are scientifically oriented, and we can sponsor more television programs that examine, in layman's language, present and future research in science and technology.

For too long now the average citizen has been suspicious of and apprehensive about the methods science uses to understand nature; therefore it is about time we opened some windows and let in some fresh air. Strengthening our lines of communication would be an excellent and a solid beginning.

## Exercise 6.1 — Spelling

**1.** Our organization is libel for the damages if our victory party gets out of control.                                                   liable

**2.** We must adapt a new method of evaluation before proceeding.          adopt

**3.** His conscience would not let him dessert his helpless comrades. — desert

**4.** Sally can breath under water for two minutes as long as she remains stationary. — breathe

**5.** Their could not be a better site for our new gymnasium. — There

**6.** The principles of mathematics are absolute. — C

**7.** This welding devise was formerly owned by the city engineering department. — device

**8.** Thelma went straight to her academic advisor for council. — counsel

**9.** Our house is situated in a quiet part of town, were there are no commercial buildings or apartment houses. — where

**10.** My yearly health examination was quite thorough, but I past with flying colours. — passed

**11.** Our high-school band, led by two drum majorettes, proceeded us into the football stadium. — preceded

**12.** Our plant personnel must be safety conscious at all times. — C

**13.** When my best friend immigrated to Australia, I felt deserted. — emigrated

**14.** We do not know whether he is threw repairing the duplicating machine. — through

**15.** I do not know were my English course is being held. — where

**16.** Danielle could not hike any further because the heel came off her boot. — farther

**17.** Please tell me whose responsible for enrolling students in their proper courses. — who's

**18.** Our school principal excepted the safety award on behalf of the staff and students. — accepted

**19.** Stella's marks were higher then Barbara's, but both their marks were lower than Olaf's. — than

**20.** I asked for a leave of absense, and my supervisor assented. — absence

**21.** I was eighteen when my first child was borne. — born

**22.** The scoutmaster led us to shelter when the lightening struck the tree, but the storm soon passed, allowing us to proceed with our hike. — lightning

**23.** Its too bad that City Council will not pass more stringent pollution regulations. — It's

**24.** You must site the sources of your quotations before turning in your essays. — cite

**25.** Our office has quite enough stationary for our immediate needs. — stationery

**26.** They're sure that we are not too late to register for next semester. — C

**27.** We have a full compliment of workers; all we need is more work. — complement

**28.** Our team is liable to loose its next game if we do not permit our athletes to use the practice field this Friday. — lose

**29.** My reasons for resigning are personal; please do not attempt to council me any further. — counsel

**30.** Of the two distinct procedures, the later proved more cost effective and adaptable. — latter

# Exercise 7.1 — Commas That Separate Independent Clauses and Elements in a Series

(Corrections underlined.)

1. Do you like to snack on pretzels, peanuts, or potato chips?     W
2. Irving has already eaten, but his brother is still waiting to be served.     W
3. Did she want both a salad and a cup of soup?     C
4. My car needs an oil change and a tune-up and a new left front tire.     C
5. We won the game but lost the match.     C
6. Initially, William resisted the pressure to have his name placed in nomination, but he finally relented after realizing that he was the overwhelming choice of the nominating committee.     W
7. The bank tellers tried to form a union, but they could not muster enough votes.     C
8. Our chairperson sent us each a memorandum and then called a general meeting.     C
9. Both Alexandria and Hector are intelligent and industrious and generous.     C
10. Last summer our province was hit by a severe drought, several small tornadoes, and a flash flood that caused millions of dollars worth of damage.     W
11. The summer sale will begin on Thursday and end on Saturday.     C
12. Tomorrow the school cafeteria will serve either hot dogs and baked beans or fish and chips.     C
13. Our entertainment committee planned the menu, rented the hall, and hired the band.     W
14. My music teacher was once a famous concert pianist, but now he rarely gives concerts.     W
15. All of the faculty members think that the school semester is too long, that classes are too large, and that the grading system is too lenient.     W
16. My father's company manufactures circuit boards, computer chips, and small batteries.     W
17. The school band plays in city parades and at half-time shows during the football season.     C
18. During our trip to Disney world we visited science exhibits, ate in a Polynesian restaurant, and went on amusement rides.     W
19. Dylan and Sean auditioned for the play, but they were not chosen for any of the major roles.     W
20. John bought the computer and then never used it.     C
21. Potato salad and cold meat and hot dogs are my favourite picnic foods.     C
22. I entered the room, closed the blinds, and then went to bed.     W
23. The film we saw last night was too long and too violent and much too juvenile.     C

**24.** Mr. Lammons sent the package last Thursday, but we never
received it until this Wednesday.                                          W

**25.** The children ran into the school yard, jumped on the swings,
climbed on the monkey bars, and then began celebrating the
beginning of their summer recess.                                         W

**26.** Our parents think that we should learn about the harmful effects
of drugs, alcohol, and tobacco.                                           W

**27.** The severe thunderstorm blew down small trees, knocked down
telephone wires, and short-circuited the power lines.                     W

**28.** Maureen's clothes are chic and well-tailored and expensive.       C

**29.** The game began on time, but half the spectators were still not seated.   W

**30.** Dr. Harrington was a famous surgeon and the first to perform
a heart transplant operation in our province.                             C

# Exercise 7.2 — Commas That Separate Coordinate Adjectives and Confusing Sentence Elements

**1.** With Michael, Lisa was quite secure.                               W

**2.** Hugh wore a light brown suit and a dark green tie.                  C

**3.** The cold, damp, dreary afternoon lowered everyone's spirits.       W

**4.** High above, the workers placed another girder on the skeleton
of the new apartment building.                                            W

**5.** They finally released the snowy white doves over the cavernous
football stadium.                                                         C

**6.** Something must be done about our slow, inefficient, outdated
transportation system.                                                    W

**7.** Inside, the factory thermometer reached 35 degrees celsius.        W

**8.** He hit a high fly ball to the speedy left fielder.                 C

**9.** The long, lonely, tedious hours that I spent on my meticulous
historical research finally paid off with an ''A'' grade on my final
term paper.                                                               W

**10.** By nine, fifty people were lined up outside the department store.  W

**11.** We stood on the shore and watched the swift, graceful sailboats
glide across the azure blue lake.                                         W

**12.** Our new computer literacy course was offered in one of our
largest, refurbished, well-lighted classrooms on the first floor.        W

**13.** Without stopping, the subway train rushed by the station platform.  W

**14.** Hurrying to greet his family in the crowded airport lounge, Henry
tripped over a small brown suitcase and broke his arm.                    C

**15.** My favourite summer drink is a long, tall, cold glass of lemonade.  W

**16.** Debbie was a quiet, shy, introverted girl before she joined our
drama club.                                                               W

**17.** Outside, the roads were covered with ice.                         W

18. The placid sea and the purple sunset made our South Sea island an ideal and a picturesque retreat.                    C

19. The green shag rug and the dark brown chesterfield blended together very well.                    C

20. Surprisingly, university graduates are not finding decent jobs.                    W

21. My favourite summer sports are sailing and water skiing.                    C

22. Loud, tumultuous cheers greeted our strong, well-conditioned athletes when they entered the crowded gymnasium.                    W

23. While cooking, the chef was annoyed by the suffocating heat in the large kitchen.                    W

24. Her long, dull, monotone speech was a major disappointment.                    W

25. Just as Bill was punting, his dog ran onto the field.                    W

26. Wilma's light blue Chevrolet was stolen by a tall woman in bright yellow running shorts.                    C

27. I missed too many valuable opportunities to acquire the necessary skills to earn a comfortable living.                    C

28. His long, sloppy, ungrammatical essay received a well-deserved failing grade.                    W

29. The hot, humid, sultry summer afternoon was not a good time of day to play tennis.                    W

30. Far below, the automobiles looked like tiny bugs.                    W

## Exercise 7.3 — Commas That Set Off Non-Restrictive Modifiers, Appositives and Introductory Phrases and Clauses

1. My father, who recently retired from the fire department, is lecturing on fire safety at our local high school.                    W

2. The running shoes that I purchased from the sporting goods store on Main Street have ripped across the heel.                    C

3. *Peter the Great* is the title of an award-winning book by Robert K. Massie.                    C

4. After completing his homework assignment, Teddy decided to play a computer game.                    W

5. After lunch Ingrid went shopping.                    C

6. Harold Baines, our Vice-President, is being transferred to Montreal.                    W

7. Tracy Kidder's novel, *The Soul of a New Machine*, is a fascinating story about computer engineers.                    W

8. Any student who wishes to apply for a student loan must fill out an application form at our Student Services Department.                    C

9. Whatever happened to Melvin Matlock, our former cost accountant?                    W

10. The woman who was driving the red Ford left her grocery cart in the parking lot.                    C

11. During the graduation ceremony our college president received the Citizen-of-the-Year award.     C

12. Our local radio announcer, Pat Carson, is retiring next month.     W

13. Students who use the library consistently will probably receive the highest grades in English Literature.     C

14. The mechanic who repaired my car's transmission did an excellent job.     C

15. Elizabeth I, the Virgin Queen, was one of the most influential monarchs in English history.     W

16. With so much work to do, how can you sit and watch television for the rest of the evening?     W

17. After class we played basketball in the schoolyard.     C

18. The Wicked Witch of the West is a character in Walt Disney's *Snow White and the Seven Dwarfs*.     C

19. *Joshua Then and Now*, by Mordecai Richler, is my favourite Canadian novel.     W

20. My sister Peggy is arriving next Wednesday.     C

21. Veronica Mitford, the chairman of our Business Department, is visiting Greece this summer.     W

22. When we arrived home after 1:00 a.m., we found our babysitter playing Trivial Pursuit with our son.     W

23. The boy wearing the green hat scored two goals for our hockey team last night.     C

24. During the play the leading lady became ill.     C

25. Abraham Lincoln, the Great Emancipator, is one of the most revered American presidents.     W

26. Having won six straight hands of poker, Jack decided to cash in his winnings and go home.     W

27. The Canadian Prairies, where I lived for many years, is having a severe drought this summer.     W

28. The story of John the Baptist is one of the most intriguing Bible stories that I have ever read.     C

29. Our local community college, which is located just north of the city, is building a new gymnasium next to the soccer field.     W

30. The English teacher who wears a rose in his lapel has just published a book of short stories.     C

## Exercise 7.4 — Commas That Set Off Sentence Modifiers, Absolute Constructions, and Contrasting Elements

1. Sheila is, in fact, a first-class soccer player.     W

2. We are obviously late for class.     C

3. Times being what they are, he is fortunate to get even a part-time job.     W

**4.** They will probably arrive about 9:00 p.m., weather permitting.    W

**5.** The actors, rehearsing without scenery or proper lighting, had to rely on their imaginations.    W

**6.** You should have bought a magazine, not a lottery ticket.    W

**7.** She is indeed a famous physicist.    C

**8.** You are certainly not eating much tonight.    C

**9.** As a rule, my organization never sponsors organized sports.    W

**10.** They were tired, but happy, after their courageous win in the Olympic trials.    W

**11.** However difficult the assignment, it must be turned in on time.    W

**12.** On the contrary, Frankie is a first-rate student as well as a remarkable athlete.    W

**13.** The young girl, swimming without supervision, almost drowned in the pool.    W

**14.** All of us, I am certain, were terrified of flying for the first time.    W

**15.** The racing turtles took a long time but finally reached their destination.    C

**16.** Recommended highly, her latest novel was a major literary disappointment.    W

**17.** Adolph is, without question, a first-class brewmaster.    W

**18.** We will resume our tennis match when the weather clears.    C

**19.** Our teacher, although a severe disciplinarian, was always willing to work with the slower students.    W

**20.** The clouds were thick and grey, yet somehow peaceful and benign.    W

**21.** To be sure you're on time, set your watch five minutes ahead.    W

**22.** Tony is a Virgo, not a Capricorn.    W

**23.** Our auction sale was not as successful as we had hoped, but we are, nevertheless, still planning our historical field trip to Quebec City.    W

**24.** All things being equal, our debating team did a respectable job.    W

**25.** We are naturally worried about our upcoming examinations.    C

**26.** Whatever the cost, we shall prevail.    W

**27.** Julia, having nowhere to go, decided to return home to her parents.    W

**28.** Our coach was loud and gruff, yet fair and understanding.    W

**29.** It seems that we bought everything at the auction but the Brooklyn Bridge.    C

**30.** Our university, in my opinion, has the best library in Eastern Canada.    W

# Exercise 7.5—Commas That Set Off Names, Speakers, Echo Questions, and Mild Interjections

1. Tell me, Fred, why did you refuse to cooperate?    W
2. "Of course," replied the police officer, "we will do everything possible to apprehend the criminal."    W
3. I almost flunked English, didn't I?    W
4. John told me that he was through with teaching.    C
5. No, Father, I haven't had the car washed yet.    W
6. "The trousers look too tight," stated the tailor.    W
7. We are not yet ready to attack, General.    W
8. I spoke to Leslie just the way I am speaking to you.    C
9. There, there, you shouldn't get so upset.    W
10. She told him to mind his own business.    C
11. No, no, don't turn on the power until the green light goes on.    W
12. Mr. Wallace will hand out our marks on Monday, won't he?    C
13. May we count on your support, Reverend, for our Cancer Fund drive?    W
14. Well, well, you have finally arrived.    W
15. The president of our student body asked the school administrators if they would keep the library open on Sundays.    C
16. "The men did their best, sir, but the river is still rising."    W
17. Jonathan said, "Whenever I exercise too long, my legs ache."    W
18. Dr. Motluk told us not to worry about our grades.    C
19. We are sorry, Mrs. Donaldson, but we cannot extend your credit.    W
20. Gee, your performance was certainly exciting to watch.    W
21. Our group leader asked us if we wanted to end our therapy session early.    C
22. "Not unless you do," we replied.    W
23. "The plane leaves in ten minutes," announced the flight steward, "so please have your boarding passes ready."    W
24. Our instructor is aware, isn't he, that next Friday is a civic holiday?    W
25. Doesn't Alice know that the show starts at eight o'clock?    C
26. You have already booked our hotel room, haven't you?    W
27. Good gracious, this is a lively party.    W
28. The old gentleman said, "My, my, you are certainly in a hurry, aren't you?"    W
29. Mr. Simpson told us that he was going into hospital for a serious operation.    C
30. "If we lose this game," said the coach, "we're out of the playoffs."    W

## Exercise 7.6 – Comma Review Exercise

1. We have sold our stocks and bonds, but we are still very much
in debt.                                                                          W

2. To succeed in college you must attend all classes, do all your
home assignments, and study for all your tests.                                   W

3. My mother and father vacationed in California and Hawaii, but
they did not have time to see the surfboard races in Honolulu or
the Olympic Games in Los Angeles.                                                 C

4. The brisk, refreshing, invigorating swim in the ocean was just
what I needed.                                                                    W

5. Unfortunately, hard liquor was served at our graduation party.                 W

6. Just after ten, thirty men showed up to apply for the part-
time job that was advertised in the newspaper.                                    W

7. My uncle, who was once a stage actor, is directing our
high-school play.                                                                 W

8. Charlie Silverman, our Vice-President of Manufacturing, has
purchased a computer for his office.                                              W

9. The truck that skidded off the icy road is being examined
by our local police.                                                             C

10. Since I last saw her on stage in Vancouver, she has aged
considerably.                                                                    W

11. She is, as matter of fact, in danger of losing her scholarship.              W

12. No, Mr. Sopinka, you may not leave the room.                                 W

13. Marge is frequently late for rehearsals.                                     C

14. Well, well, what have we here? Is it
human, animal, or vegetable?                                                     W

15. My father is a mechanical engineer, not an electrical
engineer.                                                                        W

16. We have advertised for used cars, but they seem to be rare
commodities in our small city.                                                   W

17. "You have a lovely home," replied Sandra.                                     W

18. Goodness, I didn't think our shopping trip would take this
long.                                                                            W

19. That kitten is certainly playful, isn't she?                                 W

20. Watch out for the train, Juan; it is not slowing down.                       W

21. We all attended the meeting and then met for lunch.                          C

22. "I am not giving out grades today," announced the teacher,
"and that is final."                                                             W

23. Our city is, without doubt, located in one of the most scenic
areas of Canada.                                                                 W

24. Mr. Chasen told his supervisor that the welding machine was
unsafe.                                                                          C

25. I drove to the supermarket, picked up my groceries, and then
went on a picnic.                                                                W

26. No, George, the test will not be given on Friday.                            W

27. My guidance counsellor, who was once a professional hockey player, is now working on his Ph.D. degree.  _____W_____

28. Down below, the basement of the apartment building was rapidly filling with water.  _____W_____

29. Since her last appearance on stage, she has gained weight.  _____W_____

30. Carol Hoffman, my favourite singer, is retiring next year.  _____W_____

31. After dinner we intend to play scrabble.  _____C_____

32. The school bus on which our son rides was in a minor accident last Tuesday.  _____C_____

33. The baseball game should start on time, weather permitting.  _____W_____

34. Our order will arrive next week, won't it?  _____W_____

35. The cups and saucers and dishes were all broken after the minor earthquake.  _____C_____

36. Our company is located in Quebec, not New Brunswick.  _____W_____

37. All things being equal, I believe our gymnastic team will win a gold medal.  _____W_____

38. After the last shift of coal miners returned to the surface, they decided to strike for better working conditions.  _____W_____

39. We have increased our sales but not our profits.  _____C_____

40. "You may not practise your saxophone," replied Brenda, "until your father awakens."  _____W_____

# Exercise 7.7 — The Semicolon

1. Many students eat sandwiches for lunch; some, however, prefer hot meals.  _____W_____

2. I find it difficult taking notes in class; I cannot tell what is important and what isn't.  _____W_____

3. My sister is blind in one eye; nevertheless she is still a voracious reader.  _____W_____

4. During the play Katherine misplaced her glasses, but she found them under her seat during the intermission.  _____C_____

5. She thinks that everyone is against her; perhaps she is right.  _____W_____

6. Phil Hancock, Vice-President; Sally Renke, Treasurer; and Daphne Gleeson, Executive Secretary, are responsible for organizing our budget meeting.  _____W_____

7. Thomas Klein was not asked to direct our play, although he is an experienced stage director.  _____C_____

8. I am perfectly fine; I don't need help from anyone.  _____W_____

9. Irma was late for class every day last week; she is therefore being disciplined.  _____C_____

10. After our long, hot, exhausting volleyball game, we all wanted to drive to the ocean for a swim; but Jim refused to lend us his car.  _____W_____

11. He firmly believes that his company is financially healthy; he is therefore going ahead with the business merger.  _____W_____

12. Keep your mind on your work; for example, turn off the radio while you are studying.  _____W_____

13. The troops are ready, sir; they are waiting for inspection.  _____W_____

14. We are determined to finish our hike, however difficult the terrain.  _____C_____

15. Castor, Inc., Montreal; Thomson Engineering Ltd., Toronto; and Delphin Products, Calgary, are all hiring students for the summer.  _____W_____

16. Our company is presently overextended; that is, we have no cash flow.  _____W_____

17. During the concert Marie fell asleep, but she awoke before the final song.  _____C_____

18. Our college offers technology and business courses; your college, however, concentrates on applied arts.  _____W_____

19. Morris Friedman, Howard Brubaker, and Leslie Sanders are being transferred to our store in Victoria, B.C. next month.  _____C_____

20. The jungle is dangerous and the natives are unfriendly; nevertheless we shall continue our journey.  _____W_____

21. Everyone in our small town was terrified — you wouldn't believe how terrified — because the killer was still at large; for he had promised, when he returned, to wreak vengeance on the townspeople.  _____W_____

22. He vowed to climb the mountain, however long it took.  _____C_____

23. Try being careful with your money; for example, don't charge your meals when you eat out in restaurants.  _____W_____

24. My car is almost paid for; now I am going to buy a boat.  _____W_____

25. We must reduce our inventory now, or we will have to declare bankruptcy.  _____C_____

26. Marge tried to get to the bank before it closed; however, she was too late.  _____W_____

27. Mark Boudreau, the producer; Trish Cassidy, the actress; and Harold Wood, the director, were eating together at the new French restaurant.  _____W_____

28. We will have to ask for donations; we don't have enough money yet for our baseball uniforms.  _____W_____

29. I never expected to be nominated; therefore, I must decline.  _____W_____

30. George is needed on the other side of the construction site. We had therefore better give him his messages now.  _____C_____

## Exercise 7.8 — The Colon and the Dash

1. I think we have brought all of our tools (:) we have hammers, saws, nails, pliers, and screwdrivers.  _____CN_____

**2.** She ended her talk with this statement (:) "If you can't stand the heat, get out of the kitchen."　　CN

**3.** Skiing, curling, ice skating (—) these are my favourite winter sports.　　DS

**4.** Yesterday there was an automobile accident on King Street (—) or was it Park Street (—) and the damage is estimated to be in excess of five thousand dollars.　　DS

**5.** I thought I made myself clear (:) I do not accept late assignments.　　CN

**6.** Last Saturday (—) or was it Sunday (—) our next-door neighbours moved to Vancouver.　　DS

**7.** We need only one thing to make our barbecue a success (—) good weather.　　DS

**8.** We spent the entire day preparing for our auction sale (:) we collected the promised donations, made the bidding cards, and set up the tables to hold the merchandise.　　CN

**9.** What famous historical personage made the following statement (:) "Let them eat cake"?　　CN

**10.** My favourite tree (—) it is a blue spruce (—) is being cut down by the city next week.　　DS

**11.** Global pollution (—) especially water pollution (—) is endangering the health of millions of people.　　DS

**12.** The circus is coming to town next week (—) or is it the following week?　　DS

**13.** Girls and rock music (—) that's all my sons ever think about!　　DS

**14.** The principal speaker made her point very well (:) she said fiscal responsibility must be shared by everyone.　　CN

**15.** Most of our office furniture (—) chairs, desks, file cabinets, and bookcases (—) arrived last week.　　DS

**16.** My dentist always gives out this piece of advice (:) "Preventive maintenance costs less than extraction."　　CN

**17.** Drug addiction (—) this problem is a major blight on our society.　　DS

**18.** Stephanie has three brothers (—) Kevin, Mark, and Sean (—) who are outstanding scholars.　　DS

**19.** Mr. Kozol finally settled his financial problems (:) he sold his dry-cleaning business.　　CN

**20.** Our store has an interesting collection of pottery (:) there are flower pots, mixing bowls, ashtrays, and assorted cups and saucers.　　CN

**21.** Three Canadian writers (—) Margaret Atwood, Alice Munro, and Robertson Davies (—) will be studied in our English course next semester.　　DS

**22.** Sports (—) that is all he talks about!　　DS

**23.** Which teacher made the following statement (:) "Cigarette smoking is one of the least intelligent habits that students can acquire"?　　CN

24. His solution was drastic (:) he fired half his employees.                    CN

25. I have only one thing to say before I leave (—) stay alert.                  DS

26. Our recommendations were as follows (:) expand the library, cut
    class size, hire more qualified teachers, and reduce your
    support services.                                                            CN

27. There were four limousines (—) or was it five (—) parked outside
    the luxury hotel.                                                            DS

28. Don't be concerned about Melanie (—) worry about Sophie.                     DS

29. The following items were ordered by our hospital
    administrators (:) surgical equipment, hospital beds, two dozen
    thermometers, and three wheelchairs.                                         CN

30. There are only three subjects that I am enjoying this
    semester (:) mathematics, computer science, and English.                     CN

## Exercise 7.9—Quotations and Italics

1. The title of the short story I am reading is "Henry's Cat."                    W

2. "Sorry," she said, "I didn't know you were busy."                             W

3. Just before the examination began one of our class members
   asked if she could go to the bathroom.                                        C

4. Our local theatre group is performing *The Odd Couple* next month.            W

5. The editorial in yesterday's newspaper was entitled "Can We
   Afford Foreign Aid?"                                                          W

6. Which Romantic poet wrote "Ode on a Grecian Urn"?                             W

7. When I asked Marcel how he enjoyed his camping trip, he said
   it was a "bummer."                                                            W

8. *Cecilia* is the name of our new sailboat.                                    W

9. *Hill Street Blues* is my favourite television drama.                         W

10. His dull, maudlin, monotone speech went on *ad infinitum.*                   W

11. "When can we expect to receive our order?" asked the
    purchasing agent.                                                            W

12. What famous Shakespearian tragedy contains these lines:
    "The slings and arrows of outrageous fortune"?                              W

13. The store manager told the clerk that she was rude to one of
    the store's best customers.                                                  C

14. Leonard DaVinci's famous painting, *The Mona Lisa*, is on loan
    to our national museum.                                                      W

15. *Sans Souci* is the name of our newest French restaurant.                    W

16. How many *o's* are in the word meaning to select?                            W

17. When I expressed my concern about his misfortune, he simply
    replied, "*C'est la vie.*"                                                    W

18. "No, I haven't visited Montreal for two years," said Nancy,
    "but I intend to shop there next week."                                      W

19. "Once More to the Lake" is one of E.B. White's finest stories.               W

20. Don't use the word *adapt* when you mean to take possession of.              W

**21.** I read both the *New York Times* and the *Globe and Mail* every day.  <u>W</u>

**22.** In James Thurber's collection of short stories entitled *Thurber Country*, one of my favourites is "Teacher's Pet."  <u>W</u>

**23.** What famous Canadian novelist wrote *The Stone Angel*?  <u>W</u>

**24.** His major "engineering achievement" was digging a drainage ditch.  <u>W</u>

**25.** The word "love" in tennis has a completely different meaning from its conventional usage.  <u>W</u>

**26.** The film, *Joshua Then and Now,* is being released very soon.  <u>W</u>

**27.** "The Nuclear Winter" was the lead article in this month's *Maclean's* magazine.  <u>W</u>

**28.** The space shuttle *Enterprise* has already been on two missions.  <u>W</u>

**29.** My grandfather still refers to a cigar as a "stogie."  <u>W</u>

**30.** *The Thousand Islands* is my favourite vacation area.  <u>W</u>

# Exercise 7.10 — Capitalizing Correctly

**1.** My father was just hired by <u>s</u>amson and <u>s</u>ons, a consulting firm.  Samson / Sons

**2.** Our holidays start on the first <u>t</u>uesday in <u>j</u>une.  Tuesday / June

**3.** My <u>M</u>other is doing volunteer work at the Johnsville Civic Hospital.  mother

**4.** Harold went to <u>L</u>aw <u>S</u>chool at the University of Toronto.  law school

**5.** My doctor said contentedly, "<u>y</u>ou are in perfect health."  You

**6.** My best friend is moving to Calgary, Alberta, in the <u>S</u>pring.  spring

**7.** Last summer I visited <u>e</u>pcot <u>c</u>enter, which is located near <u>d</u>isney <u>w</u>orld in Florida.  Epcot Center / Disney World

**8.** The new <u>e</u>ast <u>i</u>ndian restaurant opened last night.  East Indian

**9.** This year I am enrolled in <u>G</u>eometry, <u>H</u>istory, and French.  geometry / history

**10.** Our family dentist teaches oral hygiene at the <u>C</u>ommunity <u>C</u>ollege.  community / college

**11.** Jack's <u>B</u>rother and Ruth's <u>C</u>ousin both attend The Taylor Institute of Electronics.  brother / cousin

**12.** The road to Jackson's <u>p</u>ond is full of potholes.  Pond

**13.** We want <u>J</u>ustice—not anarchy.  justice

**14.** There is a small <u>p</u>olish community near our industrial park.  Polish

**15.** La Paz is a city in what <u>s</u>outh American country?  South

**16.** Professor Erskine said that the Canadian <u>n</u>orth is rich in minerals.  North

**17.** Easter service is being held at 5:00 a.m. in our <u>C</u>hurch.  church

**18.** Forty-<u>S</u>econd Street and Broadway is Manhattan's busiest thoroughfare.  second

**19.** Our <u>H</u>igh <u>S</u>chool is undergoing extensive structural repairs.  high school

**20.** Psychology 102, Sociology 103, and <u>s</u>panish are the only electives offered this semester.  Spanish

| | |
|---|---|
| **21.** Borden <u>c</u>rescent is being repaved this summer. | Crescent |
| **22.** The local <u>G</u>olf <u>C</u>lub is honouring its founder, Ian McShane, next Tuesday. | golf club |
| **23.** I believe that <u>f</u>ather will run in the next election. | Father |
| **24.** My university professor does not have a <u>ph.d.</u>, but he is an expert on Shakespeare's poetry. | Ph.D. |
| **25.** Is Canada a member of <u>T</u>he North Atlantic Treaty Organization? | the |
| **26.** When we informed Craig of our intention to bicycle through the Rockies, he just yawned and said, "<u>d</u>on't include me in your plans." | Don't |
| **27.** The airplane landed safely at Hanover <u>air</u> <u>f</u>ield after it was struck by lightning. | Air Field |
| **28.** Our <u>C</u>ollege has the best civil technology program in the East. | college |
| **29.** I passed <u>C</u>hemistry, but I could not achieve a passing grade in English. | chemistry |
| **30.** Is Peterborough <u>N</u>orth of Toronto? | north |

## Exercise 7.11 – The Apostrophe

| | |
|---|---|
| **1.** *Whose* going to buy lunch this time? | Who's |
| **2.** Our new car lost its hubcap on the country road. | C |
| **3.** The *mens'* room is right next to the ladies' room. | men's |
| **4.** If Soames believes that we will pay for his theatre tickets, he's very much mistaken. | C |
| **5.** Whose bike is that in our driveway? | C |
| **6.** *Someones* purse was left on the seat of Hank's boat. | Someone's |
| **7.** *Theyre* not going to the Jones' party, are they? | They're |
| **8.** I have trouble reading *you're* writing because your *t's* look like *r's* and your *n's* look like *m's*. | your |
| **9.** Shakespeare's *Coriolanus* is one of my favourite Elizabethan tragedies. | C |
| **10.** The *Ryans* roses won first prize at the flower show. | Ryans' |
| **11.** Joe's '51 Oldsmobile was bought by an antique *collectors'* wife. | collector's |
| **12.** There's no reason why Marie's *parents'* can't win the sailboat race this Saturday. | parents |
| **13.** Who's the student who's going to attend the awards ceremony on our behalf? | C |
| **14.** Our *teams* lack of motivation is not the coach's fault. | team's |
| **15.** The Bennetts have just redecorated *they're* house. | their |
| **16.** Tom *Smiths'* luggage was lost by the airline's baggage handlers. | Smith's |
| **17.** *Its* a shame that he's not allowed to participate in the school's drug rehabilitation program. | It's |
| **18.** The churches' *bells'* were all ringing at once. | bells |
| **19.** My parents' mortgage will be paid off in June of *86*. | '86 |

20. The *childrens'* bicycles were laying all over our lawn.                                      children's
21. Since Michael's brothers started working, they have become
    more responsible and less impulsive.                                                          C
22. *Lets* attend the jazz concert at the Arts Center tomorrow.                                    Let's
23. Now's the time to get *they're* attention before they leave
    the union hall.                                                                                their
24. Our *cats* food was eaten by our two cocker spaniels.                                          cat's
25. *Thats* the truck my sister's boyfriend owns.                                                  That's
26. She's very impressed by his new *cars'* interior.                                              car's
27. Tourists spend a great deal of money in southern Ontario's
    vacation resorts.                                                                              C
28. A *joggers'* exercise program has just been initiated at our
    local YM/YWCA.                                                                                 jogger's
29. Her sister's sons *wont* participate in winter sports.                                         won't
30. The *Sylvesters* farm has not made any money since '79.                                        Sylvesters'

# Exercise 7.12 — Parentheses and Brackets

1. Margaret Tillotson (*now Mrs. J. Feeney*) was a famous name
   in women's golf in the 1950's.                                                                  PR
2. The widow of Tom Warden (*1906-1953*), the founder of our club,
   is being honoured at our annual banquet.                                                       PR
3. Dr. Felix Shepherd (*he is an ex-Olympian swimmer*) will lecture
   next Tuesday on the cardio-vascular benefits of jogging.                                       PR
4. "Shakespeare's greatest tragedy [*Hamlet*] depicted a young man
   with a fine mind and a delicate sensitivity on the brink of madness."                          BR
5. "The Prime Minister of Canada resides in Ottawa, the city with
   the highest free-standing structure in the world—the CN Tower."
   [*The author has mistaken Ottawa for Toronto.*]                                                BR
6. "The Bermuda Rectangle [*sic*] has been blamed for a number of
   airplane crashes during the past ten years."                                                   BR
7. This rapidly accelerating rate of inflation (*12% last year*) must be
   stopped, or our country will experience financial ruin.                                        PR
8. "John Steinbeck's great novel of the Depression era [*The Grapes
   of Wrath*] is a perfect example of the novel as social commentary."                            BR
9. The announcer informed us of two clear signs of an impending
   heart attack: (*1*) a tightening of the chest and (*2*) difficulty breathing.                  PR
10. Our instructions were issued in point form: (*a*) assemble as a
    class in the hallway opposite our classroom, (*b*) walk calmly to
    the nearest exit, (*c*) assemble on the lawn to the rear of the
    building, and (*d*) wait for the fire bell to stop ringing before
    re-entering the building.                                                                      PR
11. Jonathan Swift (*1667-1745*) and Alexander Pope (*1688-1744*)
    are my favourite eighteenth-century poets.                                                     PR

12. As we entered the old, decrepit building (*it was built in 1786*),
    the floor creaked and a pigeon flew through a hole in the roof.      PR

13. "This incredibly brilliant preface [*Dr. Samuel Johnson's Preface to
    Shakespeare*], published before his edition of Shakespeare's plays,
    is the finest monument to genius that I have ever read."      BR

14. "The assassination of Archduke Francis Ferdinand (*June 28, 1914*)
    was purported to precipitate World War I."      PR

15. "Margaret Lawrence [*sic*] is my favourite Canadian novelist."      BR

16. "This great naval base, full of hallowed memories, [*Pearl Harbor*]
    will never be abandoned."      BR

17. Arthur Gottleib (*the movie mogul*) is being wed for the fifth time
    at a small, private ceremony in his Hollywood mansion.      PR

18. Before we were considered for the physical fitness award, we
    had to accomplish three things: (*1*) we had to jog five miles
    without stopping, (*2*) do sixty consecutive push-ups, and (*3*)
    swim five laps in three minutes.      PR

19. "Because of the new advances in medicine, our infant mortality
    rate is below two per cent." [*The figure is actually 1.05%.*]      BR

20. The last T-34 jet trainer (*affectionately known as the Pussycat*)
    was taken out of service yesterday.      PR

# Exercise 7.13 — Periods, Question Marks and Exclamation Points

1. Wipe your feet before entering the house.      W
2. Will you please step to the rear of the elevator.      W
3. Find the guilty party and then punish him.      C
4. You asked me if I know the time. I don't have a watch.      W
5. May I have your undivided attention now.      W
6. At 9:00 p.m. Mr. Samuels is giving out the door prizes.      C
7. He works at the RCA plant on Fredrick Street.      C
8. When do you finish work? At five o'clock?      W
9. Susan asked her mother if she could attend our graduation party.      W
10. Watch your step when you leave the store.      W
11. Dr. Tracy is operating at 10:00 a.m.      W
12. What did you make for supper? Baked ham?      W
13. Nelson Associates is buying Craymore Inc. next month.      W
14. We always listen to CBC stereo every Tuesday evening.      C
15. The scaffold is falling! Watch out!      W
16. Now, to get down to business.      W
17. Will someone please answer the telephone.      W
18. Well. Well, she finally paid her debts.      W
19. When is our English test scheduled? Next week?      W
20. Stuart has a Ph.D. in chemistry, and Sharon has an M.A. in history.      W
21. Mrs. Sherwood works for the RCMP.      W

22. Oh my, she certainly has a large appetite.

23. Why haven't you told your supervisor about the defective ball bearings?

24. Please take your seats and open your textbooks.

25. You managed to escape from jail. How?

26. Stand up straight when I am speaking to you.

27. Watch out for the fire engine! It's heading right for us!

28. Don't slam the door when you leave.

29. Dr. McCrory asked Mrs. Thomson if she had a YWCA card.

30. When does the show start? After the commercial?

# Exercise 7.14 — Punctuation Review Exercise

1. Find the correct file copy; then send it to the supervisor of the Personnel Department.

2. When Frank first started pitching for our team—he was only sixteen years old at the time—we never dreamed that he would someday be a star in the major leagues.

3. Please tell me the source of the following statement: ''We have nothing to fear but fear itself.''

4. Sheila cannot learn to play the saxophone, however hard she tries.

5. Three RCMP officers—Clarke, Dixon, and Hannick—are being awarded medals for bravery this afternoon.

6. Soap operas—that's all she watches on TV.

7. ''Without your moral support,'' announced the mayor, ''I could never have solved our financial problems.''

8. Some convicts refer to prison as ''the joint.''

9. *Fun Tomorrow* is the title of the biography of John Morgan Gray, a revered Canadian publisher.

10. Nell asked us where we were holding our next nuclear disarmament meeting. We told her in the church basement.

11. ''The Displaced Person'' is the title of a short story by Flannery O'Connor.

12. Travis, Inc. and Sterling Mfg.. have just signed contracts to supply the CP Hotel chain.

13. She said that we must leave.

14. I read about our budding Canadian film industry in *Saturday Night* magazine.

15. Tyrone Well, Vice-President; Joanne Bickel, Treasurer; and Harry Jerome, Sales Manager, are holding a meeting in the board room at 10:00 a.m.

16. Would you mind moving out of my way.

17. The space shuttle *Discovery* has just achieved orbit.

18. ''When is the train due to arrive?'' asked Jane.

19. Jerry is mature, dependable, honest, and industrious; that is, he can handle responsibility.

W

20. She collected our reports last Friday — or was it Thursday?

W

21. Don't try to lift the cartons yourself; wait until you have help.

W

22. We ordered the following garden supplies: fertilizer, grass seed, shears, and rakes.

W

23. *The Daisy* is the name of my father's new sailboat.

W

24. It's not a question of time; it's a question of money.

W

25. Watch out! The rock is falling!

W

26. ''*Wonderland*, the amusement park, is located just north of Ottawa, Ont.'' [It is actually located north of Toronto.]

W

27. The assassination of Robert F. Kennedy (1926-1968) shocked everyone in North America.

W

28. When shall we arrange our holiday? In the spring or fall?

W

29. The term "stonewall" was popularized during the Nixon presidency.

W

30. Sam Donat — the guy who owns *Sam's Garage* — has just won ten thousand dollars in the lottery.

W

31. We must carry on, whatever the consequences.

C

32. Please stop eating your peas with a fork.

W

33. My favourite television program, *The Avengers*, has not been renewed by the sponsors.

W

34. Physics, Spanish, and chemistry are all being taught in the new wing of our high school.

W

35. ''Pierre Burton, [*sic*] I believe, is the author of *The Last Spike*.''

W

36. Please make sure that we are provided with blankets, warm boots, earmuffs, and plenty of hot coffee.

C

37. When military men refer to weapons that kill and maim people, they use the term "ordinance."

W

38. Three surgeons — Dr. Barnett, Dr. Kravitz, and Dr. Matteo — are performing the delicate transplant operation.

W

39. Please follow this procedure: (1) make sure the transmission is in neutral; (2) pull the emergency brake; (3) turn the wheels toward the curb, and (4) lock the car doors before you leave.

W

40. What would you like for dinner? Roast beef?

W

41. Whenever Carlos finishes talking on the telephone, he signs off by saying *ciao*.

W

42. Roberta Peterson has a Ph.D. in French literature and David Samuelson has an M.Ed. from Queen's University.

W

43. We studied Shakespeare's *Macbeth* last September.

W

44. Your writing is awkward because your *i's* look like *e's* and your *w's* look like *u's*.

W

45. "Sailing to Byzantium" is one of William Butler Yeats' most famous poems.      W

46. Would everyone please walk slowly toward the fire exits.      W

47. The Gleasons' party was a huge success.      W

48. The play, *Long Day's Journey into Night*, is my favourite modern tragedy.      W

49. We toured the *Statue of Liberty* when we visited New York last September.      W

50. My pay cheque was delayed in the mail; therefore I shall have to borrow lunch money.      W

# Exercise 8.1 — Detecting Clichés

(Answers may vary.)

1. We will not agree to any of his proposals.
2. If we decide to invest in the stock market, we will wait for the right opportunity.
3. Denise's contribution was late, but certainly appreciated.
4. We discovered the hydraulic system failure just in time.
5. Thelma told us a sad story when we enquired about her health.
6. Our scoring opportunities were few; nevertheless we fought to the end.
7. Please understand when I tell you that I intend to speak plainly.
8. Today it is difficult to save money.
9. Obviously our company must increase its cash flow or it will fail.
10. We are slowly losing our freedom; therefore we must conclude this divisive debate before our young union movement is cancelled.
11. Making money in a tight money market is not easy.
12. His position on disarmament is quite clear, but we must make him change his views on taxation.
13. Even though Shirley was bitterly attacked for her opinions on women's rights, she remained quite cool.
14. Robert found a wonderful woman when he married Claudia.
15. In our organization time is valuable, so you are expected to remain quite busy.

# Exercise 8.3 — Replacing Jargon

(Answers may vary.)

1. Before we inform our competitors, let's rethink our position on long-term investments.
2. Our company must become more efficient, or the funding cutbacks will have a negative impact on our department.
3. I need her financial figures before I can estimate our expenditures next fall.
4. If he approves our budget, perhaps then we can meet with our marketing people next week.
5. Next semester we will hire an engineer to teach a construction course.
6. If we do not soon discuss wages, we will have a strike on our hands.
7. I can understand your position, but can you, in turn, appreciate my special circumstances?
8. When we provide George with our information, how long will it take him to make a change in his department?
9. How long do you estimate the cutback in production you mentioned will last?

10. We must coordinate our two marketing strategies.
11. Our estimates, at this time, are inexact.
12. The point of her proposal was meant to help you achieve a closer relationship with your staff.
13. If you meet with our representative in Montreal, he will speak to our advertising agency next week.
14. What kind of response did you get from your workshop on communications?
15. Ladies and gentlemen, I know you realize the importance of the new office complex to our image, so let me show you an artist's sketch of the proposed building.

## Exercise 8.5 – Making Sentences Concise

1. Our delivery date was delayed because our production line was shut down for two days.
2. We finally found our lost dog near the old churchyard.
3. They opened their broken safe with a welding torch.
4. For clarity we shall give each of you a translation of our business memoranda.
5. Our company adopted a new order-processing system to increase sales.
6. Marg seldom eats fatty foods.
7. If I get an opportunity I shall participate in the student exchange program.
8. We will process your request for maternity leave immediately.
9. Our company's decision to diversify was, in my opinion, a big mistake.
10. We have nothing to contribute to the conversation.
11. They will inform us later about our request for a salary advance.
12. Even though Herman won the race, he is still not considered a significant athlete.
13. We have received your letter and intend to follow your recommendations.
14. I cannot respond to your proposal until I have all the pertinent information.
15. On our twentieth wedding anniversary we went on an ocean cruise.

## Exercise 8.6 – Removing Redundancies

1. The drug store was giving out (free) gifts of disposable razors as part of its promotion campaign.
2. There was a (complete and) total blackout last night that lasted for two hours.
3. My son always disappears (from view) when it is time for supper.
4. Martha's collection of antique jewellery is (very) unique.
5. We must maintain (strict) accuracy when we announce our budget for next year.
6. If we collect (together) enough household donations we can have a successful garage sale.
7. After our students connected (up) the high speed printer to the terminal outlet, we all breathed a sigh of relief.
8. The (end) result of his deliberations was the abolition of our advertising department.
9. My sister and I bought the same (identical) dress in different stores.
10. Ted's new car is red (in colour).
11. Our golf course was much too difficult for the (new) beginner.
12. We had a (serious) crisis at school yesterday when our chemistry laboratory caught fire.
13. The used-car dealer seemed sincere (and earnest) when he told us that one of his cars was never driven in the winter.

**14.** Our new car may be small (in size), but it is certainly comfortable.

**15.** If you want my (personal) opinion about her sudden promotion, just ask me when there is no one around.

# Exercise 8.7 — Revising for Effective Diction

At times we tend to forget that we have the potential to be excellent communicators, for we each have an innate ability to express our thoughts with clarity and precision. But we seem to be put off by the fundamentals of grammar and lose our focus on the more rewarding skills of sentence and paragraph construction.

Using our native language is altogether a matter of common sense, since many of the rules are obvious and logical. For instance, if we realize that we must use a verb each time we form an idea, our attitude toward sentence construction might change; for after all, a sentence is, finally, a small idea, generated by a verb and completed by other parts of speech. Also many of the rules of punctuation reflect our habits of speech — the tone we employ, the emphasis we place, and the natural hesitations we use.

Therefore, if we can begin perceiving the construction rules of grammar and syntax not as artificial and mechanistic adjuncts to communication, but as necessary guidelines that allow us to think clearly and precisely, we will soon gain a new respect for our native tongue.

# Exercise 9.1 — Preparing an Outline

**#1**

**(a)** I Sports Apparel
    A Summer
        1. Golf shoes
        2. Golf glove
        3. Tennis skirt
        4. Bathing suit
        5. Sailing cap
    B Winter
        1. Ski jacket
        2. Hockey pants
        3. Ski boots
        4. Hockey helmet
        5. Curling shoes
        6. Ice skates
        7. Toque

**(b)** I Home Entertainment
    A Radio
    B Stereo set
        1. Tapes
        2. Records

    C Television
    D Games
        1. Card games
            a. Euchre
            b. Bridge
            c. Poker
        2. Board games
            a. Monopoly
            b. Chess
            c. Trivial
               Pursuit

**(c)** I Meat
    A Beef
        1. Steaks
            a. Sirloin
            b. T-Bone
            c. Porterhouse
            d. Cube

2. Roasts
   a. Rump
   b. Eye of the round
   c. Cross-rib
3. Ground meat
   a. Meat loaf
   b. Hamburgers

(d)  I Foods of the World
  A North America
    1. Mexico
       a. Tortilla
       b. Tacos
    2. Canada
       a. Pea soup
       c. Tortiere
    3. United States
       a. Hot dogs
       b. Hamburgers
  B Europe
    1. France
       a. Chicken
          Cordon Bleu
       b. Crepes
          suzettes
    2. Italy
       a. Spaghetti
       b. Lasagna
    3. Germany
       a. Sauerkraut
       b. Weiner
          schnitzel
  C Asia
    1. China
       a. Chow mein
       b. Chop suey


#2.
(a)  I Home Tools
  A Hand
    1. Hammers
    2. Pliers
    3. Screwdrivers
    4. Wrenches
       a. Socket
       b. Crescent
       c. Pipe

B Power
  1. Drills
  2. Sanders
  3. Saws
     a. Band
     b. Jig
     c. Circular
II Garden Tools
  A Hand
    1. Rakes
    2. Hoes
    3. Shovels
  B Power
    1. String trimmer
    2. Hedge trimmer
    3. Cordless grass shear

(b)  I Literature
  A Fiction
    1. Novels
    2. Short stories
    3. Poems
       a. Lyric
       b. Narrative
    4. Children's stories
       a. Fairy tales
       b. Nursery rhymes
  B Non-fiction
    1. Biographies
    2. Journals
    3. Essays
       a. Personal
       b. Scientific
       c. Political

(c)  I Sports
  A Summer
    1. Golf
       a. Birdie
       b. Par
    2. Tennis
       a. Love
       b. Let
       c. Serve
    3. Baseball
       a. Steal
       b. Double play
       c. Walk

B Fall
  1. Football
    a. Blitz
    b. Safety
    c. Quarterback sneak
C Winter
  1. Basketball
    a. Dribble
    b. Dunk
    c. Hook shot
  2. Hockey
    a. Hat trick
    b. Slapshot
    c. Cross-check

**(d)** I Universities
  A Science
    1. Physics
    2. Chemistry
    3. Computer
  B Engineering
    1. Civil
    2. Electrical
    3. Chemical

C Humanities
  1. Literature
    a. Canadian
    b. British
    c. American
  2. History
    a. World
    b. Canadian
  3. Philosophy
    a. Logic
    b. Epistemology

II Community Colleges
  A Applied arts
    1. Child-care worker
    2. Mental retardation
      counsellor
  B Business
    1. Accounting
    2. Marketing
  C Technology
    1. Electronic
    2. Civil
    3. Chemical

**#3**

**(a)** I **To Socialize**
  A Enjoy outings with other families
    1. Picnics
    2. Walking tours
  B Meet people from different cultural backgrounds
    1. Engage in stimulating conversation
    2. Learn different customs and attitudes
  C Meet opposite sexes

II **To Escape**
  A Get away from family pressures
  B Get away from big-city living
    1. Traffic noise
    2. Overcrowded apartment buildings
    3. High crime rate

III **To Participate in Leisure Activities**
  A Tour night clubs
  B Visit museums
  C Attend concerts and plays
  D Play sports
    1. Golf
    2. Tennis
    3. Badminton

4. Skiing
   a. Downhill
   b. Cross-country

**(b) I Family environment**
   A Single-parent family
   1. There may be discipline problems
   2. There may be a lack of ethical or moral direction
   B Severe tension between mother and father
   1. The spouses may not be compatible
   2. Alcoholism may be in the family

**II Economic Environment**
   A Severe poverty
   1. There may be no jobs available
   2. The family may be on welfare
      a. Lacking self-esteem
      b. Lacking hope and ambition

**III Educational Environment**
   A Overcrowded classes
   B Overworked and unmotivated teachers
   C No school counsellors

**IV Social Environment**
   A No social services available
   1. Lack of day-care centers
   2. Lack of recreational facilities
   3. Lack of organized clubs or sports programs
   B Poor choice of companions
   1. Street gangs
   2. High-school dropouts
   3. Drug dealers

**#4**

**(a) I Itinerary Preparation with a Travel Agent**
   A List number of tourist attractions to be seen in each country
   B Arrange guided tours to specific tourist areas in each country
   C Determine time to be spent in each country

**II Language Preparation**
   A Learn key words and phrases
   B Learn how to read road signs and maps

**III Financial Preparation**
   A Purchase travellers' cheques
   B Learn exchange rates for each country
   C Learn tipping customs for each country

**IV Travel and Accommodation Preparation**
   A Land transportation
   1. Car rental
   2. Tour bus
   3. Train

     B  Accommodations
       1. Hostels and camping sites
       2. Hotels and motels
       3. Bed and breakfast establishments

**(b)**  **I**  **Construction**
     A  Bricklayer
     B  Carpenter
     C  Heavy-equipment operator
     D  Ironworker

  **II**  **Sports**
     A  Football
       1. Referee
       2. Coach
     B  Skiing
       1. Ski instructor
       2. Lift-tow operator
     C  Golf
       1. Caddy
       2. Greenskeeper

 **III** **Conservation**
     A  Game warden
     B  Forest ranger
     C  Water quality inspector

**#5**

**I**  **By Automobile**
  A  Advantages
    1. Costs less than a plane or a train
     a. Riders share transportation and food costs
     b. Accommodations are inexpensive
       i. Sharing motel rooms
       ii. Staying in camping areas
    2. Able to see countryside
     a. Make unscheduled side trips
     b. Visit historic sites
     c. See tourist areas
    3. Opportunity to meet different people en route
  B  Disadvantages
    1. Must stop often
    2. Cramped quarters; not enough room to move around
    3. Takes long time to reach destination
    4. Hazardous weather and road conditions occur
     a. Snowstorms
     b. Icy roads
     c. Fog and rain
    5. Mechanical failure can happen
    6. Higher accident rate than plane or train

## II By Train
A Advantages
  1. Room to move around
  2. Seats more comfortable than an automobile
  3. Better social surroundings
  4. Can see countryside from the window
  5. Faster than an automobile
  6. Sleeping accommodations part of the fare
B Disadvantages
  1. Travel at night
  2. Much slower than a plane
  3. Confined to a rigid schedule and a designated route
     a. Train routes are not always the most scenic
     b. Departure and arrival times may not be convenient
  4. Noise level may be high
  5. Weather conditions cause many delays
  6. Food not always well prepared
  7. Costs more than an automobile

## III By Plane
A Advantages
  1. Planes are faster than both trains and automobiles
  2. Weather is not a factor; planes fly above bad weather
  3. Passengers can see a film in flight
  4. Planes have a better safety record than autos and trains
  5. Food is served at your seat
B Disadvantages
  1. Cramped space
     a. No head room
     b. Seats smaller than seats on the train
     c. Aisles narrow and restrooms small
  2. Cannot see the countryside
  3. No opportunity to socialize
  4. High level of boredom
  5. Menus usually limited

**#6** (Answers will vary.)

**(a)** THESIS STATEMENT: *Before you go for a job interview, there are a number of planning stages that you should consider.*

  I   Learn all you can about the career choices, the advancement opportunities, and the salary scale of your chosen occupational area.
  II  Learn everything you can about the company that has advertised the job.
      A. Find out its age and size.
      B. Find out if it is a national or a multi-national company and how many branches it has within Canada.
      C. Also, learn how it is organized and managed, how many products it manufactures, and who its competitors are.

III Learn about the desirable requirements for the job.
   A. For instance, do the educational requirements include a university degree, a community-college diploma, or any specialized skill training?
   B. What employment experience do you need, if any, and are there community involvement requirements?
IV Do a complete personal checklist.
   A. For example, try to answer the following questions as honestly as you can:
     1. What are my major strengths and weaknesses?
     2. Why should the company hire me over someone else with similar qualifications?
     3. Do I work well with people?
     4. What are my salary needs?
     5. What are my long-term goals?
     6. Am I ready to accept responsibility and make decisions?
V Next, you should prepare a resume or data sheet.
   A. Make sure the resume contains a heading, your educational background and work experience, a personal information section, and a list of references.
     1. The heading must include your name and address, your telephone number, and the title of the job you are applying for.
     2. Your educational background and work experience must be comprehensive.
       a. Your education information should include both secondary and post-secondary schooling, and any other specialized training received outside of public institutions.
       b. Your work experience information should include both full-time and part-time jobs, with your last job listed first, and including all the starting and finishing dates.
     3. Your personal information may include your height and weight, age, marital status, the condition of your health, and a list of your hobbies and interests.
     4. The last section of your resume should contain a list of people who can attest to your personal qualities, your educational background, and your work experience.
VI Finally, you may prepare for the interview by rehearsing, either by yourself before a mirror, or with a friend.


**(b)** THESIS STATEMENT: *There are six major areas that one should consider when evaluating a speech.*
  I When judging speeches one must consider the following areas of evaluation: content, organization, language, diction, physical behaviour, and communication.
   A. Content evaluation includes the topic, purpose, and development details of the speech.
     B. Organization evaluation always includes the proper development of the introduction, the body, and the conclusion.
     C. Language evaluation includes the vocabulary used, the usage and style, and the tone of the speech.
     D. Diction evaluation covers articulation and pronunciation of words, phrasing and emphasis, and tempo and voice control.

E. Physical behaviour evaluation focusses on the speaker's poise, gestures, eye contact, and facial expressions.

F. Communication evaluation considers the speaker's projection, the audience's response, and the overall impression made by the speech.

# Exercise 10.1 — Paragraph Unity

1. I cannot remember when I had a more enjoyable outing. The weather was perfect and the picnic food delicious. The softball game we played was full of laughs and unexpected excitement, and our marshmallow toast at dusk was the perfect ending of a perfect day. I hope we do it all again next year.

2. Many of us feel that our football team has a good chance to win our division title. We have the best quarterback and the best line-backing crew in our division. Furthermore, most people agree that our head coach is second to none. If we do not win the title, it won't be because we lack the talent.

3. Driving large, gas-guzzling cars is no longer a symbol of prestige, but a sign of irresponsibility. With such a premium placed on energy conservation in Canada, it is almost criminal to drive an inefficient automobile. Because many people still associate bigness with social importance, they simply ignore the necessity for fuel conservation. Unfortunately, many of them can afford to be wasteful and irresponsible; but the question is, can we afford their irresponsibility? I think not. Therefore, we must force our North American car-makers to scale down the size of their cars and to manufacture more fuel-efficient engines. If responsible behaviour cannot be freely demonstrated by our citizens, then our government will have to legislate it.

4. My favourite reading matter is science fiction because I enjoy using my imagination. When I involve myself in fantastic situations in the distant future, my mind seems to open up, and I feel more alive; my imagination is full of space ships, time warps, anti-matter, and black holes. I know that scientific and technological progress is made by people who dream and imagine and speculate—who live at least a part of their lives in the future. That is why I recommend science fiction to anyone interested in developing his creative abilities.

5. Your good intentions can sometimes get you into trouble; I learned this valuable lesson when I was only thirteen. My older brother was on our high-school basketball team, and I was on my way to see him play. As I approached a busy intersection, I noticed an old lady who seemed afraid to cross the street because of the heavy traffic. Her glasses were extremely thick, and she seemed to be squinting at the traffic. Feeling sorry for her, I decided to lend her a hand across the street. Boy was that a mistake! As soon as I touched her arm, she hit me over the head with her "five-ton" purse and kicked me in the shins. Then she screamed for help. When the traffic cop came running over to where we were standing, she accused me of trying to molest her, and demanded my arrest. After a long and involved explanation, I finally convinced the police officer that I had

made an honest mistake; but he cautioned me to be more careful in the future. You see, the old woman wasn't so helpless after all; in fact, she was working for the city monitoring traffic—she had a traffic counter in her right hand. The lesson I learned was never to offer assistance to anyone unless I was absolutely certain it was needed and would be gratefully accepted.

## Exercise 10.2 — Selecting the Topic Sentence

**(a)** 2. Ottawa offers many attractions for the summer tourist.

**(b)** 3. Skiing in the spring has many advantages over skiing during the months of December and January.

**(c)** 3. Modern marriage is quite different from the traditional marriage of my grandparents.

**(d)** 2. There is quite a difference between ice hockey and field hockey.

**(e)** 3. Personal essays are more satisfying to write than expository essays.

**(f)** 1. My job in the factory is boring.

**(g)** 2. Since Sue has changed the style and colour of her hair, she seems to have undergone a personality change.

**(h)** 1. I love Broadway musicals.

**(i)** 3. Hang gliding is a dangerous sport.

**(j)** 1. Why do people smoke cigarettes?

**(k)** 3. John cannot decide what he wants out of life.

**(l)** 2. Collecting rare books is more satisfying and more expensive than collecting match covers.

**(m)** 1. I will never eat in this restaurant again.

**(n)** 3. There are a number of reasons for the decline of literacy in our society.

**(o)** 2. I think Canada should do more to protect its natural resources.

## Exercise 10.3 — Position of the Topic Sentence

5

1 and 4

1 and 5

4

1

## Exercise 10.4 — Paragraph Types

**A.** INTRODUCTORY STATEMENT

**1.** Our store stocks a full line of sporting equipment.

**2.** My cat has many human characteristics.

**3.** Our city is noted for its excellent ethnic restaurants.

**4.** My English and math teachers use different teaching techniques.

**5.** The novel I have just read is boring and poorly written.

**B.** TRANSITIONAL STATEMENT

**1.** On the other hand, my physics course is an academic disaster.

**2.** But our military budget is far from adequate.

**3.** The frustration of some of the fans, however, developed into violence.

**4.** Also, our educational system must adapt to this computer revolution.

**5.** Monastic communism, however, is significantly different from Russian communism.

**C.** CONCLUDING STATEMENT

**1.** The organization committee should be congratulated for doing such a superb job.

**2.** The companies that manufacture and sell electrical appliances need to place more emphasis on quality control.

**3.** If our management does not soon improve, we may have to close the area.

**4.** We must band together and vote these incompetent politicians out of office.

**5.** It is obvious that our college does not consider technology to be a high-priority subject.

# Exercise 10.5 — Topic Sentence and Patterns of Development

**1.** Cause and Effect

**2.** Narration and Description

**3.** Classification

**4.** Definition

**5.** Comparison and Contrast

**6.** Definition

**7.** Example

**8.** Process Description

**9.** Comparison and Contrast

**10.** Definition

**11.** Narration and Description

**12.** Classification

**13.** Enumeration by Details

**14.** Comparison and Contrast

**15.** Classification

**16.** Narration and Description

**17.** Example

**18.** Process Description

**19.** Enumeration by Details

**20.** Comparison and Contrast

# Index